Ius Gentium: Comparative Perspectives on Law and Justice

Volume 141

Ius Gentium is a book series which discusses the central questions of law and justice from a comparative perspective. The books in this series collect the contrasting and overlapping perspectives of lawyers, judges, philosophers and scholars of law from the world's many different jurisdictions for the purposes of comparison, harmonisation, and the progressive development of law and legal institutions. Each volume makes a new comparative study of an important area of law. This book series continues the work of the well-known journal of the same name and provides the basis for a better understanding of all areas of legal science.

The *Ius Gentium* series provides a valuable resource for lawyers, judges, legislators, scholars, and both graduate students and researchers in globalisation, comparative law, legal theory and legal practice. The series has a special focus on the development of international legal standards and transnational legal cooperation.

Aslı Alkış Tümtürk

Online Privacy and Data Protection of Children in the European Union and the United States

Springer

Aslı Alkış Tümtürk
Budapest, Hungary

ISSN 1534-6781 ISSN 2214-9902 (electronic)
Ius Gentium: Comparative Perspectives on Law and Justice
ISBN 978-3-032-27533-2 ISBN 978-3-032-27534-9 (eBook)
https://doi.org/10.1007/978-3-032-27534-9

This work was supported by Tempus Közalapítvány.

This Springer imprint is published by the registered company Springer Nature Switzerland AG
The registered company address is: Gewerbestrasse 11, 6330 Cham, Switzerland

Acknowledgement I would like to express my heartfelt gratitude to the many individuals who have guided, supported, and inspired me throughout the course of this research and the creation of this book.

First and foremost, I am deeply indebted to my professors at the University of Szeged who played pivotal roles in the success of this research. My sincere thanks to Prof. Dr. Attila Badó, the Director of the Institute of Comparative Law, for his kind encouragement and guidance throughout my Ph.D. journey and for his support in embarking on this publishing process.

I owe immense gratitude to my supervisors, Dr. Szilvia Váradi, Dr. Kertészné, and Dr. Zsolt Nagy, whose unwavering support and valuable insights have been instrumental in shaping my academic path. A special note of thanks to Prof. Dr. Hajdu József for his invaluable contributions and guidance throughout my Ph.D. studies.

I would also like to extend my appreciation to my thesis reviewers, Dr. Julien Rossi and Dr. Dániel Eszteri, whose constructive feedback and deep expertise significantly enhanced the quality and readiness of my research.

On a more personal note, I wish to express my sincere gratitude to my beloved family. Without the spiritual and material support of my dear late father, may he rest in peace, I would not have had the opportunity to pursue this research. My mother's constant support has been a pillar of strength throughout this journey, and I am forever grateful for her.

I am thankful to my brother, whose encouragement sustained me during moments of doubt and exhaustion. To my husband, whose exceptional qualities of compassion, empathy, and unwavering support have been a source of constant inspiration. His love and belief in me have been invaluable as I navigated the challenges of researching and composing this book.

I would also like to extend my gratitude to my parents-in-law and my brother-in-law for their encouragement and support throughout this journey. Their kindness and belief in me have meant so much, and I am appreciative of their presence in my life.

To my cherished family: *İyi ki varsınız, canım ailem.* Your faith in me has been the cornerstone of my perseverance and success.

Finally, I am also grateful for my dear friends who have always provided me with encouragement through times of adversity and have also been there to celebrate my accomplishments.

Aslı Alkış Tümtürk

Competing Interests The author has no competing interests to declare that are relevant to the content of this manuscript.

Contents

Abbreviations

AI	Artificial Intelligence
APPI	Act on the Protection of Personal Information (Japan's Data Protection Law)
BCRs	Binding Corporate Rules
BIPA	Biometric Information Privacy Act
BND	Bundesnachrichtendienst
CA	Court of Appeal
CCPA	California Consumer Privacy Act
CDC	Centres for Disease Control and Prevention
CFR	Charter of Fundamental Rights of the European Union
CJEU	European Court of Justice
CLPO	Civil Liberties Protection Officer in the Office of the Director of National Intelligence
COPPA	Children's Online Privacy Protection Act
DPA	Data Protection Authority
DPF	Data Privacy Framework
DPIA	Data Protection Impact Assessment
DPRC	Data Protection Review Courts
ECHR	European Convention on Human Rights
ECtHR	European Court of Human Rights
EDPB	European Data Protection Board
EDPS	European Data Protection Supervisor
eID	European Digital Identities
EPRS	European Parliamentary Research Service
EU	European Union
GDPR	General Data Protection Regulation
FERPA	Family Educational Rights and Privacy Act
FRA	European Union Agency for Fundamental Rights
FTC	Federal Trade Commission
HIPPA	the Health Insurance Portability and Accountability Act
ISS	Information Society Services

ITA	International Trade Administration
ML	Machine Learning
NAIH	Nemzeti Adatvédelmi és Információszabadság Hatóság (Hungarian Data Protection Authority)
NCMEC	National Centre for Missing and Exploited Children
NSA	National Security Agency
PIA	Privacy Impact Assessment
SCCs	Standard Contractual Clauses
TCPA	Telephone Consumer Protection Act
UK	United Kingdom
UNCRC	United Nations Convention on the Rights of the Child
US	United States
WP12	Article 29 Data Protection Working Party: Working Document. Transfers of Personal Data to Third Countries: Applying Articles 25 and 26 of the EU Data Protection Directive
WP29	Article 29 Data Protection Working Party
WP254	Article 29 Data Protection Working Party: Working Document on Adequacy Referential

Chapter 1
Introduction

Abstract This research compares the General Data Protection Regulation (GDPR) and Children's Online Privacy Protection Act (COPPA) and their practices regarding children's online data protection and privacy in the European Union (EU) and the United States (US) in several areas. It starts with investigating the historical and legal basis of both regimes, their interplay, and the impact on the regulation of children's personal data in online contexts. Afterwards, it assesses the effectiveness of parental consent concepts and requirements in both legislations, the efficacy of age thresholds for granting consent and age-verification methods and overall age assurance mechanism. Additionally, it considers whether children's privacy rights should be exercised directly or through parental mediation. Subsequently, data controllers' responsibilities when processing children's personal data will be explored. It examines the gap between textual legal requirements and their practical implementation, using real-world examples and civil and criminal case law. The research, using comparative legal analysis and investigating multidisciplinary perspectives, questions if the strong reliance on parental consent effectively protects children's privacy. It aims to propose and promote more child-centred and efficient regulatory and enforcement approaches that prioritises the best interest of the children. In the final chapter, the research analyzes recent developments and emerging challenges, highlighting the need to shift primary responsibility for providing children with a safe online environment from parental supervision to privacy and security-focused design and system architecture. This approach is supported by real-world examples, industry practices, and legal cases stemming from rapid advancements in AI-related technologies.

The concept of privacy has a rich historical foundation, dating back to Code of Hammurabi, ancient Greek and Roman laws when the sanctity of the household was highly regarded.[1] This notion that one's home is a private and safeguarded area remains a fundamental component of contemporary privacy discourse.[2]

---

[1] Dash (2004, p. 9).

[2] Charter of Fundamental Rights of the European Union, OJ C 326, 26.12.2012, pp. 391–407, Article 7: "Everyone has the right to respect for his or her private and family life, home and communications."

A. Alkış Tümtürk, *Online Privacy and Data Protection of Children in the European Union and the United States*, Ius Gentium: Comparative Perspectives on Law and Justice 141, https://doi.org/10.1007/978-3-032-27534-9_1

Despite the widespread acknowledgement of privacy rights both historically and currently, privacy does not have a universally agreed-upon definition. Its definition is dynamic, adapting to the changing social, cultural, and economic circumstances of various regions and eras. However, the primary approaches to privacy in the European Union (EU) and the United States (US) can be comprehended by examining a variety of prominent definitions.

The idea of the "right to be let alone" proposed by Louis Brandeis and Samuel Warren in 1890 is largely seen as a crucial milestone in the evolution of the modern understanding of privacy.[3] Moreover, the law professor Alen Westin made a valuable contribution to the idea that individuals should have the freedom to decide both the content and the amount of information they share with others.[4] These specifications affected privacy law in the US, and as a result, privacy has frequently been viewed as a component of liberty, the right to be free from governmental intrusions in the US.[5]

Following the aforementioned developments in the US, the EU created a new sort of protection. In the EU's approach to privacy, in addition to the right to be let alone, the right to private life, right to be autonomous, and have a control over one's own information play a crucial role.[6] The data protection stemming from the right to privacy covers specifically any information belonging to an identified or identifiable natural person in the EU.[7] As technology and the Internet improved, the EU data

---

European Convention for the Protection of Human Rights and Fundamental Freedoms, as amended by Protocols Nos. 11 and 14, 4 November 1950, ETS 5, Article 8(1): "Everyone has the right to respect for his private and family life, his home and his correspondence".

U.S. Const. amend. IV.: "The right of the people to be secure in their persons, houses, papers, and effects, against unreasonable searches and seizures, shall not be violated, and no Warrants shall issue, but upon probable cause, supported by Oath or affirmation, and particularly describing the place to be searched, and the persons or things to be seized."

U.S. Const. amend. XIV section 1.1: "All persons born or naturalized in the United States, and subject to the jurisdiction thereof, are citizens of the United States and of the State wherein they reside. No State shall make or enforce any law which shall abridge the privileges or immunities of citizens of the United States; nor shall any State deprive any person of life, liberty, or property, without due process of law; nor deny to any person within its jurisdiction the equal protection of the laws."

[3] Warren and Brandeis (1890, p. 205).

[4] Westin (1967, p. 7).

[5] U.S. Const. amend. IV.

[6] CFR, Article 7.

ECHR, Article 8(1).

Regulation (EU) 2016/679 of the European Parliament and of the Council of 27 April 2016 on the protection of natural persons with regard to the processing of personal data and on the free movement of such data, and repealing Directive 95/46/EC (General Data Protection Regulation), OJ 2016 L 119, 04.05.2016, pp. 1–88, Recital 7: "[…] Natural persons should have control of their own personal data.[…]" and Article 12-23 (Right of the data subject).

[7] GDPR, Article 4(1): "'personal data' means any information relating to an identified or identifiable natural person ('data subject'); an identifiable natural person is one who can be identified, directly or indirectly, in particular by reference to an identifier such as a name, an identification number,

subjects who provide their personal data became more aware of the limited control over their personal data.[8]

Although the data-driven society raises numerous concerns, this research concentrates on a critical and specific aspect of these issues: the privacy and data protection of children in the digital age. The online presence of children has increased significantly due to the spread of social media platforms and various digital tools, rendering them especially vulnerable to privacy risks.

We have observed that one in three internet users worldwide are children[9] and that 80% of children in developed Western countries have digital footprints before the age of two, largely due to the actions of their families.[10] Lawmakers may not be sufficiently prioritising this problem, perhaps because they prioritise economically more attractive issues, such as data transfers and profiling,[11] over protecting vulnerable data subjects who would not contribute as much to the Digital Single Market economically.[12] Similarly, websites, particularly social media networks, ignore the existence of children on their platforms and turn a blind eye to the fact that children under the age of consent are utilising their services.[13]

The General Data Protection Regulation (GDPR) of the European Union[14] and the Children's Online Privacy Protection Act (COPPA) of the US[15] took vital measures since, rather than disregarding the internet presence of children, they

location data, an online identifier or to one or more factors specific to the physical, physiological, genetic, mental, economic, cultural or social identity of that natural person".

[8] Custers et al. (2019, p. 1).

[9] UNICEF, More than 175,000 children go online for the first time every day, tapping into great opportunities, but facing grave risks (6 February 2018), https://www.unicef.org/press-releases/more-175000-children-go-online-first-time-every-day-tapping-great-opportunities.

[10] United Nations, Children's right to privacy in the digital age must be improved (15 July 2021) https://www.ohchr.org/en/stories/2021/07/childrens-right-privacy-digital-age-must-be-improved.

[11] GDPR defines profiling as follows: "[...] any form of automated processing of personal data consisting of the use of personal data to evaluate certain personal aspects relating to a natural person, in particular to analyse or predict aspects concerning that natural person's performance at work, economic situation, health, personal preferences, interests, reliability, behaviour, location or movements".

GDPR, Article 4(4).

[12] Macenaite and Kosta (2017, p. 160).

[13] Auxier et al. (2020) Children's engagement with digital devices, screen time. Pew Research Center, p. 2. https://www.pewresearch.org/internet/2020/07/28/childrens-engagement-with-digital-devices-screen-time/.

[14] Regulation (EU) 2016/679 of the European Parliament and of the Council of 27 April 2016 on the protection of natural persons with regard to the processing of personal data and on the free movement of such data, and repealing Directive 95/46/EC (General Data Protection Regulation), OJ 2016 L 119, 04.05.2016, pp. 1–88.

[15] 16 CFR Part 312 Children's Online Privacy Protection Act; Final Rule, 15 U.S.C. §§ 6501–6506, Federal Register Vol. 64, No. 212, 03.11.1999, pp. 59888–59915.

created provisions mentioning them.[16] However, they both rely on parental responsibility regarding protecting children's online safety. In situations when parents lack awareness regarding the potential hazards and repercussions associated with their children's online activities, depending only on parental accountability may exacerbate the well-being concerns regarding children. Besides, these requirements are not comprehensive. For instance, neither the GDPR nor the COPPA impose any restrictions with respect to parental sharing. The difference between the legal text and its application in practice is another issue we have identified, which will be further examined in the subsequent chapters.

In this research, we intend to compare the COPPA and the GDPR and their practices regarding children's online data protection and privacy in the EU and the US in a number of areas. The comparison is justified given that the US was among the first jurisdictions to enact targeted federal legislation addressing children's online privacy through COPPA and Article 8 of the GDPR partially adopted the COPPA's approach to children's data protection. It is evident that the two legislations share similarities since, both the GDPR, and the COPPA hold parents/legal guardians[17] accountable for their children's online actions and require parental consent for sharing children's personal data online. Additionally, they implement a similar age of digital consent for children.[18] There are also some conceptual differences, for example, the term "personal information" is employed by COPPA, instead of "personal data" used in GDPR. Although the concepts are similar, the GDPR adopts a broader and more open-ended definition. Personal information is determined by an enumerated and closed list of identifiers under COPPA.[19] However, the scope can be slightly expanded;

---

[16] 16 CFR Part 312 Children's Online Privacy Protection Act; Final Rule, 15 U.S.C. §§ 6501–6506, Federal Register Vol. 64, No. 212, 03.11.1999, pp. 59888–59915 and Regulation (EU) 2016/679 of the European Parliament and of the Council of 27 April 2016 on the protection of natural persons with regard to the processing of personal data and on the free movement of such data, and repealing Directive 95/46/EC (General Data Protection Regulation), OJ 2016 L 119, 04.05.2016, pp. 1–88, Article 8.

[17] GDPR employs the phrase "the holder of parental responsibility over the child." In this study, the word "parent" will be employed henceforth, as it represents the usual scenario. Nevertheless, it is important to note that any of these terms might be substituted with the phrase "legal guardians or holders of parental responsibility."

[18] GDPR, Article 8 and 16 CFR 312.2 "Child".

[19] 16 CFR 312.2 "Personal information": "means individually identifiable information about an individual collected online, including:

(1) A first and last name;

(2) A home or other physical address including street name and name of a city or town;

(3) Online contact information as defined in this section;

(4) A screen or user name where it functions in the same manner as online contact information, as defined in this section;

(5) A telephone number;

(6) A government-issued identifier, such as a Social Security, State identification card, birth certificate, or passport number;

(7) A persistent identifier that can be used to recognize a user over time and across different websites or online services. Such persistent identifier includes, but is not limited to, a customer

for example, information obtained about a child (such as hobbies, interests, or preferences) may also be considered personal information if combined with a unique identifier from the list.[20] By making these comparisons, we will attempt to highlight both the weaknesses and strengths, and in doing so, we will provide remedies for the flaws and seek the ideal solutions.

The research begins by examining the historical and legal developments that led to the creation of the COPPA and Article 8 of the GDPR, assessing the reciprocal impact of these frameworks and their prospective influences moving forward. It then explores the scope of the parental consent mechanism and whether the threshold ages for parental consent set under both regulations are reasonable and effective in practice. This debate leads us to investigate whether it is possible to strike a balance between reliability and respect for children's privacy in age verification methods. The research will also focus on whether privacy rights should be exercised directly by children or remain the responsibility of parents. In addition, the research evaluates whether the GDPR and the COPPA adequately address the legal responsibilities of data controllers when processing children's data, and explores how data controllers can interact with children in a way that respects both their privacy and their developmental needs. It also explores the impact of the GDPR and the COPPA on the policies of online service providers and parental sharing practices of social media platforms.

Finally, with the help of these findings the overarching question will be addressed: Does an excessive reliance on parental consent and accountability effectively protect the personal data and privacy of children? This research aims to evaluate, through comparative legal analysis, literature review and examination of practical application, the effectiveness of the parental consent mechanism and whether it necessitates reconsideration. It will also examine who is primarily responsible for the processing of children's data by AI-related technologies. Besides, it offers practical suggestions for enhancing the balance between protecting children and facilitating their secure participation in the online environment. It will also incorporate numerous legal cases from civil law and criminal law and multidisciplinary perspectives, including sociological research, surveys, and real-world examples, to enhance its conclusions.

Our long-term goal is to promote and encourage legal reforms, including more stringent regulations on AI systems that process children's data. Therefore, we expect

---

number held in a cookie, an Internet Protocol (IP) address, a processor or device serial number, or unique device identifier;

(8) A photograph, video, or audio file where such file contains a child's image or voice;

(9) Geolocation information sufficient to identify street name and name of a city or town;

(10) A biometric identifier that can be used for the automated or semi-automated recognition of an individual, such as fingerprints; handprints; retina patterns; iris patterns; genetic data, including a DNA sequence; voiceprints; gait patterns; facial templates; or faceprints; or

(11) Information concerning the child or the parents of that child that the operator collects online from the child and combines with an identifier described in this definition."

[20] 16 CFR 312.2 "Personal information": "[...] Information concerning the child or the parents of that child that the operator collects online from the child and combines with an identifier described in this definition."

that our research will help to the future creation of more child-friendly and child-centred policies, as well as more child-friendly social media rules and restrictions. In addition, we will emphasise that these laws and restrictions must always be implemented and enforced with the best interests of children in mind.

References

Auxier B, Anderson M, Perrin A, Turner E (2020) Children's engagement with digital devices, screen time. Pew Research Center, p 2. https://www.pewresearch.org/internet/2020/07/28/childrens-engagement-with-digital-devices-screen-time/

Custers B, Sears AM, Dechesne F, Georgieva I, Tani T, Van der Hof S (2019) EU personal data protection in policy and practice, vol 29. TMC Asser Press, Springer, The Hague, pp 1–249

Dash S (2004) The intruders: Unreasonable searches and seizures from King John to John Ashcroft. Rutgers University Press, New Brunswick, p 9

Macenaite M, Kosta E (2017) Consent for processing children's personal data in the EU: following in US footsteps? Inf Commun Technol Law 26(2):146–197

Warren SD, Brandeis LD (1890) Right to privacy. Harv Law Rev 4(5):193–220

Westin AF (1967) Privacy and freedom. Atheneum, New York, p 7

Chapter 2
The Historical Context and Background of the GDPR Article 8 and the COPPA

Abstract In this chapter, we examine the history of privacy and data protection in the US and the EU, as well as how the concepts of privacy and data protection have developed through time due to economic and social changes. Later, we argue that technological advances and computer innovations gave rise to a new right, data protection, which was derived from the protection of private life. We explain the background of the GDPR and the COPPA and we conclude the Chapter 2 by mentioning the parts that should be improved, such as the consent age threshold (which should be uniform and well-justified across all EU Member States) and the introduction of effective and innovative methods for obtaining parental consent (some of the methods for verifying parental consent of the COPPA might be transplanted into the GDPR Article 8) as well as methods for verifying children's age when accessing websites, particularly websites that contain age-restricted content. This chapter contributes to the literature by providing a deductive comparison of the historical roots of the COPPA and Article 8 of the GDPR.

Even though privacy became a widely recognised right in the nineteenth and twentieth centuries, its origins date back much further. In the *Code of Hammurabi*, for instance, domestic life was protected against invasions and the protection of the house is strongly supported by religion at the time. The concept that the house is sacred was also prevalent in ancient Greece and Roman law.[1]

The distinction between the private and public gives birth to the notion of privacy. This separation essentially stems from his/her goods versus theirs and himself/herself versus the others. Nevertheless, the concept and understanding of privacy evolve with time.[2] In the Roman era, even though the house was a private area, there were no toilets within the homes. One or two out of every five people may have had toilets at home, but the majority used the public toilets, where seats are adjacent to one another and there are no signs of dividers between the seats.[3] Researchers have questions

[1] Dash (2004, p. 9).

[2] Lukács (2016, p. 257).

[3] Wald (2016, p. 457).

A. Alkış Tümtürk, *Online Privacy and Data Protection of Children in the European Union and the United States*, Ius Gentium: Comparative Perspectives on Law and Justice 141, https://doi.org/10.1007/978-3-032-27534-9_2

such as whether or not public restrooms were socializing places where people sat half-naked close to one another, had a chat and made friends which is quite the contrary of the modern sense of privacy.[4]

We may infer that as society and the economy evolve, so does the concept of privacy. As a result of the economic and social changes of the nineteenth century and urbanisation, for instance, people began to live in crowded cities, resulting in a loss of physical space and privacy. Notwithstanding, in contrast to the village life, they were able to experience a new type of mental privacy and freedom, in the sense that who they were living with, where they were working, and what they were doing were no longer concerns of their neighbours. The development of newspapers and photo-journalism, however, has resulted in the emergence of a new form of surveillance, which has a particularly negative impact on famous persons and families.[5]

In 1890, one of the most famous law review articles titled "Right to Privacy",[6] was written by *Samuel Warren* and *Louis Brandeis* in response to these sociological and technological advancements and new forms of privacy loss. The article describes how the press disregards and violates the boundaries of individuals' private lives, and how these violations of privacy impair the well-being of individuals.[7]

It is widely accepted that Warren's dislike of Boston's print media in general and his perception of its invasion of social privacy inspired this article and with Brandeis's sophisticated contribution resulted in a landmark paper. The idea of developing this article, the article's poignant focus on human sensitivities, and its definition of privacy as the "right to be let alone" all contributed to the establishment of the modern fundamental right to privacy.[8]

The introduction of personal computers during the 1970s[9] prompted inquiries into the adequacy of the right to privacy in protecting private life.[10] Consequently, advancements in technology led to the emergence of a new right known as the right to data protection, which also encompasses the protection of private life.[11]

Consequently, Alan Westin's publication titled *Privacy and Freedom* in 1967 contributed to define the global field of privacy and data protection as he asserts that privacy grants individuals the right to determine the content, manner and extent of the information they share with others.[12] Privacy and Freedom became the reference book for the upcoming informational privacy, and it was believed that this article was the first which examined the coming issues regarding data privacy and data protection.[13]

---

[4] Wald (2016, p. 458).

[5] Lukács (2016, p. 257).

[6] Warren and Brandeis (1890, pp. 193–220).

[7] Warren and Brandeis (1890, p. 196).

[8] Bratman (2002, p. 629), Barron (1979, p. 876), Palmer (2011, p. 71).

[9] Ceruzzi (1996, pp. 1–31).

[10] Lukács (2016, p. 259).

[11] Lukács (2016, p. 259).

[12] Westin (1967, pp. 1–487).

[13] Clearwater and Hughes (2013, p. 899).

The aforementioned improvements to the right to privacy and data protection first arise in the US, followed by the EU, which developed a new type of protection.[14] Hence, a comparative analysis of these two jurisdictions on each side of the Atlantic will be conducted in this research, with a focus on their respective historical developments as a starting point for enhanced clarity and understanding.

Privacy rights first appeared in common law torts in the US, where criminal and civil remedies existed for the exploitation of an individual's personal name and image for advertising purposes. It initially appears in a New York legislation classifying the use of the name, portrait, or image of any person for "advertising purposes or for the purposes of trade" without obtaining their written consent as both a misdemeanour and a tort.[15] In the amended version of this statute, it is still stated, without omitting the children's privacy rights, as follows:

> "A person, firm, or corporation that uses the name, portrait, or picture of a living person for advertising or commercial purposes without first obtaining the written consent of that person, or if a minor, of his or her parent or guardian, is guilty of a misdemeanour."[16]

Afterwards, in Griswold v. Connecticut, the Supreme Court has recognised privacy rights as constitutional rights. A Connecticut statute prohibited the use of any substance or medication to prevent conception. Therefore, the plaintiffs in that case argued that the enacted Connecticut statute violated the Fourteenth Amendment. The ruling was sustained by an intermediate court of appeal and the state's highest court. The Fourteenth Amendment states that "[…] No State shall make or enforce any law which shall abridge the privileges or immunities of citizens of the United States […]"[17] the Supreme Court ruled that the Connecticut law in question violated the fundamental right to privacy surrounding marriage and for the first time recognised marital privacy as a constitutional right.[18]

As previously noted, the increasing use of computers and technological developments have resulted in the establishment of a new right known as the right to data protection, and individuals are most concerned about the government's power to access, use, analyse, and store personal information. In response to these concerns, the United States Congress adopted the Privacy Act of 1974.[19] The Privacy Act of

---

[14] Szabó (2005, p. 44).

[15] N.Y. Sess. Laws 1903, ch. 132, §§ 1–2, amended by N.Y. Civ. Rights Law, §§ 50–51 (McKinney 1909) cited in Keeton et al. (1984, pp. 850–851).

[16] N.Y. Civ. Rights Law, §§ 50 (McKinney 1909).

[17] U.S. Const. amend. XIV Sect. 1.1: "All persons born or naturalized in the United States, and subject to the jurisdiction thereof, are citizens of the United States and of the State wherein they reside. No State shall make or enforce any law which shall abridge the privileges or immunities of citizens of the United States; nor shall any State deprive any person of life, liberty, or property, without due process of law; nor deny to any person within its jurisdiction the equal protection of the laws."

[18] Griswold v. State of Connecticut, 381 U.S. 479 (1965) 484–86. https://tile.loc.gov/storage-services/service/ll/usrep/usrep381/usrep381479/usrep381479.pdf. See also: Hong (2005, pp. 76–77) and Talley (2019, p. 143).

[19] Privacy Act of 1974, Pub. L. No. 93–579, 88 Stat. 1896, as amended 5 U.S.C.§ 552a. See also: Talley (2019, p. 143).

1974 aims to restrict government violations of citizens' personal information while maintaining the government's legitimate efficiency goals. This statute prohibits the collection, use, and storage of personally identifiable information without the individual's consent. There are, however, numerous government-beneficial exceptions to this restriction.[20]

However, the Privacy Act of 1974 is not the same as the GDPR, the EU's overarching regulation, because it only applies to the processing of personal information by the federal government. Therefore, after the Privacy Act of 1974, several laws targeting different sectors and data subject groups were enacted, including the Health Insurance Portability and Accountability Act (HIPPA),[21] the Family Educational Rights and Privacy Act (FERPA),[22] Telephone Consumer Protection Act of 1991 (TCPA)[23] and most significantly for our research, the Children's Online Privacy and Protection Act (COPPA).[24,25]

In May 1996, a consumer watchdog group known as the Centre for Media Education filed a complaint with the FTC regarding the KidsCom.com (KidsCom) conduct because the KidsCom acquired children's information without correctly disclosing the purpose of collection. Moreover, KidsCom sold the collected personal information such as name, email address, home address or phone numbers of children to third parties without giving the adequate notice to the parents and providing them with the opportunity to control over their children's personal information.[26]

In 1997, the FTC investigated and published its findings in a letter that involves several principles. They suggested that those principles should apply generally to the collection of personal information from children online. In this letter, the FTC staff argued that KidsCom's information gathering practises violated Section 5 of the Federal Trade Commission Act[27] due to its practices were deceptive or unfair. Furthermore, this letter states that parental approval should be obtained before disclosing children's information to any third party.[28]

For the first time, the FTC announced its criteria for collecting personal information from children in this letter.[29] Following these developments, the FTC delivered

---

[20] 5 U.S.C.§ 552a(b)-(f). For detailed Overview of the Privacy Act of 1974: Hong (2005, pp. 81–85).

[21] Health Insurance Portability and Accountability Act. Pub. L. No. 104–191, 110 Stat.1936 (1996).

[22] Family Educational Rights and Privacy Act of 1974, 20 U.S.C. § 1232 g (1974).

[23] Telephone Consumer Protection Act of 1991, 47 U.S. Code § 227 (1991).

[24] 16 CFR Part 312 Children's Online Privacy Protection Act; Final Rule, 15 U.S.C. §§ 6501–6506, Federal Register Vol. 64, No. 212, 03.11.1999, pp. 59,888–59,915.

[25] Hall (2018, p. 132) cited in Talley (2019, pp. 143–144).

[26] Warmund (2000, pp. 192–193).

[27] 15 U.S.C. § 45(a)(1) (1994): "Unfair methods of competition in or affecting commerce, and unfair or deceptive acts or practices in or affecting commerce, are hereby declared unlawful."

[28] Federal Trade Commission, FTC Staff Sets Forth Principles For Online Information Collection From Children, July 1997, https://www.ftc.gov/news-events/news/press-releases/1997/07/ftc-staff-sets-forth-principles-online-information-collection-children.

[29] Warmund (2000, p. 193).

its Privacy Online Report to Congress in 1998 concerning the online collection of children's personal information.[30]

In light of the survey results in this report, the FTC informed Congress of the necessity for parental consent while collecting children's personal information. This report suggests that consent from parents should be obtained for the collecting of personal information from children aged 12 and younger due to their vulnerability to overreaching by the marketers.[31] In reaction to this report, Congress established the COPPA,[32] the first federal law protecting children's online privacy, in 1998.[33] Recognising the analysis of the report, Congress decided that the act's provisions would only apply to children under the age of 13.[34]

In the meantime, following advancements in the right to privacy in the US, two critical international treaties developed at the regional level in Europe: The European Convention on Human Rights (ECHR) was established by the Council of Europe in 1950,[35] and the Charter of Fundamental Rights of the European Union was officially declared by the European Parliament, the European Council, and the European Commission in 2000.[36]

Yet, before delving into those international treaties, we shall note the world's first data protection law, the *Hessisches Datenschutzgesetz* of 1970.[37] This law was enacted by the German federal state of Hesse in order to protect personal information stored in public bodies' files. However, the right to private and family life provided by Article 8 of the ECHR was not included in the *Hessisches Datenschutzgesetz*.[38]

According to Article 8 of the ECHR, "Everyone has the right to respect for his private and family life, his home and his correspondence."[39] Later the same right

---

30 Federal Trade Commission, Privacy Online: A report to Congress, June 1998, https://www.ftc.gov/sites/default/files/documents/reports/privacy-online-report-congress/priv-23a.pdf.

31 Federal Trade Commission, Privacy Online: A report to Congress, June 1998, 42 https://www.ftc.gov/sites/default/files/documents/reports/privacy-online-report-congress/priv-23a.pdf.

32 16 CFR Part 312 Children's Online Privacy Protection Act; Final Rule, 15 U.S.C. §§ 6501–6506, Federal Register Vol. 64, No. 212, 03.11.1999, pp. 59,888–59,915.

33 Warmund (2000, p. 194).

34 Federal Trade Commission, Complying with COPPA: Frequently Asked Questions, Q9. Why does COPPA apply only to children under 13? What about protecting the online privacy of teens?, https://www.ftc.gov/business-guidance/resources/complying-coppa-frequently-asked-questions#A.%20General%20Questions.

35 Council of Europe, European Convention for the Protection of Human Rights and Fundamental Freedoms, as amended by Protocols Nos. 11 and 14, 4 November 1950, ETS 5, https://www.echr.coe.int/documents/convention_eng.pdf.

36 Charter of Fundamental Rights of The European Union, OJ C 364, 18.12.2000, pp. 1–22. It became legally binding as EU primary law with the Lisbon Treaty(*) in 1 January 2009.

(*) Treaty of Lisbon, Amending the Treaty on European Union and the Treaty establishing the European Community, OJ C 306, 17.12.2007, pp. 1–271.

37 Hessisches Datenschutzgesetz of 7 October 1970, Gesetz- und Verordnungsblatt für das Land Hessen Teil I, No. 41, 625 of 12 October 1970.

38 Naef (2023, p. 21).

39 Council of Europe, European Convention for the Protection of Human Rights and Fundamental Freedoms, as amended by Protocols Nos. 11 and 14, 4 November 1950, ETS 5, Article 8(1).

appeared in the CFR almost identically as "Everyone has the right to respect for his or her private and family life, home and communications".[40]

However, because these articles are not very thorough and do not define what is privacy or how it should be legally guaranteed, the decisions of European Court of Human Rights (ECtHR) could offer these answers.[41]

Nonetheless, the ECtHR has stated in its case law that there is no exhaustive concept of privacy since the ECHR's reach is so expansive and technological progress necessitates constant changes to the terms and definitions of privacy.[42] Even though the list is not exhaustive, we may still enumerate some of the examples that the European Court of Human Rights has deemed to be an intrusion of private life under Article 8 of ECHR, such as the protection of personal data,[43] wiretapping,[44] sexual life,[45] profession or domicile,[46] and the protection against the environmental nuisances (e.g., noise nuisance).[47] It is ideal to develop a flexible approach to privacy since, as stated previously, the concept of privacy is changing as technology improves and society evolves.[48]

Case law from the European Court of Human Rights (ECtHR) had a significant effect on the European Union's Court of Justice (CJEU). This significant effect can be explained in a few ways: as we mentioned above, Article 7 of the CFR is substantially identical to Article 8 of the European Convention on Human Rights.[49] Besides, according to Article 52 of the CFR, the extent and meaning of the rights

---

[40] Charter of Fundamental Rights of The European Union, OJ C 364, 18.12.2000, pp. 1–22, Article 7.

[41] Gellert and Gutwirth (2013, p. 524).

[42] Niemietz v. Germany judgment on 16 December 1992, no. 13710/88 para. 29: "The Court does not consider it possible or necessary to attempt an exhaustive definition of the notion of "private life"[...]".

[43] Leander v. Sweden judgment of 26 March 1987, no. 9248/81 para. 46–48.

[44] Klass and Others v. Germany judgment on 6 September 1978, no. 5029/71 para. 41.

[45] Dudgeon v. the United Kingdom judgment on 22 October 1981, no. 7525/76 para. 40–41.

[46] Niemietz v. Germany judgment on 16 December 1992, no. 13710/88 par. 28–33.

[47] Powell and Rayner v. the United Kingdom judgment of 21 February 1990, no. 9310/81, para. 41.

[48] For further information regarding the cases and the interpretation: Lukács (2016, p. 260) and Gellert and Gutwirth (2013, pp. 524–527).

[49] Case C-450/06 Varec [2008] ECR I-581, EU:C:2008:91, para. 48: "One of the fundamental rights capable of being protected in this way is the right to respect for private life, enshrined in Article 8 of the ECHR, which flows from the common constitutional traditions of the Member States and which is restated in Article 7 of the Charter of fundamental rights of the European Union, proclaimed in Nice on 7 December 2000 (OJ 2000 C 364, p. 1) (see, in particular, Case C-62/90 Commission v Germany [1992] ECR I-2575, paragraph 23, and Case C-404/92 P X v Commission [1994] ECR I-4737, paragraph 17). It follows from the case-law of the European Court of Human Rights that the notion of 'private life' cannot be taken to mean that the professional or commercial activities of either natural or legal persons are excluded (see Niemietz v Germany, judgment of 16 December 1992, Series A No 251-B, §29; Société Colas Est and Others v France, No 37971/97, §41, ECHR 2002-III; and also Peck v The United Kingdom No 44647/98, §57, ECHR 2003-I). Those activities can include participation in a contract award procedure."

included in the CFR that were inspired by the ECHR are the same as those secured by the ECHR:

> "[...] In so far as this Charter contains rights which correspond to rights guaranteed by the Convention for the Protection of Human Rights and Fundamental Freedoms, the meaning and scope of those rights shall be the same as those laid down by the said Convention. This provision shall not prevent Union law providing more extensive protection."[50]

As technology improved and the impacts of the digitisation became abundantly apparent, the EU acknowledged the need for data protection.[51] Although the right to data protection derives from the right to privacy, it is more specific in ensuring the fair collection, use, and storage of personal information by both the private and public sectors. Data protection encompasses all personally identifiable information, including names, birth dates, photographs, videos, postal addresses, email addresses, telephone numbers, and biometric data (e.g., fingerprints). IP addresses, cookies, and location data are also considered personal information, as they enable the identification of individuals through their devices.[52] The concept of data protection is not limited to privacy; it also safeguards individuals through their personal data, even if it is not a violation of privacy but a violation of other fundamental rights, such as when the data subject is threatened with discrimination.[53]

Besides the right to respect for private and family life (Article 7),[54] the CFR recognises the right to the protection of personal data (Article 8)[55] and the related core concepts. It specifies that the processing must be lawful, fair, and limited to the stated purposes (either consent or other legitimate interests laid down by the law). Moreover, Article 8 of the CFR provides that individuals have the right to access and rectify their personal data.[56] The CFR elevates the right to data protection to the status of a fundamental right under EU law. Article 8 of the CFR, which was drafted

---

[50] CFR, Article 52(3).

[51] Pearce and Platten (1998, p. 531).

[52] Article 29 Data Protection Working Party, Opinion 4/2007 on the concept of personal data, 01,248/07/EN.

WP 136, Adopted on 20th June 2007, pp. 1–26.

[53] CFR, Article 21: "1. Any discrimination based on any ground such as sex, race, colour, ethnic or social origin, genetic features, language, religion or belief, political or any other opinion, membership of a national minority, property, birth, disability, age or sexual orientation shall be prohibited. 2. Within the scope of application of the Treaties and without prejudice to any of their specific provisions, any discrimination on grounds of nationality shall be prohibited."

ECHR, Article 14: "The enjoyment of the rights and freedoms set forth in this Convention shall be secured without discrimination on any ground such as sex, race, colour, language, religion, political or other opinion, national or social origin, association with a national minority, property, birth or other status."

See also: Raphael Gellert and Serge Gutwirth: The legal construction of privacy and data protection, Computer Law & Security Review 29, no. 5 (2013), 526.

[54] CFR, Article 7.

[55] CFR, Article 8.

[56] CFR, Article 8(2).

some years after Convention 108 and the Directive 95/46/EC,[57] shall be interpreted as a continuation of pre-existing EU data protection legislation.[58]

Initially, ECtHR case law issued data protection within Article 8 of the ECHR,[59] but in 1981, the Council of Europe established the Convention for the Protection of Individuals with regard to Automatic Processing of Personal Data (Convention 108). Convention 108 was the first international treaty with legal force in the field of data protection. Under the terms of this convention, the parties have agreed to alter their domestic legislation to conform to the requirements and principles, and they will guarantee that the fundamental rights of all individuals relating to the processing of personal data are protected by their domestic laws.[60]

With Convention 108, the Council of Europe was successful in raising the concept of data protection and defining the main principles of data protection; however, it was not successful in harmonising the legal framework across the Member States, as the entry into force dates were not consistent.[61] Besides, the Member States' data protection approach was not uniformed. In terms of data protection, some Member States had very strict legislation while others had almost none at all.[62]

The EU's Member States also had different data protection standards, which had restricted free data flow within the EU and hindered trade among the Member States. The European Commission proposed an EC regulation in 1990 to address the need for data protection rules to be harmonised across Member States in order to create a fully united market.[63] However, due to the poor language and numerous inconsistencies in this first draft, the EC published an amended proposal to replace it in 1992.[64] Afterwards, in October 1995, the European Union's Directive 95/46/EC

---

[57] Directive 95/46/EC of the European Parliament and of the Council of 24 October 1995 on the protection of individuals with regard to the processing of personal data and on the free movement of such data, OJ L 281, 23.11.1995, pp. 31–50.

[58] European Union Agency for Fundamental Rights, Council of Europe, European Court of Human Rights, European Data Protection Supervisor: Handbook on European data protection law (2018), 28, https://www.echr.coe.int/Documents/Handbook_data_protection_ENG.pdf.

[59] Leander v. Sweden judgment of 26 March 1987, no. 9248/81 para. 46–48.

[60] Council of Europe, Convention for the Protection of Individuals with Regard to the Automatic Processing of Individual Data, 28.01.1981, ETS No. 108 amended as Council of Europe, Convention 108 + Convention for the protection of individuals with regard to the processing of personal data, ETS No. 108 (2018) https://www.coe.int/en/web/data-protection/convention108-and-protocol.

[61] Council of Europe, Chart of signatures and ratifications of Treaty 108, https://www.coe.int/en/web/conventions/full-list?module=signatures-by-treaty&treatynum=108.

[62] Mei (1993, p. 305).

[63] European Commission, Proposal for a Council Directive Concerning the Protection of Individuals in Relation to the Processing of Personal Data, COM(90) 314 final – SYN 287, OJ C 277/3, 5.11.1990, pp. 3–12.

[64] European Commission, Amended Proposal for a Council Directive on the Protection of Individuals with Regard to the Processing of Personal Data and on the Free Movement of Such Data, Preamble, COM(92) 422 final - SYN 287, OJ C 311/30, 27.11.1992, pp. 30–61.; See also: Mei (1993, p. 309).

was enacted[65] with the stated goal of harmonising data protection legislation at the national level within the European Union.[66]

Nevertheless, according to Article 288 of the Treaty on the Functioning of the European Union (TFEU), directives are not directly applicable in the Member States once they come into force at the Union level, since they need EU Member States to incorporate them into national law in order to accomplish the directive's intended results. As stated in the TFEU, directives are legally binding on Member States, but it is up to national authorities to choose the form and means of attaining the intended results.[67] In this regard, the European Court of Justice has concluded that directives do not have a direct effect on horizontal relations, even though the state can be held liable for failing to apply a rule that is clear precise, unconditional, and leaves no room for the Member State to exercise discretion.[68] Therefore, adopting the directives into domestic legislation does not result in completely uniform national laws across the Member States.

In the meantime, the technology had developed since the Directive 95/46/EC was adopted, as well as technological advancements such as cloud computing, personalised advertising, and social networking platforms, geo-location apps created several privacy and data protection challenges. In addition, because of globalisation, cross-border data flows and data processing have expanded. Besides, Article 16 of the

[65] "Member States shall bring into force the laws, regulations and administrative provisions necessary to comply with this Directive at the latest at the end of a period of three years from the date of its adoption."

Directive 95/46/EC of the European Parliament and of the Council of 24 October 1995 on the protection of individuals with regard to the processing of personal data and on the free movement of such data, OJ L 281, 23.11.1995, pp. 31–50, Article 32(1).

[66] Directive 95/46/EC of the European Parliament and of the Council of 24 October 1995 on the protection of individuals with regard to the processing of personal data and on the free movement of such data, OJ L 281, 23.11.1995, pp. 31–50, Article 1: "1. In accordance with this Directive, Member States shall protect the fundamental rights and freedoms of natural persons, and in particular their right to privacy with respect to the processing of personal data. 2. Member States shall neither restrict nor prohibit the free flow of personal data between Member States for reasons connected with the protection afforded under paragraph 1."

[67] Consolidated version of the Treaty on the Functioning of the European Union, OJ C 326, 26.10.2012, pp. 47–390, Article 288.

[68] "The Commission recalls the three tests which must be satisfied before a provision of a directive may have direct effect: (i) a clear and precise obligation, (ii) not accompanied by conditions, (iii) with no margin of discretion left to the Member State." Case 148/78, Pubblico Ministero v Ratti [1979] ECR 1629, EU:C:1979:110, p. 1636.

"[...] according to settled case-law, a directive cannot of itself impose obligations on an individual and cannot therefore be relied upon as such against an individual. It follows that even a clear, precise and unconditional provision of a directive seeking to confer rights or impose obligations on individuals cannot of itself apply in proceedings exclusively between private parties." Case C-80/06, Carp v. Electricité de France (EDF) [2007] ECR I-4473, EU:C:2007:327, para. 20 cited in Craig (2011, p. 335).

TFEU's[69] coming into effect ushered in a new era for data protection and established a sound legal foundation for a comprehensive data protection legislation in the EU.[70]

Accordingly, the European Data Protection Supervisor published an opinion on the European Commission's Communication in June 2011 regarding a need for "a comprehensive approach on personal data protection in the EU".[71] This need was met by enacting a regulation rather than a directive, which are legal actions that apply directly and entirely to all EU Member States as soon as they enter into force, without the need for transposition into national law.[72]

Following its adoption by the European Parliament and the Council of the European Union, the General Data Protection Regulation (GDPR) went into effect in 2016. As of May 25, 2018, compliance is required for any controller or processor that processes personal data and established in the EU, regardless of whether the processing occurs in the EU or not.[73] In addition, it applies if data subjects are in one of the Member States in the EU and the data controller or processor is based outside the EU, but the providing of goods and services to such data subjects in the EU or monitoring of their behaviour occurs within the EU.[74] Consequently, we may infer that the GDPR created a wide territorial scope.

Additionally, the GDPR strengthened data protection and privacy rights. At this moment, we only discuss a few of the most significant amendments, but in the following chapters, we will examine in depth the provisions relevant to our topic. For instance, data portability is a new right introduced by the GDPR.[75] Besides, the right to be forgotten, initially articulated by the CJEU,[76] is incorporated into the GDPR as a separate data subject right.[77] Moreover, the concept of consent is defined under the GDPR as:

> "any freely given, specific, informed and unambiguous indication of the data subject's wishes by which he or she, by a statement or by a clear affirmative action, signifies agreement to the processing of personal data relating to him or her".[78]

---

69 TFEU, Article 16.

70 TFEU, General Part, Context, para. 13–16.

71 European Data Protection Supervisor (EDPS), Opinion on the Communication from the Commission on "A comprehensive approach on personal data protection in the European Union", OJ C 181/01, 22.06.2011, p.1, https://edps.europa.eu/data-protection/our-work/publications/opinions/comprehensive-approach-personal-data-protection_en.

72 Consolidated version of the Treaty on the Functioning of the European Union, OJ C 326, 26.10.2012, pp. 47–390, Article 288.

73 GDPR, Article 3(1).

74 GDPR, Article 3(2).

75 GDPR, Article 20.

76 Case C-131/12 Google Spain SL and Google Inc. v Agencia Española de Protección de Datos (AEPD) and Mario Costeja González EU:C:2014:317 and Case C-507/17 Google LLC v Commission nationale de l'informatique et des libertés (CNIL) EU:C:2019:772.

77 GDPR, Article 17 and Recital 66.

78 GDPR, Article 4(11).

On one hand, the core concept of consent is quite similar to that of Directive 95/46/EC,[79] and it remains one of the lawful bases for processing personal data.[80] On the other hand, the GDPR gives further guidance on how the data controller should comply with the consent's main components (e.g., demonstrating the given consent, to ensure that consent is freely given and there is no imbalance of power between the data subject and the data controller).[81] It also includes instructions on how the data subject may exercise more control over their data, such as by withdrawing their consent at any time, which must be as simple as giving consent in the first place.[82]

Furthermore, fines for the GDPR violations increased to a maximum of €20 million, or 4% of the company's global turnover of the preceding financial year.[83] Likewise, the controller or processor shall compensate any individual who has suffered material or non-material harm as a direct result of the controller's or processor's violation of the GDPR.[84] Overall, the GDPR merged twenty-eight different data protection laws emanating from the Directive 95/46/EC into one single legislation that is stricter and more effective with enhanced data protection rights, concepts, and remedies in the case of a breach of the GDPR.[85]

There were no particular requirements for the protection of children's personal data in the Directive 95/46/EC. The GDPR, however, did not turn a blind eye to children's online activities and Article 8 of the GDPR provided special protection for the processing of children's personal data.[86] However, the history of Article 8 did not reveal well-reasoned and well-justified requirements, as the majority of debates focused on articles with direct economic impact (e.g., articles related to data transfers, profiling) rather than the vulnerable data subjects who will not contribute economically to the Digital Single Market.[87] For instance, it is not well-reasoned why the age of consent barrier may be lowered to 13, and as if that were not enough, the Commission stated that for commercial purposes they adopted the US age of consent, which is 13.[88] Nonetheless, Member States might raise the age of consent

---

[79] Directive 95/46/EC defines the consent as: "any freely given specific and informed indication of his wishes by which the data subject signifies his agreement to personal data relating to him being processed." Article 7 further states that personal data shall be processed only if: "data subject has unambiguously given his consent".

[80] GDPR, Article 6(1)(a) and Directive 95/46/EC, Article 7(a).

[81] GDPR, Article 7 and Recitals 32, 33, 42, 43.

[82] Article 29 Working Party, Guidelines on consent under Regulation 2016/679 17/EN WP 259 rev.01, Adopted on 28 November 2017, Last Revised and Adopted on 10 April 2018, 1–31, 4–5.

[83] GDPR, Article 83(6).

[84] GDPR, Article 82(1).

[85] Sebastian (2014–2015, pp. 222–223).

[86] GDPR, Article 8.

[87] Macenaite and Kosta (2017, p. 160).

[88] "[…] The specific rules on consent in the online environment for children below 13 years – for which parental authorisation is required – take inspiration for the age limit from the current US Children Online Data Protection Act of 1998 and are not expected to impose undue and unrealistic burden upon providers of online services and other controllers. […]" Commission Staff Working

to 16, which could lead to a lack of uniformity and validity issues when data is transferred to another country or even within the EU. In that scenario, the opposite would occur when we consider the original objective of the EU about the free flow of personal data.[89]

Besides, the GDPR does not indicate any methods for obtaining parental consent as the COPPA does[90]; however, for data controllers to have legal certainty, there must be guidance on how to verify such parental consent.

Since the GDPR does not specify any particular procedure, the burden lies on the data controllers by obliging them to make reasonable efforts, taking into account the available technology, to determine if the consent is granted by the authorised parents.[91] It is unclear, however, how much work would be considered reasonable and how this should be proven and confirmed.[92]

The methods employed to verify parental consent under the COPPA do not have to be directly transplanted to the GDPR as they may become ineffective over time as technology advances. However, it may be possible to create a rule as a general norm that is technology neutral (as in Article 32 of the GDPR[93]). However, it may still include certain instances, such as the measures stated in Article 32 in relation to data security requirements.[94]

Paper, Impact Assessment, SEC (2012) 72 final, p. 68, https://www.europarl.europa.eu/cmsdata/59702/att_20130508ATT65856-1873079025799224642.pdf.

[89] GDPR, Article 1(3): "The free movement of personal data within the Union shall be neither restricted nor prohibited for reasons connected with the protection of natural persons with regard to the processing of personal data."

[90] 16 CFR COPPA 312.5(b)(2): "(i) Providing a consent form to be signed by the parent and returned to the operator by postal mail, facsimile, or electronic scan;(ii) Requiring a parent, in connection with a monetary transaction, to use a credit card, debit card, or other online payment system that provides notification of each discrete transaction to the primary account holder; (iii) Having a parent call a toll-free telephone number staffed by trained personnel; (iv) Having a parent connect to trained personnel via video-conference; (v) Verifying a parent's identity by checking a form of government-issued identification against databases of such information, where the parent's identification is deleted by the operator from its records promptly after such verification is complete; or (vi) Provided that, an operator that does not "disclose" (as defined by § 312.2) children's personal information, may use an email coupled with additional steps to provide assurances that the person providing the consent is the parent. Such additional steps include: Sending a confirmatory email to the parent following receipt of consent, or obtaining a postal address or telephone number from the parent and confirming the parent's consent by letter or telephone call. An operator that uses this method must provide notice that the parent can revoke any consent given in response to the earlier email."

[91] GDPR, Article 8(2).

[92] GDPR Article 8(2) and Macenaite and Kosta (2017, p. 177).

[93] GDPR, Article 32.

[94] GDPR, Article 32: "Taking into account the state of the art, the costs of implementation and the nature, scope, context and purposes of processing as well as the risk of varying likelihood and severity for the rights and freedoms of natural persons, the controller and the processor shall implement appropriate technical and organisational measures to ensure a level of security appropriate to the risk, including inter alia as appropriate: (a) the pseudonymisation and encryption of personal data; (b) the ability to ensure the ongoing confidentiality, integrity, availability and resilience of processing systems and services; (c) the ability to restore the availability and access to personal data in a timely

We may draft a sample rule like this:

> Taking into consideration the state of the art, the controller and the processor should adopt adequate technologies to guarantee the consent is given or authorised by the holder of parental responsibility over the child, including inter alia as appropriate:
>
> (a) conducting a video conference with the parents to verify their official IDs
>
> (b) confirming the electronic identification (eID) credentials of the parents compared with the eID attributes of the children
>
> (c) Where the processing is unlikely to pose a high risk (e.g., subscribing to a newsletter), consent can also be given through email.[95]

The European Commission's European Digital Identity framework[96] will be examined in Chapter 3.4, which addresses online age verification methods; therefore, a detailed discussion is not included here. Nevertheless, it is important to note that the framework, which includes eID credentials and the European Digital Identity (EUDI) Wallet,[97] may also support parental consent verification mechanisms. EUDI Wallet could enable individuals to present verified attributes, such as proof of identity or parental responsibility, through privacy-preserving mechanisms that limit unnecessary disclosure of personal information. It would be ideal if the children's digital identity solutions included parental information (such as their names and surnames) so that data controllers could conduct secure and reliable verification accordingly.

In the next chapter on the notion of parental consent, we will analyse in depth all of the aforementioned topics, including the general concept of consent, parental consent under the GDPR and COPPA, the minimum age for parental consent, and online age verification methods.

References

---

manner in the event of a physical or technical incident; (d) a process for regularly testing, assessing and evaluating the effectiveness of technical and organisational measures for ensuring the security of the processing."

[95] The author developed this sample rule in light of the suggestions of her PhD thesis reviewers, Dr. Dániel Eszteri and Dr. Julien Rossi, as well as resembling the requirements of GDPR Articles 8 and 32.

[96] Regulation (EU) 2024/1183 of the European Parliament and of the Council of 11 April 2024 amending Regulation (EU) No 910/2014 as regards establishing the European Digital Identity Framework, OJ 2024 L 1183, 30.04.2024, pp. 1–64.

[97] "'European Digital Identity Wallet' means an electronic identification means which allows the user to securely store, manage and validate person identification data and electronic attestations of attributes for the purpose of providing them to relying parties and other users of European Digital Identity Wallets, and to sign by means of qualified electronic signatures or to seal by means of qualified electronic seals."

Regulation (EU) 2024/1183 of the European Parliament and of the Council of 11 April 2024 amending Regulation (EU) No 910/2014 as regards establishing a framework for a European Digital Identity, Article 1(3)(j), inserting Article 3(42).

Barron JH (1979) Warren and Brandies, the right to privacy. Harv Law Rev 4:193; (1890) Demystifying a landmark citation. Suffolk Univ Law Rev 13(4): 876
Bratman B (2002) Brandeis and Warren's the right to privacy and the birth of the right to privacy. Tenn Law Rev 69(3):629
Ceruzzi P (1996) From scientific instrument to everyday appliance: the emergence of personal computers 1970–77. Hist Technol Int J 13(1):1–31
Clearwater A, Hughes JT (2013) In the beginning—an early history of the privacy profession. Ohio St. Law J 74(6):899
Craig P (2011) The evolution of EU law, 2nd edn. Oxford University Press, Oxford, p 335
Dash S (2004) The intruders: unreasonable searches and seizures from King John to John Ashcroft. Rutgers University Press, New Brunswick, p 9
Gellert R, Gutwirth S (2013) The legal construction of privacy and data protection. Comput Law Secur Rev 29(5):524
Hall HK (2018) Oversharenting; is it really your story to tell. John Marshall J Inf Technol Priv Law 33(3):132
Hong H (2005) Dismantling the private enforcement of the privacy act of 1974: Doe v. Chao. Akron Law Rev 38(1):76–77
Keeton WP et al (1984) Prosser and Keeton on the law of torts, 5th edn. West Publishing Co., St. Paul Minn, pp 850–851
Lievens E, Verdood V (2018) Looking for needles in a haystack: key issues affecting children's rights in the General Data Protection Regulation. Comput Law Secur Rev 34(2):274
Lukács A (2016) What is privacy? The history and definition of privacy. In: Gábor K (ed) Tavaszi Szél 2016 Tanulmánykötet I., Budapest, Doktoranduszok Országos Szövetsége, p 257
Macenaite M, Kosta E (2017) Consent for processing children's personal data in the EU: following in US footsteps? Inf Commun Technol Law 26(2):146–197
Mei P (1993) The EC proposed data protection law. Law Policy Int Bus 25(1):305
Naef T (2023) The global reach of the right to data protection. In: Data protection without data protectionism. European Yearbook of International Economic Law, vol 28. Springer, p 21
Palmer VV (2011) Three milestones in the history of privacy in the United States. Tulane Eur Civil Law Forum 26:71
Pearce G, Platten N (1998) Achieving personal data protection in the European Union. JCMS 36(4):531
Sebastian MJ (2014–2015) The European Union's general date protection regulation: how will it affect non-EU enterprises. Syracuse J Sci Tech Law 31:222–223
Szabó MT (2005) Kísérlet a privacy fogalmának meghatározására a magyar jogrendszer fogalmaival. Információs Társadalom: Társadalomtudományi Folyóirat 5(2):44
Talley VAM (2019) Major flaws in minor laws: improving data privacy rights and protections for children under the GDPR. Indiana Int Comp Law Rev 30(1):143
Wald C (2016) The secret history of ancient toilets. Nature 533(7604):457
Warmund J (2000) Can COPPA work—an analysis of the parental consent measures in the children's online privacy protection act. Fordham Intell Prop Media Ent Law J 11(1):192–193
Warren SD, Brandeis LD (1890) Right to privacy. Harv Law Rev 4(5):193–220
Westin AF (1967) Privacy and freedom. Atheneum, New York, pp 1–487

Chapter 3
Concept of Parental Consent in the GDPR and the COPPA

Abstract In this chapter, the concept of parental consent, when it is required, and how to verify it before processing children's personal data are covered. The COPPA provides data controllers with various non-exhaustive methods to get parental consent. Whereas the GDPR lacks this guidance. We recommend that the GDPR transplant these COPPA sample methods under Article 8. We discuss how and why the GDPR partially transplanted the COPPA's threshold age of online consent. Considering the research and surveys conducted in the EU and the US, we question the appropriateness of these threshold ages in the GDPR and the COPPA. We also examine the age assurance mechanisms for implementing Internet restrictions for children. Online age verification methods would help provide a solution that protects children's privacy, even from their parents, while protecting them from harmful content. This can be achieved not only by parental intervention, but also by data controllers and service providers providing the essential services.

3.1 Concept of Consent in the GDPR

Article 8 of the Charter of Fundamental Rights of the EU (CFR) highlights the importance of consent as a lawful basis for processing personal data and stipulates that everyone should have control over their data.[1] In accordance with the CFR, consent is one of the six legal grounds for processing personal data under the GDPR[2] and is defined as:

> " [...] any freely given, specific, informed and unambiguous indication of the data subject's wishes by which he or she, by a statement or by a clear affirmative action, signifies agreement to the processing of personal data relating to him or her".[3]

[1] CFR, Article 8.

[2] GDPR, Article 6(1).

[3] GDPR, Article 4 (11).

A. Alkış Tümtürk, *Online Privacy and Data Protection of Children in the European Union and the United States*, Ius Gentium: Comparative Perspectives on Law and Justice 141, https://doi.org/10.1007/978-3-032-27534-9_3

According to the Preamble of the GDPR, it is one of the main goals of the GDPR to ensure the data subjects' control, which is why data controllers must ensure that they collect personal data based on consent obtained in complete accordance with the CFR and the GDPR. Otherwise, the processing of the collected personal information would be unlawful.[4]

Article 6 of the GDPR lists the lawful bases for processing personal data. These include the data subject's consent to the processing of his or her personal data for one or more specific purposes, the performance of a contract, compliance with a legal obligation, protection of the data subject's or other natural persons' vital interests, processing by public authorities, and the data controller's or a third party's legitimate interest.[5] Since our research focuses on Article 8 of the GDPR, which relates to conditions applicable to children's and parents' consent in regard to information society services, we shall concentrate on consent as the legal basis where data is processed in relation to information society services.[6]

Where data processing is not related to information society services,[7] we should consult national civil legislation to see whether parental consent is necessary. Medical examinations or treatment at a doctor's office using electronic equipment, for

---

[4] Article 29 Working Party, Guidelines on consent under Regulation 2016/679 17/EN WP 259 rev.01, 10 April 2018, 1–31, 3.

[5] GDPR, Article 6(1) (b-f).

[6] GDPR, Article 8(1).

[7] Indicative list of services not regarded as Information Society Services shall be found under the Annex I of Directive (EU) 2015/1535:

> "1. Services not provided 'at a distance' Services provided in the physical presence of the provider and the recipient, even if they involve the use of electronic devices: (a) medical examinations or treatment at a doctor's surgery using electronic equipment where the patient is physically present; (b) consultation of an electronic catalogue in a shop with the customer on site; (c) plane ticket reservation at a travel agency in the physical presence of the customer by means of a network of computers; (d) electronic games made available in a video arcade where the customer is physically present. 2. Services not provided 'by electronic means' — services having material content even though provided via electronic devices: (a) automatic cash or ticket dispensing machines (banknotes, rail tickets); (b) access to road networks, car parks, etc., charging for use, even if there are electronic devices at the entrance/exit controlling access and/or ensuring correct payment is made, — offline services: distribution of CD-ROMs or software on diskettes, — services which are not provided via electronic processing/inventory systems: (a) voice telephony services; (b) telefax/telex services; (c) services provided via voice telephony or fax; (d) telephone/telefax consultation of a doctor; (e) telephone/telefax consultation of a lawyer; (f) telephone/telefax direct marketing. 3. Services not supplied 'at the individual request of a recipient of services' Services provided by transmitting data without individual demand for simultaneous reception by an unlimited number of individual receivers (point to multipoint transmission): (a) television broadcasting services (including near-video on-demand services), covered by point (e) of Article 1(1) of Directive 2010/13/EU; (b) radio broadcasting services; (c) (televised) teletext."

Directive (EU) 2015/1535 of the European Parliament and of the Council of 9 September 2015 laying down a procedure for the provision of information in the field of technical regulations and of rules on Information Society services OJ L 241, 17.9.2015, Annex I.

example, would not be considered information society services,[8] and we should consult national laws to determine the age at which a child can consent to his or her medical treatment without parental consent. It would be the age of majority (18) in countries such as Hungary and Italy, and 16 in countries such as Portugal and Spain, but in countries such as Germany and Sweden, it would be based on maturity rather than a fixed age.[9]

Other issues, such as the role of parents in data processing based on a contractual relationship, are outside the scope of this research and would necessitate a review of national civil laws. Nevertheless, this research will provide instances from civil law to clarify relevant issues, as case law concerning data protection, especially with children's personal data, remains limited. The focus points of this research from the standpoint of the lawful basis of data processing are highlighted in bold font in Fig. 3.1 below.

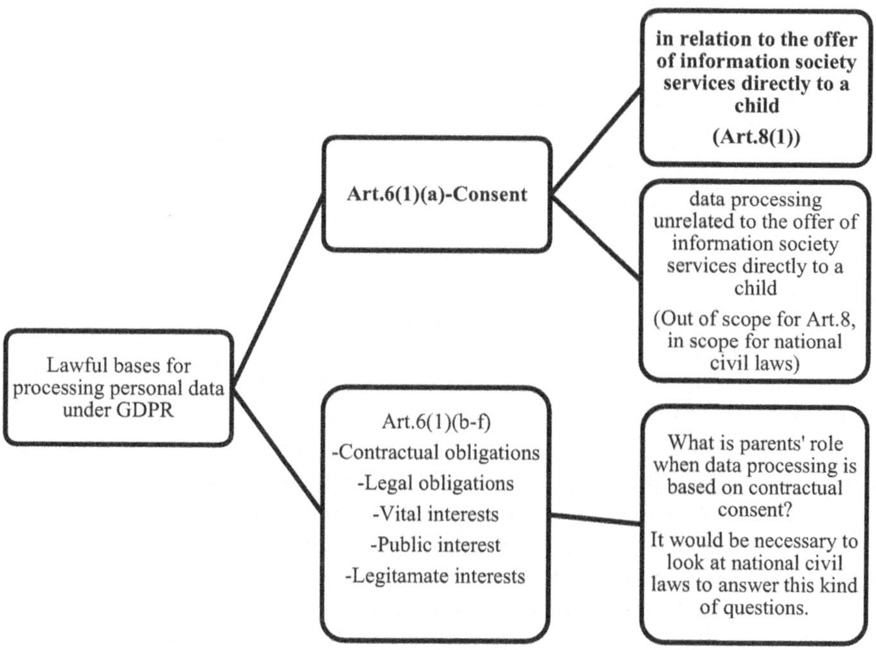

Fig. 3.1 Lawful bases of data processing under the GDPR[10]

---

[8] Directive (EU) 2015/1535 of the European Parliament and of the Council of 9 September 2015 laying down a procedure for the provision of information in the field of technical regulations and of rules on Information Society services OJ L 241, 17.9.2015, Annex I(1)(a).

[9] FRA (European Union Agency for Fundamental Rights), Consenting to medical treatment without parental consent, https://fra.europa.eu/en/publication/2017/mapping-minimum-age-requirements-concerning-rights-child-eu/consenting-medical-treatment-without-parental-consent#:~:text=However%2C%20where%20a%20medical%20intervention,is%20set%20at%2015%20years.

[10] The author created this schema based on the Articles 6 and 8 of the GDPR.

Furthermore, the GDPR and COPPA's concepts of children's and parents' consent and the definition of information society services will be examined in depth in the next subchapter (3.2). In this chapter, we will rather examine the GDPR's concept of consent by examining its definition.

First and foremost, consent should be freely given, which implies that the data subject should have a genuine choice. For example, if online content cannot be accessible without consent, there is no real choice, and hence the consent-obtaining process would be unlawful.[11]

Second, consent should be granted for one or more specific purposes. Therefore, the necessity for specific consent should be considered in light of the purpose limitation principle, which states that personal data must be "collected for specified, explicit and legitimate purposes and not further processed in a manner that is incompatible with those purposes".[12] For instance, in the scenario where the data subject has provided consent to YouTube for the collection of personal data with the purpose of receiving recommendations for similar content videos, if YouTube were to thereafter let third parties provide adverts related to the content being seen, it would be necessary to get a new consent for this additional purpose.[13]

In light of the GDPR's transparency principle, consent should be informed.[14] The data controller must inform the data subject of their identity, contact information, the purpose for collecting personal data, the type of data collected and used, the data subject's right to withdraw consent, and the appropriate safeguards in the event of data transfers to a third country or international organisation.[15] These details should be written in a clear and simple manner that everyone can comprehend, not only lawyers. If children are the intended audience, privacy policies should be age appropriate. For example, it might be illustrated with simple and fun animated movies or vivid drawings.[16]

Consent should be unambiguous and given by the data subject in the form of a clear statement or affirmative action. As a result, pre-ticked or opt-out consent options are not allowed by the GDPR since consent must be obtained prior to the collection of personal data. Consent can be granted via several means, such as by signing a document, writing a clear statement, expressing orally by phone or video call, or actively ticking an optional box declaring "I agree", "I consent". For example, if consent is obtained by ticking boxes, the boxes should have the same size, shape, and colour. If the "I consent" button is overly eye-catching, it would confuse the data

---

[11] Article 29 Working Party, Guidelines on consent under Regulation 2016/679 17/EN WP 259 rev.01, 10 April 2018, 1–31, 5–6.

[12] GDPR, Article 5(1)(b).

[13] Article 29 Working Party, Guidelines on consent under Regulation 2016/679 17/EN WP 259 rev.01, 10 April 2018, 1–31, 11–12.

[14] GDPR, Article 5(1)(a).

[15] GDPR, Article 15.

[16] Article 29 Working Party, Guidelines on consent under Regulation 2016/679 17/EN WP 259 rev.01, 10 April 2018, 1–31, 13–15.

subject and mislead them. Thus, that deceived consent cannot be regarded as clear and unambiguous.[17]

Moreover, before collecting personal data, the data controller should determine the legal basis that would be relied on at the time of collection. In the case of issues arising about consent, such as the data subject's choice to withdraw consent, the data controller is not permitted to replace the aforementioned legal bases with the data subject's consent.[18]

Nonetheless, if the data subject is a child, the processing might pose a high risk to the data subject's interests or fundamental rights and freedoms, even if the processing is based on a lawful basis. For this reason, the GDPR Recital 75 highlights that:

> "The risk to the rights and freedoms of natural persons, of varying likelihood and severity, may result from personal data processing which could lead to physical, material or non-material damage, in particular: [...] where personal data of vulnerable natural persons, in particular of children, are processed".[19]

Data Protection Authorities may also publish some processes for which mandatory data protection impact assessments (DPIAs) are required.[20] For example, the Hungarian Data Protection Authority (NAIH) requires DPIA where personal data processing involves biometrics for the purpose of uniquely identifying natural persons, particularly vulnerable persons such as children.[21] Additionally, a DPIA is required where large amounts of personal data related to vulnerable persons, including children, are processed for purposes other than the original purpose of the processing.[22] Furthermore, if children's personal data are processed for the purpose of profiling and automated decision making, a DPIA is also necessary.[23]

Likewise, the UK DPA requires a mandatory DPIA when using the personal data of children or other vulnerable persons in the context of marketing, profiling, other automated decision-making activities, or when offering online services directly to children.[24]

---

[17] Article 29 Working Party, Guidelines on consent under Regulation 2016/679 17/EN WP 259 rev.01, 10 April 2018, 1–31, 15–18.

[18] Article 29 Working Party, Guidelines on consent under Regulation 2016/679 17/EN WP 259 rev.01, 10 April 2018, 1–31, 23.

[19] GDPR, Recital 75.

[20] GDPR, Article 35(4).

[21] Nemzeti Adatvédelmi és Információszabadság Hatóság (NAIH), GDPR 35 (4) Mandatory DPIA List, List of Processing Operations Subject to DPIA GDPR 35 (4), point (2), https://www.naih.hu/data-protection/gdpr-35-4-mandatory-dpia-list.

[22] Nemzeti Adatvédelmi és Információszabadság Hatóság (NAIH), GDPR 35 (4) Mandatory DPIA List, List of Processing Operations Subject to DPIA GDPR 35 (4), point (19), https://www.naih.hu/data-protection/gdpr-35-4-mandatory-dpia-list.

[23] Nemzeti Adatvédelmi és Információszabadság Hatóság (NAIH), GDPR 35 (4) Mandatory DPIA List, List of Processing Operations Subject to DPIA GDPR 35 (4), point (20), https://www.naih.hu/data-protection/gdpr-35-4-mandatory-dpia-list.

[24] Information Commissioner's Office (ICO), When do we need to do a DPIA?, What does the ICO consider likely to result in high risk?, point (9), https://ico.org.uk/for-organisations/uk-gdpr-guidance-and-resources/accountability-and-governance/data-protection-impact-assessments-dpias/when-do-we-need-to-do-a-dpia/.

3.2 Children and Parental Consent in the GDPR Comparing with the COPPA

According to Article 8 of the GDPR,

> "[…] in relation to the offer of information society services directly to a child, the processing of the personal data of a child shall be lawful where the child is at least 16 years old. Where the child is below the age of 16 years, such processing shall be lawful only if and to the extent that consent is given or authorised by the holder of parental responsibility over the child. Member States may provide by law for a lower age for those purposes provided that such lower age is not below 13 years."[25]

As a result, because children are vulnerable, GDPR necessitates an additional measure of protection. The rationale for this additional protection is indicated in Recital (38), which emphasizes their vulnerability by stating that "[…] they may be less aware of the risks, consequences and safeguards concerned and their rights in relation to the processing of personal data […]".[26]

There are two conditions that must be met in order to apply Article 8 of the GDPR: first, this provision is "in relation [only] to the offer of information society services directly to a child"[27]; and second, the processing should be based on consent.[28] Contracts and other services concluded or delivered online, such as applications, search engines, social media platforms, online streaming services, online games, news, and educational services, are examples of information society services.[29] Furthermore, the phrase "offered directly to a child" means that Article 8 does not

---

[25] GDPR, Article 8(1).

[26] GDPR, Recital 38.

[27] GDPR, Article 8(1).

[28] According to Article 4(25) of the GDPR the Information Society Service means a service as defined in point (b) of Article 1(1) of Directive 2015/1535:"[…]any service normally provided for remuneration, at a distance, by electronic means and at the individual request of a recipient of services. For the purposes of this definition: (i) 'at a distance' means that the service is provided without the parties being simultaneously present; (ii) 'by electronic means' means that the service is sent initially and received at its destination by means of electronic equipment for the processing (including digital compression) and storage of data, and entirely transmitted, conveyed and received by wire, by radio, by optical means or by other electromagnetic means; (iii) 'at the individual request of a recipient of services' means that the service is provided through the transmission of data on individual request. […]".

Directive (EU) 2015/1535 of the European Parliament and of the Council of 9 September 2015 laying down a procedure for the provision of information in the field of technical regulations and of rules on Information Society services OJ L 241, 17.9.2015, p. 1, Article 1(b).

[29] Article 29 Working Party, Guidelines on consent under Regulation 2016/679 17/EN WP 259 rev.01, 10 April 2018, 1–31, 24.

"The ECJ held that information society services cover contracts and other services that are concluded or transmitted on-line. Where a service has two economically independent components, one being the online component, such as the offer and the acceptance of an offer in the context of the conclusion of a contract or the information relating to products or services, including marketing activities, this component is defined as an information society service, the other component being the physical delivery or distribution of goods is not covered by the notion of an information society

apply to service providers who explicitly state that they are offering their services to adults, unless it is proven otherwise (for example, while the service provider states that it does not provide services for children, its content includes cartoons, toys, and online children games).[30]

Whereas the COPPA covers commercial websites or online services directed to children under the age of 13 that collect information from children or have actual knowledge that they collect information from children, as well as a website or online service that has actual knowledge that it is collecting personal information directly from users of another website or online service directed to children.[31]

Thus, the COPPA expanded the definition of "services offered directly to a child" by including the term *having actual knowledge* that children's personal information is being gathered. However, this phrase was not specified in terms of how the operators might demonstrate their knowledge.

The April 2025 amendments to COPPA broaden the considerations for determining whether a website, online service, or any part thereof is aimed at children. In making this determination, the FTC will evaluate several factors, including subject matter, visual content, animated characters, child-appealing music, language used, child-attracting celebrities, and advertising offered on the platform or online service.[32]

However, while considering everyday life occurrences, it should be clear that the social media network operators (e.g., Facebook, Instagram) have actual knowledge that children under the age of 13 have accounts by simply lying about their age. It is clear from their profile photos, activities, and interactions with other users. Even so, their services are not considered to be provided directly to children. Accordingly, we claim that the enhanced definition is not yet fully functional in practice.

---

service. The online delivery of a service would fall within the scope of the term information society service in Article 8 GDPR." EDPB, Guidelines 05/2020 on consent under Regulation 2016/679 Version 1.1, Adopted on 4 May 2020, Updated on 13 May 2020, 1–33 para. 129.

[30] Article 29 Working Party, Guidelines on consent under Regulation 2016/679 17/EN WP 259 rev.01, 10 April 2018, 1–31, 25.; The GDPR does not define a child, but Convention on the Rights of the Child does: "For the purposes of the present Convention, a child means every human being below the age of eighteen years unless under the law applicable to the child, majority is attained earlier." Assembly, UN General, Convention on the Rights of the Child, United Nations, Treaty Series 1577, no. 3 (1989), pp. 1–23.

[31] 16 CFR Part 312 Children's Online Privacy Protection Act; Final Rule, 15 U.S.C. §§ 6501–6506, Federal Register Vol. 64, No. 212, 03.11.1999, p. 59,888–59,915, at part §312.2.

[32] 16 CFR 312.2(1): "In determining whether a website or online service, or a portion thereof, is directed to children, the Commission will consider its subject matter, visual content, use of animated characters or child-oriented activities and incentives, music or other audio content, age of models, presence of child celebrities or celebrities who appeal to children, language or other characteristics of the website or online service, as well as whether advertising promoting or appearing on the website or online service is directed to children. The Commission will also consider competent and reliable empirical evidence regarding audience composition and evidence regarding the intended audience, including marketing or promotional materials or plans, representations to consumers or to third parties, reviews by users or third parties, and the age of users on similar websites or services."

The COPPA also requires website and online service operators to obtain parental consent before collecting, using, or disclosing their children's personal information, as Article 8 of the GDPR does. Furthermore, the COPPA requires operators to make reasonable efforts to obtain parental consent, taking into account the available technology.

The real-world impact of this obligation was particularly emphasised in December 2022, when Epic Games reached a settlement with the Federal Trade Commission that included a $275 million civil penalty. The FTC found that Epic had collected personal information from children under the age of 13 without first obtaining verifiable parental consent, contrary to one of COPPA's central obligations. This lack of parental involvement also had wider consequences, as it meant that children were able to use the platform with default privacy and communication settings that could expose them to contact with strangers. At the time, the FTC described the penalty as the largest ever imposed for a COPPA violation. Under the terms of the settlement, Epic was required to introduce stronger mechanisms for obtaining parental consent, adjust default settings for child users, and delete previously collected children's data unless valid parental consent could be verified.[33]

Unlike Article 8 of the GDPR, the COPPA provides some examples of methods for verifying parental consent. These include providing parental consent through e-mail or electronic scan; if there is a monetary transaction using a credit card that provides notification, having a parent phone or video-conference with authorised personnel, and verifying the parent's identification by checking their government-issued ID.[34]

These methods are not exhaustive; there may be more methods developed by the operators and approved by the Federal Trade Commission (FTC) in light of the currently available technology. To employ an alternative method, operators do not need FTC approval. However, some operators desire FTC approval to guarantee that their process complies with the COPPA regulation. For example, the FTC has approved a novel method of asking knowledge-based challenge questions that only the children's parents can correctly answer.[35] There is also the *email plus* approach, which is solely appropriate for the operators' internal use without disclosing the collected data. These consist of three steps: The operator first requests consent from the parent by e-mail, and the parent responds by giving consent. Finally, the operator

[33] Federal Trade Commission, Fortnite Video Game Maker Epic Games to Pay More Than Half a Billion Dollars over FTC Allegations of Privacy Violations and Unwanted Charges, Press Release (19 December 2022) https://www.ftc.gov/news-events/news/press-releases/2022/12/fortnite-video-game-maker-epic-games-pay-more-half-billion-dollars-over-ftc-allegations.

United States of America (on behalf of the Federal Trade Commission) v. Epic Games, Inc. Case No. 5:22-cv-00518-BO (U.S. District Court for the Eastern District of North Carolina).

[34] 16 CFR COPPA 312.5(b)(2).

[35] FTC, Complying with COPPA: Frequently Asked Questions, QI.4., Complying with COPPA: Frequently Asked Questions | Federal Trade Commission (ftc.gov) and FTC, Verifiable Parental Consent and the Children's Online Privacy Rule, https://www.ftc.gov/business-guidance/privacy-security/verifiable-parental-consent-childrens-online-privacy-rule.

confirms that they have received the parental consent, which is the so-called *plus* factor of this method.[36]

The COPPA's non-exhaustive methods are appropriate examples of how data controllers might get parental consent in order to comply with the rule. If the methods had been exhaustive, they would have been restricted given how quickly technology advances, and they would have fallen behind the developments. However, it is beneficial that the FTC may constantly updated its list by adding new methods, and also that providers of online services have the option of not obtaining FTC approval and still using their own method.[37]

As stated above, unlike the COPPA, the GDPR does not define any method and instead leaves that solution to data controllers, requiring them to do all reasonable measures to verify the given consent was granted legitimately by those who have parental responsibility, considering the available technology. We suggest that providing some instances for verifying parental consent would be good for both parents and data controllers as guidance.[38] Nonetheless, there is still the possibility to adjust and adopt methods of the COPPA in compliance with the EU's legal system. This might pave the path for a useful example of legal transplanting in the digital era.[39]

There are exceptions to prior parental consent under the COPPA. For instance, a one-time response to a child's request could be an example if the operator not using any personal information and immediately deleting the collected information after replying to the request. Another example would be replying to a child's request multiple times (e.g., monthly newsletters), in which case the operator should notify the parents and guarantee that they have the choice to unsubscribe from the website/online service. Moreover, such information may be collected in order to protect children's safety, public safety, or the security or integrity of a website/online service.[40]

Whereas the only exception to the necessity of parental consent indicated in GDPR Article 8 is the preventive or counselling services offered directly to children, because they seek to protect the best interests of the child.[41] For example, if a child goes to

---

[36] 16 CFR COPPA 312.5(b)(2)(vi).

[37] FTC, Verifiable Parental Consent and the Children's Online Privacy Rule, https://www.ftc.gov/business-guidance/privacy-security/verifiable-parental-consent-childrens-online-privacy-rule.

[38] See the sample rule created by the author at Chapter 2:

"Taking into consideration the state of the art, the controller and the processor should adopt adequate technologies to guarantee the consent is given or authorised by the holder of parental responsibility over the child, including inter alia as appropriate:

(a) conducting a video conference with the parents to verify their official IDs.

(b) confirming the electronic identification (eID) credentials of the parents compared with the eID attributes of the children.

(c) Where the processing is unlikely to pose a high risk (e.g., subscribing to a newsletter), consent can also be given through email."

[39] For more information see: Alkis Tümtürk A (2022, pp. 235–243).

[40] For more information about the exceptions see: 16 CFR 312.5(c).

[41] GDPR, Recital (38).

his/her school's counselling service to discuss problems with his/her classmates and bullying, and the counsellor collects and records the student's personal information for further research and performance to help the student, this processing does not require parental consent. Then again, this exception does not exclude contacting parents in order to gain their cooperation in the best interests of the child.

Comparing the two legislations in terms of these exceptions, we argue that legitimate interests of online services should not be served as an excuse for not obtaining parental consent before processing children's personal data, since Article 6 states that when the data subject is a child, such interests might well be overridden by the children's best interests.[42] However, if a child's vital interests or a public task are involved, processing without parental consent may be lawful, as mentioned in the same article.[43]

Furthermore, the exemptions granted by the COPPA, which allow operators to collect children's personal information without parental consent under some circumstances, do not qualify as an exception under the GDPR. To avoid any confusion, it is important to note that Article 8 of the GDPR does not use the term collection as the COPPA does.[44] The COPPA defines the collection as:

> "[t]he gathering of any personal information from a child by any means, including but not limited to:
>
> (1) Requesting, prompting, or encouraging a child to submit personal information online;
>
> (2) Enabling a child to make personal information publicly available in identifiable form;
>
> (3) Passive tracking of a child online."

Therefore, *collection* under the COPPA is similar to the concept of *processing* under the GDPR, since processing also involves the collection of personal information.[45] Yet, one may argue that processing is more comprehensive than collection. Since, for example, processing includes the deletion or restriction of data, but collection under the COPPA does not cover deletion if the operator takes reasonable measures to delete them prior to their public availability.[46]

The COPPA does not include the preventive or counselling service exception, as the GDPR does, and the reason for this would be that the legislators did not consider the importance of these services, or the legislators assumed that these services could

---

[42] GDPR, Article 6(1)(f).

[43] GDPR, Article 6(1)(d) and (e).

[44] Instead GDPR uses the term "processing" and it is defined under the Article 4(2) as "[a]ny operation or set of operations which is performed on personal data or on sets of personal data, whether or not by automated means, such as collection, recording, organisation, structuring, storage, adaptation or alteration, retrieval, consultation, use, disclosure by transmission, dissemination or otherwise making available, alignment or combination, restriction, erasure or destruction."

[45] GDPR, Article 4(2). "'processing' means any operation or set of operations which is performed on personal data or on sets of personal data, whether or not by automated means, such as collection, recording, organisation, structuring, storage, adaptation or alteration, retrieval, consultation, use, disclosure by transmission, dissemination or otherwise making available, alignment or combination, restriction, erasure or destruction."

[46] 16 CFR COPPA 312.2(2).

not behave in the best interests of the children more than parents do. However, in some cases, qualified counsellors may be more knowledgeable about pedagogy, digital literacy, and privacy education than average-educated parents. For example, with the increasing use of social media networks, parents now have more opportunities to share their children's intimate moments in public, and they typically do not obtain their children's approval before revealing their privacy. Most of cases it is because of these parents' lack of education and risk-analysis abilities. According to a survey, teens find their parents' sharing embarrassing and useless.[47] Consequently, parental sharing might result in (cyber)bullying among the teens' classmates. Therefore, we assert that it would be beneficial for children if the COPPA contained an exception for obtaining prior parental consent when offering preventative or counselling services directly to children. Because there could be occasions in which children report their parents' inappropriate behaviour towards them to school counselling services. Thus, this exception would allow children to express themselves and seek online assistance from school counsellors/teachers.

The observed discrepancy could also possibly be attributed to the differing extents of applicability of various legislations. The scope of COPPA is limited to the Internet, but the GDPR is not restricted by technology and applies to the processing of personal data regardless of the method employed, whether it be online or offline. It is conceivable that at the time of the enactment of the COPPA in 1998, the legislators may not have foreseen the emergence of online counselling services.

In this subchapter, we analysed the concept of parental consent, the methods for verifying parental consent prior to processing, and the exceptions to this verification, comparing the GDPR and the COPPA. In the next subchapter, we will analyse the threshold age at which parental consent must be obtained in accordance with the GDPR and the COPPA. We will analyse the relevance of the concept of a threshold age and whether or not it is necessary for protecting the personal data and privacy of children.

3.3 Threshold Age for Parental Consent Under the GDPR and the COPPA

Children under the age of 13 are more vulnerable to the hazards and consequences of their online behaviours and interactions, according to the FTC.[48] Hence, the COPPA defines the term "child" as an individual under the age of 13.[49] Can one argue that

[47] Verswijvel et al. (2019, p. 104,407).

[48] Complying with COPPA: Frequently Asked Questions, Why does COPPA apply only to children under 13? What about protecting the online privacy of teens? https://www.ftc.gov/business-guidance/resources/complying-coppa-frequently-asked-questions.

[49] 16 CFR COPPA 312.2 "Child: means an individual under the age of 13."

a child of 12 years old is vulnerable, but a child of 13 years old is not? In everyday life, children aged 12 and 13 frequently have similar abilities.[50]

Moreover, would not it be better if the rule cover at least the adolescent years of the children? Senator *Edward Markey* of the US revealed that subject matter in his initial draft. He classified a child as anyone under the age of 16, but they changed it to 13 for some economic reasons. Some e-commerce companies did not want to lose this attractive adolescent market. He now admits that the age threshold of 13 years was too low, but he claims that it was the best he could do, because not only e-commerce companies, but also civil liberties groups, were opposed to the age threshold of 16 years old.[51]

However, for similar economic reasons, the EU has followed in the footsteps of the US and implemented a remarkably similar age threshold with its partial legal transplanting. We suggest it is partly because, while the EU raised the age to 16 in order to protect teenagers, it also allows the Member States to lower it till the age of 13. Furthermore, the age of 13 was chosen as the standard age based on the COPPA since it would otherwise be a burden on websites and online service providers, as stated directly by the European Council.[52] According to this reasoning, we claim that economic considerations appear to be more important than adolescents' online data protection and privacy.

The Table 3.1 below compares the ages of consent of the Member States in different scenarios: accessing the realm of digital platforms, entering the labour market and receiving medical care, including diagnosis and surgery, engaging in sexual activities with others lawfully.

As seen in the table, the highest ages of consent thresholds are found in areas where children receive medical care. Getting a diagnosis or having surgery without parental consent is legal in ten of the EU Member States only from the age of 18, and it is legal in seven of them depending on the child's maturity. The child maturity test indicates that doctors should make decisions on a case-by-case basis. This maturity test would not be achievable in the digital world, because even if some questions were asked to assess the children's maturity, such questions may be passed by coincidence.

---

[50] Talley (2019, p. 145).

[51] The Wall Street Journal, Julie Jargon, How 13 Became the Internet's Age of Adulthood? (18 June 2019), https://www.wsj.com/articles/how-13-became-the-internets-age-of-adulthood-11560850201.

[52] European Commission, Commission Staff Working Paper, Impact Assessment, Accompanying the document Regulation of the European Parliament and of the Council on the protection of individuals with regard to the processing of personal data and on the free movement of such data (General Data Protection Regulation) and Directive of the European Parliament and of the Council on the protection of individuals with regard to the processing of personal data by competent authorities for the purposes of prevention, investigation, detection or prosecution of criminal offences or the execution of criminal penalties, and the free movement of such data, SEC (2012) 72 final, p. 68, https://www.europarl.europa.eu/cmsdata/59702/att_20130508ATT65856-1873079025799224642.pdf. For more information regarding the mentioned legal transplantation: Asli Alkis Tümtürk: The Threshold Age for Children's Online Consent in Light of the Watson/Legrand Debate: Is Legal Transplant Possible in the Digital Era?, The Journal of Comparative Law vol. 17/1 (2022), 243.

Table 3.1 Age of consent in the member states

	Digital platforms[53]	Part-time work[54]	Medical treatments[55]	Sexual activity[56]
Austria	14	15	Depends on maturity	14
Belgium	13	15	Depends on maturity	16
Bulgaria	14	15	18	14
Croatia	16	15	16	15
Cyprus	14	14	18	17
Czech Republic	15	15	Depends on maturity	15
Denmark	13	13	15	15
Estonia	13	13	Depends on maturity	14
Finland	13	14	18	16
France	15	14	18	15
Germany	16	15	Depends on maturity	14
Greece	15	15	18	15
Hungary	16	16	18	14
Ireland	16	14	16	17
Italy	14	16	18	14
Latvia	13	13	14	16
Lithuania	14	14	16	16
Luxembourg	16	15	Depends on maturity	16
Malta	13	16	18	18
Netherlands	16	13	16	16

(continued)

[53] EuConsent, Digital Age of Consent under the GDPR, https://euconsent.eu/digital-age-of-consent-under-the-gdpr/#:~:text=As%20per%20Article%208%20of,at%20least%2016%20years%20old'.

[54] FRA (European Union Agency for Fundamental Rights), Minimum age requirements related to rights of the child in the EU, Social rights; Employment; Education; Alternative care; LGBTI and Mobility, https://view.officeapps.live.com/op/view.aspx?src=https%3A%2F%2Ffra.europa.eu%2Fsites%2Fdefault%2Ffiles%2Ffra_uploads%2Ffra-2018-social-rights-lgbti-specific-data_en.xlsx&wdOrigin=BROWSELINK.

[55] FRA, Consenting to medical treatment without parental consent, https://fra.europa.eu/en/publication/2017/mapping-minimum-age-requirements-concerning-rights-child-eu/consenting-medical-treatment-without-parental-consent#:~:text=However%2C%20where%20a%20medical%20intervention,is%20set%20at%2015%20years.

[56] FRA, Minimum age requirements related to rights of the child in the EU, Marriage and sexual consent; Citizenship; Political Participation; Religion; Health, https://view.officeapps.live.com/op/view.aspx?src=https%3A%2F%2Ffra.europa.eu%2Fsites%2Fdefault%2Ffiles%2Ffra_uploads%2Ffra-2017-status-religion-health-specific-data_en.xlsx&wdOrigin=BROWSELINK.

Table 3.1 (continued)

	Digital platforms	Part-time work	Medical treatments	Sexual activity
Poland	16	16	16	15
Portugal	13	16	16	14
Romania	16	16	18	15
Slovakia	16	15	18	15
Slovenia	15	15	15	15
Spain	14	16	16	16
Sweden	13	13	Depends on maturity	15

Given that health data is classified as a special category of personal data according to Article 9 of the GDPR,[57] it is justifiable to set higher age thresholds for obtaining digital consent for the use of health data. In the GDPR's Preamble, it is stated that processing personal data which are sensitive by their nature poses a significant risk to the fundamental rights and freedoms of individuals.[58] Therefore, they require specific protection and the Article 9 prohibits processing data with sensitive nature (e.g., health data) unless one of these conditions is met[59]: data subject provides explicit consent; data subject's data with sensitive nature is processed in the context of employment, social security and social protection (on the basis of law); vital interests of data subject is in place; processing is necessary for the legitimate activities of non-profit bodies; the data is made public by the data subject; processing is necessary for the establishment of legal claims or judicial acts; processing is necessary for reasons of public interest (on the basis of law); processing is necessary for the purposes of health or social care (on the basis of law); processing is necessary for reasons of public health (on the basis of law); or processing is necessary for archiving, research and statistics purposes (on the basis of law).

Nevertheless, internet service providers profit from the processing of individuals' personal data; even if the personal data falls under the special categories,[60] they choose to share it with interested organizations (such as advertising companies). The MyFitnessPal app, for example, indicates in its privacy policy that they process users' personal data for "internet-based and cross-app, cross-device advertising."[61] In terms of data with sensitive nature, users can choose not to provide them; however, in this case, they will be unable to access some of the services and features, meaning that the app would not function fully.[62] Individuals under the age of eighteen are not

[57] GDPR, Article 9(1).

[58] GDPR, Recital 51.

[59] GDPR, Article 9(2) (a-j).

[60] For more detailed information regarding the potential legal basis for processing of health data: Váradi (2021, pp. 358–362).

[61] MyFitnessPal Privacy Policy, https://www.myfitnesspal.com/privacy-policy.

[62] MyFitnessPal Privacy Policy, https://www.myfitnesspal.com/privacy-policy.

permitted to register for the MyFitnessPal app; however, there are several health-related applications that enable children to register.

For example, the Happify that promises to improve well-being of users, measure their emotional happiness, and reduce their stress and anxiety levels. It allows children aged 16 and older to register their app. They also state that they give opt-in or opt-out options for data with sensitive nature before sharing it with third parties.[63] A 16-year-old child, though, may not be mature enough to understand the consequences of sharing sensitive information with third parties. Doctors, however, should keep their patients' personal information and diagnoses private, unlike internet service providers.[64]

Interestingly, a 16-year-old child in Hungary, for example, cannot go to a doctor on his/her own, but he/she may download a health-related app (e.g., Happify) on his/her phone that collects and processes data with sensitive nature and might even share this data for profit. Even though, considering the risks associated with both options, the first scenario should be considerably more secure and confidential, given that doctors must adhere to the physician–patient privilege.

When it comes to another sensitive area of children's data, their sexual lives, the age of consent ranges between 14 and 16 in the Member States. So, the threshold ages are not as high as the medical treatments, and oddly, the maturity test for the age of consent for children's sexual activity is not required. Furthermore, some nations allow children to participate in sexual behaviours before they may engage in internet activities. For example, a 14-year-old child in Hungary or Germany can have sexual intercourse, but he or she cannot create a social media account without the consent of his or her parents.

On the one hand, there are these sensitive areas in individuals' lives, and on the other, there is the labour market, which people may participate in once they reach maturity. The legal age of consent for children to enter the labour market part-time may also be found in the table above, and the ages are quite similar among the Member States, ranging from 13 to 16. However, it might still be perplexing for a child at the age of 13, for example, in the Netherlands, where he or she can choose to work part-time after school and earn his or her own money but cannot obtain an e-mail account without the consent of his or her parents.

These differing consent ages for different matters do not appear to be well-reasoned or consistent. Thereby, this might cause confusion for a child's abilities between the physical world and the online realm. A child may easily assume that lying about his/her age is the best option to avoid these online restrictions that he/she does not have in real life or has less of in comparison to his/her online activities.

Furthermore, in most situations, the age verification process to register for an app or enter a website is too simple since the applications or websites merely ask

---

[63] Happify, Legal, Happify™ Privacy Policy: Last Updated July 2022, https://www.happify.com/public/legal/#legal.

[64] European Council of Medical Orders, European Charter of Medical Ethics, Ethical Principles, Principle 5: "The physician is the patient's essential confidant. He betrays this confidence on revealing what he has learned from the patient." https://www.ceom-ecmo.eu/en/ethics-and-deontology.

children to type their ages themselves. For example, the MyFitnessPal app stated above just needs a child to input their age/birth date before proceeding with the registration procedure, and then they can create an account with the help of their e-mail address.[65] It is also straightforward for a child to get a Gmail account. A child may simply provide an age that is appropriate in their country to open a Gmail account.[66] This method makes it very easy for a child to lie. This issue will be covered in-depth in the next chapter.

Children may also get social media accounts by registering with the proper age requirement in their jurisdiction. Considering children under the age of 13 (or in some jurisdictions up to 16) cannot legally register for certain social media networks (e.g., Facebook,[67] Instagram[68]), they appear to be lying about their ages in order to register for those platforms, as seen below in the Pew Research Center's 2020 surveys conducted in the US.[69] The ages of children who access social networking sites are decreasing till they are less than two years old. Among the younger children, those aged 9 to 11 had the highest rate. It appears that some parents in the US are still allowing their children to have social media accounts even though the vast majority of them agree that children under the age of 12 should avoid using such sites due to the risks they pose (including exposure to sexual content, violent content, cyberbullying, and harassment).[70]

---

[65] MyFitnessPal, Sign Up, https://www.myfitnesspal.com/account/create.

[66] Google, Sign Up, https://accounts.google.com/signup/v2/webcreateaccount?flowName=GlifWebSignIn&flowEntry=SignUp.

[67] Facebook Help Center, How to Report Things, How do I report a child under the age of 13 on Facebook?, https://www.facebook.com/help/157793540954833/?helpref=uf_share.

[68] Instagram Help Center, How to Report Things, Report a child under 13 on Instagram, https://help.instagram.com/2922067214679225/?helpref=hc_fnav.

[69] In "Complying with COPPA: Frequently Asked Questions" FTC answers the question regarding the responsibility of operators for children's lie in general audience sites as: "The Rule does not require operators of general audience sites to investigate the ages of visitors to their sites or services. See 1999 Statement of Basis and Purpose, 64 Fed. Reg. 59,888, 59,892. However, operators will be held to have acquired actual knowledge of having collected personal information from a child where, for example, they later learn of a child's age or grade from a concerned parent who has learned that his child is participating on the site or service."

Federal Trade Commission, Complying with COPPA: Frequently Asked Questions, H. General Audience and Teen Sites or Services, 1, https://www.ftc.gov/business-guidance/resources/complying-coppa-frequently-asked-questions#I.%20Verifiable%20Parental%20Consent.

It should be also noted that the COPPA broadens the definition of "services offered directly to a child" by including the phrase having actual knowledge that children's personal information is being gathered. As mentioned before, while considering everyday life occurrences, it should be clear that the social media network operators (e.g., Facebook, Instagram) have actual knowledge that children under the age of 13 have accounts by simply lying about their age. It is clear from their profile photos, activities, and interactions with other users. Moreover, there exist study findings and statistical data that confirm the presence of underage children within social media networks.

[70] Auxier et al. (2020, pp. 2–4). https://www.pewresearch.org/internet/2020/07/28/childrens-engagement-with-digital-devices-screen-time/.

As observed in the surveys conducted in EU countries, and similar to the findings obtained in the US, children who use social media networks include not only legally permitted children but also children who are underage.[71]

We advocate that considering Table 3.1 above, the varying digital ages of consent in different European countries have no significant effect on children's access to social media networks. According to a research (2019) conducted by Better Internet for Kids (BIK)[72] about children's age of consent for data processing across the Europe, the selected countries' justifications for decreasing/increasing the online age of consent (as permitted by the GDPR) are often based on two factors: First, those that do not lower the age of consent online argue that they do so for the safety of children.[73] Second, those who reduce the internet age of consent (to as low as 13) justify their actions by claiming that they respect children's right to freedom of speech and press.[74]

Yet, based on the referred studies, we may conclude that raising the legal age of consent does not give further protection and that decreasing it has no direct influence on children's online behaviour. According to mentioned report of BIK, Spain asserted that age-based restrictions on access to the Internet and its services might reduce the chances of the children to have sufficient Internet skills and cope with the difficulties of the digital life. Hence, Spain's data protection legislation sets the age of consent for the processing of a child's personal information at 14.[75] Nonetheless, based on the data shown in the EU Kids Online survey (2020) mentioned above, daily visits to social media networks by children aged 9–16 in Spain are below average.[76] It seems that decreasing the age requirement has no immediate effect on children's motivation to participate in online activities.

In Spain, where the threshold age for parental consent is 14, children use social media networks at a lower rate than in Germany, where the threshold age is 16. Additionally, according to EU Kids Online survey, children aged 9 to 16 in Germany experience higher online victimisation than children in Spain. Furthermore, if we compare Finland (where the threshold age for parental consent is 13) and Norway examples (where the threshold age for parental consent is 16), we can observe that Finland has the lowest rates, while Norway has one of the highest rates of online victimisation, particularly among children aged 9–11.[77] These findings from the BIK report and EU Kids Online survey (2020) suggest that variances in the digital age of consent have no direct effect on use or online safety in practise.

Another noteworthy observation is that the age of children who claim to be harmed by online victimization is unrelated to their age. In other words, encountering harm is not exactly proportional to the age of children. In Switzerland, for example, children

[71] Smahel et al. (2020, p. 30).

[72] Milkaite and Lievens (2019, pp. 1–7).

[73] See the examples: Milkaite and Lievens (2019, pp. 4–6).

[74] See the examples: Milkaite and Lievens (2019, pp. 3–6).

[75] Milkaite and Lievens (2019, p. 5).

[76] Smahel et al. (2020, p. 30).

[77] Smahel et al. (2020, p. 58).

aged 15–16 were the most affected by online victimization as compared to younger children. However, as observed in the Slovak Republic, the youngest children, aged 9 to 11, are the most harmed.[78]

In order to make comparative conclusions about the age of digital consent, some Member States, according to the findings of the same report of BIK, referred to various legal disciplines and articles in their draft laws on personal data protection. For instance, explanatory part of the Draft Law of the Slovenian Personal Data Protection Act asserts that the age of 15 was chosen in accordance with the Slovenian Family Law Code, which allows a 15-year-old child to take legal action alone.[79] Similarly, as shown in Table 3.1 above, the minimum age for beginning part-time employment, receiving medical care, or engaging in sexual activity is 15 in Slovenia.

A similar example is provided by the Polish draft law on the protection of personal data, which explains that the age of 13 was selected due to the similar age threshold provided by the Polish Civil Code, which states that a person who has reached the age of 13 has limited legal capacity and can therefore enter into "minor contracts of daily life." Nevertheless, unlike the draft law, the final law does not mention children and the age was set at 16 years.[80]

Another interesting example stated by the Czech Republic in their explanatory note on the draft law (*Dôvodová Správa*) is that teens may get driving licences (types of motorcycles) at the age of 15, despite the riskier and more difficult nature of these vehicles. Hence, this note claims that it may be improper to restrict email services, social networks, and other comparable forms of online communication. It is recommended that education should be used to address the risks of online activities. Ergo, the age of 15 was chosen as the digital consent age.[81] In the Czech Republic, the minimum age for beginning a part-time work or engaging in sexual behaviour is similarly 15, as shown in Table 3.1 above.

The practice of comparing the age of digital consent to that of other law fields is, in our view, appropriate. It clarifies the legislative intention and gives relative consistency, as shown by Slovenia and the Czech Republic. Hence, we may suggest that all Member States adopt a uniform age of digital consent and provide appropriate justifications for their choice. A uniform age threshold for digital consent online would offer clarity, consistency, and simplicity of compliance inside the EU for both individuals and companies. They may utilise the comparative method to determine the age threshold considering European legal culture and customs. Chapter 6 of this research will include further suggestions on the standardised age at which children may provide digital consent. Establishing a uniform age is also crucial for transferring data not only to third countries but also inside the Union. This topic will be discussed in Chapter 5.

---

[78] Smahel, Machackova, Mascheroni, Dedkova, Staksrud, Ólafsson, Livingstone, and Hasebrink (2020, p. 132).

[79] Milkaite and Lievens (2019, p. 5).

[80] Milkaite and Lievens (2019, p. 5).

[81] Milkaite and Lievens (2019, p. 2).

Moreover, setting age restrictions, we believe, can direct and guide parents, but in the digital era and with growing technology, it appears hard to keep children away from these digital platforms. Furthermore, there are certain advantages to participating in online activities such as online libraries, opportunity to learn different cultures and languages, instructive documentaries, and brain-boosting games. As previously indicated, the countries participated in BIK's research also emphasised the significance of children using the Internet to enhance their digital skills and exercise their right to information[82] and freedom of expression.[83]

On one hand, parents cannot and should not keep their children away from these beneficial internet activities. On the other hand, according to the GDPR and the COPPA, parents have the responsibility to protect their children's privacy and online safety.[84] We suggest that policymakers should review whether imposing age limits is useful or whether there would be other solutions.[85]

An alternative and optimal method would be to achieve a good balance with the aid of digital education and literacy. Another alternative would be the combination of parental supervision with the use of a software solution that limits inappropriate content and websites.[86] Furthermore, ethical design principles could be adopted by data controllers and online service providers (e.g., third-party suppliers who do not determine the processing purposes but offer online platforms). These principles would entail the inclusion of child-friendly content that considers the specific online needs of children.

However, currently, we should implement legal age restrictions on the Internet as mandated by the GDPR and the COPPA. In the next chapter, we will examine age-verification solutions that are designed to comply with the legal age of consent for using digital platforms.

3.4 Online Age Verification Methods

According to the COPPA and the GDPR, as indicated above, parents are primarily responsible for their children's safety. However, in the natural course of events, parents cannot be expected to constantly monitor and supervise their children. Thus,

[82] Article 17 of the UNCRC guarantees the right to information of children.
UN Commission on Human Rights, Convention on the Rights of the Child, E/CN.4/RES/1990/74, 07.03.1990, Article 17.

[83] Article 13 of the UNCRC protects the right of children to freedom of expression.
UN Commission on Human Rights, Convention on the Rights of the Child, E/CN.4/RES/1990/74, 07.03.1990, Article 13.

[84] GDPR, Article 8 and 16 CFR COPPA 312.5.

[85] Smahel, Machackova, Mascheroni, Dedkova, Staksrud, Ólafsson, Livingstone, and Hasebrink (2020, p. 132).

[86] For more information regarding the software solutions for parental control: Alkis (2021, p. 17).

attempts are being undertaken to develop internet tools that would make it simpler to monitor children when the parents are physically absent.[87]

Thereby, age verification has the potential to be a beneficial method for making the Internet safer for children. The goal of age verification systems is to impose a technological instrument that checks if the internet user is of legal age to access age-restricted content.[88]

The Digital Services Act (DSA) also references age verification as a risk mitigation measure in addition to parental control tools.[89] Article 35 of the DSA also states that the risk mitigation instruments, including age verification, should be appropriate, proportionate, reasonable, and effective.[90] Therefore, it should be as minimally intrusive as feasible. Age verification tools should be dedicated solely to confirming the age and should not extend beyond this specific purpose.

Furthermore, given that age verification itself typically presents significant risks to the rights and freedoms of data subjects, the DPIA should be conducted by the service provider prior to the commencement of processing. The DPIA should evaluate the necessity and proportionality of the processing. And it should recognize risks and address them through suitable measures. Technical and organizational measures should be implemented appropriately to ensure compliance. For instance, if content or services do not pose any risks to the audience and are deemed suitable for all age groups, age verification would be unnecessary and should not satisfy the proportionality and necessity criteria.[91]

Online age verification systems may present significant challenges and concerns that policymakers, data controllers, and parents should be aware of and work to address to improve them. It is important to remember that there is no such thing as a flawless age verification mechanism. The assumption that the age verification method would keep children safe from any harmful content may cause a false feeling of security.[92]

When it comes to existing age verification methods, none of them are perfect but there are some features that make some of them preferred. The European Commission recently has issued a blueprint for an age verification system to encourage the creation of a safer online environment for children. According to the blueprint, the age verification methods should be privacy-preserving, user-friendly, free of charge,

---

[87] Alkis (2021, p. 8).

[88] Van der Maelen (2019, p. 115).

[89] Regulation (EU) 2022/2065 of the European Parliament and of the Council of 19 October 2022 on a Single Market for Digital Services and amending Directive 2000/31/EC (Digital Services Act) OJ L 277, 27.10.2022, pp. 1–102, Article 35(1)(j).

[90] Regulation (EU) 2022/2065 of the European Parliament and of the Council of 19 October 2022 on a Single Market for Digital Services and amending Directive 2000/31/EC (Digital Services Act) OJ L 277, 27.10.2022, pp. 1–102, Article 35(1).

[91] EDPB Statement, Statement 1/2025 on Age Assurance Adopted on 11 February 2025, p. 1–11, at para. 13–14.

[92] Thierer (2007, p. 3).

secure, harmonized across the Europe, and compatible with the European Digital Identity Wallet.[93]

The technical solution should be designed to ensure that the application is available for installation from the app store, and that age verification is conducted using tools such as national identification documents or other adequate alternatives. Following the verification of age, the link between the proof provider and the user should be cut off and no additional information should be transferred. Furthermore, proof of age should not contain any other identifiable information that could facilitate tracing. Subsequently, the user requests access from the online service provider that offers age-restricted content. In order to access, the user shall present an anonymous proof of age. The validation should be conducted by the online service provider in a privacy-preserving manner, ensuring that no information is disclosed to the proof of age provider. Ultimately, access should be authorized following thorough validation.[94] We will also examine here an EU-funded pilot product later aimed at implementing this formula. However, prior to that, we will enumerate and assess the verification methods employed within the online environment.

First, there is the self-verification method, which is the most often employed by websites and applications and is based on the internet user writing their birth date (e.g., Facebook)[95] or clicking a yes or no box (e.g., mralkohol.hu)[96] as proof that they are of legal age. That is affordable and extremely simple to require for the operators; yet it is very easy for a child to lie in order to gain access to or create an account for certain websites, applications, or social media networks.[97]

Recently, it has not been regarded as a proper age verification method nor as an effective means of age assurance. As it is a trust-based method, no further proofs are required beyond the confirmation itself. In fact, European Commission's Better Internet for Kids project's report on age assurance typologies also identified self-declaration as a distinct classification from age verification and age estimation methods, although all are encompassed within the broader category of age assurance techniques.[98] Similarly, the Online Safety Act of the UK also stipulates

[93] European Commission, Blueprint for an age verification solution to help protect minors online (9 October 2025) https://digital-strategy.ec.europa.eu/en/factpages/blueprint-age-verification-solution-help-protect-minors-online.

[94] European Commission, Blueprint for an age verification solution to help protect minors online (9 October 2025) https://digital-strategy.ec.europa.eu/en/factpages/blueprint-age-verification-solution-help-protect-minors-online.

[95] Facebook, Sign Up: https://www.facebook.com/signup.

[96] Mr.Alkohol (Coctails&Drinks), https://mralkohol.hu/.

[97] Polonetsky (2009, pp. 3–4).

[98] European Commission, Directorate-General for Communications Networks, Content and Technology, Center for Law and Digital Technologies (eLaw) and LLM, Mapping age assurance typologies and requirements – Research report, Publications Office of the European Union, 2024, pp. 1–64, https://data.europa.eu/doi/10.2759/455338, at 7.

that self-declaration shall not be considered as a form of age verification or age estimation.[99]

The second method is the peer-based verification, which is based on the peers' ratings of internet users who intend to attend a website. However, these ratings should be based on offline interactions with these Internet users, rather than their online profiles. This strategy can be effective in social media networks since it is simple to rate peers based on their profile pictures and it is also cost-effective for operators. However, there is the potential of creating fake accounts and verifying them with each other, which may render the verification technique ineffective. This method is relatively more reliable than self-verification, although there is still the possibility of fraud without much effort.[100]

Third, there is the use of a credit card, debit card, or other online payment systems as an age verification method.[101] Moreover, under the COPPA, this is also a verification system for obtaining parental consent, but it is only allowed in connection with a monetary transaction.[102] We agree that this should be the case, because providing credit card information for other purposes, such as creating a social network account is not reasonable. Besides, children may also have bank accounts and as a result, distinguishing a child from an adult could be difficult.[103] Even if it is feasible to detect that it is a child bank account, the question remains as to how we can determine the precise age from the bank account or credit card number.

Moreover, some children steal or borrow credit cards from their parents and use them online without their parents' knowledge.[104] Furthermore, while not all adults or children use credit or debit cards, requiring them and assuming that everyone has or should have one might be discriminatory to those who do not prefer to use credit cards or cannot afford them at all.[105] Even if they have one, some people may be reluctant to provide their credit card information due to some reasonable security concerns.

Fourth, providing personal IDs such as a passport or driver's license might be an option for age verification, and it would be relatively easy to distinguish a child from an adult. However, this could lead to plenty of privacy issues because, on the Internet today, if you share a piece of information, it could be shared with untrustworthy third parties in a fraction of a second, either voluntarily because the parties have

---

[99] Online Safety Act 2023 (UK), 2023 c. 50, received Royal Assent on 26 October 2023, available at https://www.legislation.gov.uk/ukpga/2023/50/pdfs/ukpga_20230050_en.pdf, at Part 12, Sect. 230(4).

[100] Polonetsky (2009, p. 4).

[101] Polonetsky (2009, p. 5).

[102] 16 CFR COPPA 312.5(b)(2)(ii).

[103] Children may also have bank accounts with the consent of their parents or guardians. For instance: HSBC, Children's Bank Accounts, https://www.hsbc.co.uk/current-accounts/products/children/.

[104] The Guardian, Boy, 12, Steals Credit Card and Goes on Bali Holiday after Fight with Mother (23 April 2018) https://www.theguardian.com/australia-news/2018/apr/23/boy-12-steals-credit-card-and-goes-on-bali-holiday-after-fight-with-mother cited in Van der Maelen (2019, p.117).

[105] Van der Maelen (2019, pp. 117–118).

some economic interest in doing so or through malicious cyber-attacks. It might be reliable as an age verification tool, but it could easily go beyond its purpose and generate some data protection difficulties. As a result, personal IDs should not be used unless there are very secure and trustworthy government websites such as systems that enable access to public services from a single website (e.g., Ügyfélkapu[106] in Hungary).[107]

Fifth, as previously stated, there is a knowledge-based authentication method for verifying parental consent that has been approved by the FTC. It can, in fact, be used as an age verification method since it can distinguish between children and adults. (However, this rule may not be applicable to adults with intellectual disabilities, since they may have the cognitive functioning of underage children.)[108] Nevertheless, some of the EU Member States, including Hungary, require data controllers to get parental consent if the children are under the age of 16. In this case, a 16-year-old child and an 18-year-old adult cannot always be distinguished by knowledge-based questions since 16-year-olds often have the similar levels of maturity as 17/18-year-olds.[109]

Sixth, fingerprints, bone density, characteristic markings on the surface of the eye, or other biologically unique identifiers may be used to determine the age of users. There are not just physical biometrics, but also behavioural biometrics that may be used to determine a user's age, such as typing style.[110] Biometric data, however, is classified as sensitive information about an individual under the GDPR, and "…the processing of genetic data, biometric data for the aim of uniquely identifying a natural person…"[111] is prohibited. This means that biometric data cannot be used for any purpose if there is no explicit consent or other legal bases (e.g., "processing is necessary to protect the vital interests of the data subject or another natural person"[112]). Therefore, data controllers should ensure that their data policy explains the risks and consequences of collecting and processing biometric data clearly, and they should get the explicit consent of underage children's parents for lawfully processing their biometric data.

Even if parents trust the website, there is always the potential of cyber-attacks, and if a malicious third-party acquires a child's biometric data, such as his/her fingerprint, they may access any service that needs a fingerprint (e.g., verifying a passport, unlocking a phone's screen). Eventually, the consequences would be extremely dangerous, given that a fingerprint, like other biometric data, is a unique characteristic

---

[106] Ügyfélkapu, https://ugyfelkapu.gov.hu/.

[107] Polonetsky (2009, p. 7).

[108] Patel et al. (2020, pp. 23–35).

[109] Van der Maelen (2019, pp. 119–120).

[110] Polonetsky (2009, p. 11).

[111] GDPR, Article 9(1).

[112] GDPR, Article 6(1)(d).

of an individual. Furthermore, fake fingerprints may imitate real ones in today's technology.[113] Biometrics provide a false sense of security since they are unique features, but that does not mean that current technology cannot reproduce them. According to a study presented at a security conference in Los Angeles, artificial fingerprints called "DeepMasterPrints" by New York University researchers may fool 77% of the subjects in the dataset with a 1% mismatch rate.[114] So, in today's digital age, unique does not imply secrets, and passwords can be changed if they are hacked, but what if fingerprints are stolen? As a result, before exposing biometric information in the cybersphere, one should proceed with caution.

A person's voice and facial features can be used as biometric data since these distinguishing characteristics can also be used to identify a person if they are processed using a specific technological measures.[115] There are voice recognition artificial intelligence (AI) solutions that might be used for verifying the age of individuals, such as Apple's Siri,[116] which detects the users' voice and assists them with vocal instructions, or voice signatures,[117] which are currently used to access one's own bank account via telephone banking. When it comes to face-matching AI solutions, one might consider the iPhone's Face ID tool, which is used for unlocking the screen and accessing certain applications (e.g., Internet banking apps, e-wallet) on users' phones.[118]

However, many AI systems can only determine an age range rather than the specific age of a child. Because a 12-year-old child and a 13-year-old child may sound and look alike, an AI cannot determine a child's actual age.[119] Therefore, we suggest that verifying/estimating the age via voice recognition tools is not an appropriate solution, and it can also cause the same security problems with fingerprints as we mentioned above. There is always the risk of having those unique features stolen by malicious attackers. Matching Face IDs and voice signatures with individuals'

[113] The Guardian, Fake fingerprints can imitate real ones in biometric systems – research, 15 November 2018, https://www.theguardian.com/technology/2018/nov/15/fake-fingerprints-can-imitate-real-fingerprints-in-biometric-systems-research.

[114] Bontrager et al. (2018, p. 2) cited in The Guardian, Fake fingerprints can imitate real ones in biometric systems – research, 15 November 2018, https://www.theguardian.com/technology/2018/nov/15/fake-fingerprints-can-imitate-real-fingerprints-in-biometric-systems-research.

[115] GDPR, Recital 51: "The processing of photographs should not systematically be considered to be processing of special categories of personal data as they are covered by the definition of biometric data only when processed through a specific technical means allowing the unique identification or authentication of a natural person."

Van der Maelen (2019, pp. 119–120).

[116] Apple, Siri, https://www.apple.com/siri/.

[117] For instance: HSBC Voice ID, https://www.hsbc.com.hk/ways-to-bank/phone/voice-id/.

[118] Apple, Use Face ID on your iPhone or iPad Pro, https://support.apple.com/en-us/HT208109#:~:text=Tap%20Set%20Up%20Face%20ID,your%20head%2C%20tap%20Accessibility%20Options.

[119] Alkis (2021, pp. 16–17).

personal IDs might pose a significant risk since it may provide access to sensitive personal information, such as bank accounts[120] and phone access.

None of the aforementioned methods are flawless. On the one hand, there are precise ways for estimating a child's age, but they are not privacy-friendly by default, such as personal ID or biometric characteristics (e.g., fingerprint) scanning. On the other hand, there are technologies that may breach data privacy but are ineffective for estimating an individual's precise age, such as voice recognition and facial ID tools. Moreover, there are methods that are privacy-friendly yet completely useless since they are so simple to deceive, such as self-verification and/or peer-verification. There is also a knowledge-based authentication method that does not violate privacy but is ineffective in identifying exact age. Moreover, as previously mentioned, this method seems to be unhelpful for adults with intellectual disabilities. There is no middle ground solution that protects children's personal information while also protecting them from harmful content.[121]

As previously stated, many underage children disclose personal information online, according to Pew Research Center research and EU Kids Online survey results (e.g., social media network sites). As many websites only require self-verification methods, children may easily deceive the system. These legislative threshold ages and age verification procedures appear to be ineffective in preventing children from accessing inappropriate online content. In this case, it should be noted that, in addition to the legal requirements and the restrictions imposed by data controllers and operators, additional supporting solutions are necessary.

It is important to note at this point that euCONSENT is an ongoing EU-funded project comprised of twelve partners including academic institutions, NGOs, and technology providers[122] that aims to design and provide an EU-wide network that is trying to complete age verification systems and secure online parental consent when children share their personal data online. The primary purpose of this initiative is to safeguard children from potential damage when they access age-restricted adult content online, while also advocating their rights to access appropriate online content that the Internet provides for children.[123]

The first large-scale pilot of this project was completed between February 17th and March 3rd, 2022. More than 2000 people from five countries in Europe took part in the study, including Greece, the United Kingdom, Germany, Cyprus, and Belgium. In this first part of the project, they aimed to understand the current situation in the online sphere, such as how businesses (e.g., social media channels, online shops, etc.) obtain parental consent and verify the age of the children, how they implement

---

[120] Children may also have bank accounts with the consent of their parents or guardians. For instance: HSBC, Children's Bank Accounts, https://www.hsbc.co.uk/current-accounts/products/children/.

[121] Alkis (2021, p. 21).

[122] UpcoMinds, AgeCheck, JusProg, Lisal Expert, Revealing Reality, AGEify, Aston University, London School of Economics and Political Science, Leiden University, Digie, AVPA, John Carr, University of Exeter, https://euconsent.eu/partners/.

[123] euCONSENT, FAQ: What is euCONSENT ASBL?, https://euconsent.eu/faq/.

requirements of the GDPR, and what children and parents expect in terms of the safety and security of their personal data.[124]

To analyse them, they assigned specific missions to project members to perform. Each participant was required to accomplish three tasks and then complete the questionnaires connected to these missions. For example, the first mission was to access the dummy alcohol seller website, and in order to do so, the children should verify their age using one of the methods provided. Subsequently, the website should redirect the users to the secure website, where they will be notified that they are underage to visit the aforementioned adult material website. The second objective was to access the dummy social networking platform. However, due to being recognised as underage in the previous task, they needed parental consent to proceed. The final task was gaining entry to a dummy chat website, which likewise required obtaining parental consent in order to successfully complete the mission. Other scenarios included a dummy knife seller website and a dummy dating site.[125]

According to the statistics, over 81% of the participants completed at least two missions, and 63% finished all three missions while following the instructions. The research indicated that face recognition was by far the most often used method for age verification by 68% of all participants due to its quickness and simplicity, whereas credit card verification was chosen by only 3% of all participants. The research also revealed that while 91% of parents thought it was vital for them to offer consent each time their children wished to disclose personal data online, 74% of them displayed willingness in real-life settings.

In our perspective, having such a study to assess the existing situation and provide suggestions to EU legislators using the findings of these surveys is a critical step, and it may serve as an example for other countries around the world. Nonetheless, there are certain gaps in the initial phase of this project. For example, the project shows that the most commonly used age verification method is facial age estimation preferred by 68% of all participants. However, we do not deduce how effective it was in completing the missions, because, as previously stated, facial recognition cannot be accurate in cases where, for example, a 16-year-old may appear to be 18 years old and have access to age-restricted consent simply because he/she seems to be 18 years old. It is a simple method to use, as stated on the project website, however, it would have been ideal to illustrate the obstacles and challenges of the procedures as well. Furthermore, the least popular method was the use of credit cards as a means of age verification with only 3% of participants in the euCONSENT project, but the reason behind this is not mentioned.[126]

---

[124] euCONSENT, euCONSENT's first large scale pilot (18 March 2022) https://euconsent.eu/euconsents-first-large-scale-pilot/.

[125] euCONSENT, euCONSENT's first large scale pilot: What did the participants have to do? (18 March 2022) https://euconsent.eu/euconsents-first-large-scale-pilot/.

[126] euCONSENT, A summary of the achievements and lessons learned of the euCONSENT project and what comes next (7 December 2022) https://euconsent.eu/a-summary-of-the-achievements-and-lessons-learned-of-the-euconsent-project-and-what-comes-next/.

Furthermore, within the scope of this project, the only way to gain parental consent was to contact them through email using parental consent provider applications JusProg and Upcom.[127] It would have been preferable, however, to include other parental consent-granting methods in order to compare them and identify which method is the most and least popular among parents. Thus, we might have gained insight into the relative efficacy of the indicated parental consent providing methods.

Following the completion of the project's initial phase, European data protection authorities expressed increased interest in the system and proposed more precise specifications for the age verification mechanisms. The French CNIL, for example, proposed a "double-blind" cryptographic solution, which will be explained with an example below, that enables age certificates to be received by age-restricted websites without allowing them to track user activities or identify the users. Spanish AEPD favoured the "device-based" approach to minimize the risk of the age verification system becoming a tool that enables predators to locate children online.[128]

To meet these new requirements and transition the pilot project into operational deployment, the Safe Online fund was utilized to proceed to the second phase of the project, and euCONSENT ASBL, a non-profit organization, was established.

Since then, they have developed a system called AgeAware, a tokenized and anonymized age verification record that enables other age assurance providers to access it for a limited period. This approach eliminates the need for users to perform new age checks each time they visit different websites or applications. They have collaborated with three age verification providers to develop this software system known as AgeChecked, VerifyMy, and Yoti.[129]

In practice, when a user wishes to access an age-restricted website or application, the age assurance provider contracted by the website offers several methods available within the AgeAware system, such as facial estimation verification, traditional ID checks, digital ID verification, or credit card verification.[130]

After the verification is completed, the user can get to the website without having to create an AgeAware account. However, if users choose to create an account, they can use the token stored on their device repeatedly with a quick face ID check, as long as the first age check was done recently enough. This method ensures that the website or app cannot figure out who the user is, and the age verification service cannot determine which sites their users are visiting. This is known as the "double-blind" solution.[131]

---

[127] euCONSENT, euCONSENT's first large scale pilot: How about parental consent? Which Parental Consent Providers were involved? How was the process? (18 March 2022) https://euconsent.eu/euconsents-first-large-scale-pilot/.

[128] euCONSENT, Building a Safer Internet: The Journey to AgeAware® (9 January 2025) https://euconsent.eu/building-a-safer-internet-the-journey-to-ageaware/

[129] euCONSENT, Building a Safer Internet: The Journey to AgeAware® (9 January 2025) https://euconsent.eu/building-a-safer-internet-the-journey-to-ageaware/

[130] euCONSENT, Interoperability through AgeAware from euCONSENT (24 June 2025) https://euconsent.eu/interoperability-through-ageaware-from-euconsent/

[131] euCONSENT, Interoperability through AgeAware from euCONSENT (24 June 2025) https://euconsent.eu/interoperability-through-ageaware-from-euconsent/

Meanwhile, The European Commission also acknowledged that age verification methods and parental consent tools, notwithstanding the implementation of the GDPR, are ineffective. This is due to the fact that most users are only required to submit their birth date or just tick a box during the registration process.[132] As a result, in accordance with its European Digital Identity proposal,[133] the Commission encouraged the Member States to implement effective age-verification methods.[134] Finally, the European Digital Identity Framework came into effect in May 2024. Each Member State will provide at least one version of the EU Digital Identity (EUDI) Wallet by 2026.[135] The EUDI Wallet will enable users to exercise control over their data through "selective disclosure" mechanism allowing them to share only the minimal amount of information necessary with digital service providers (e.g., banks, universities, employers, etc.) for the intended purpose.

One of the functions of the EUDI Wallets could be age verification, and the potential for interoperability between EUDI Wallets and privacy-preserved ecosystems could be investigated to enhance the user experience in the upcoming months. Particularly, in matters concerning parental consent verification, the EUDI should be involved, as identity verification is essential for this process.

On one hand, age assurance through digital identity solutions would be a trustworthy solution, because it would be based on reliable government databases.[136] On the other hand, it may result in discrimination against those who do not wish to participate in this system; thus, this system would be preferable if it remained a voluntary choice.[137] To ensure this voluntary participation, service providers should implement some of the aforementioned age verification alternatives that do not depend on digital identity solutions, especially in low-risk situations, also referred to as a risk-based approach, thereby respecting user preferences and upholding fundamental rights standards.

---

[132] European Commission, Communication from the Commission to the European Parliament, The Council, The European Economic and Social Committee and the Committee of the Regions a Digital Decade for children and youth: the new European strategy for a better internet for kids (BIK +), Brussels, 11.5.2022 COM (2022) 212 final, p. 6.

[133] European Commission, Proposal for a Regulation of the European Parliament and of the Council amending Regulation (EU) No 910/2014 as regards establishing a framework for a European Digital Identity, Brussels, 3.6.2021 COM (2021) 281 final 2021/0136 (COD).

[134] European Commission, Proposal for a Regulation of the European Parliament and of the Council amending Regulation (EU) No 910/2014 as regards establishing a framework for a European Digital Identity, Brussels, 3.6.2021 COM (2021) 281 final 2021/0136 (COD), pp. 11–12.

[135] Regulation (EU) 2024/1183 of the European Parliament and of the Council of 11 April 2024 amending Regulation (EU) No 910/2014 as regards establishing the European Digital Identity Framework, OJ 2024 L 1183, 30.04.2024, pp. 1–64.

[136] Jules Polonetsky, Online Age Verification for Our Children A Report on the Tools and Resources Available for Safeguarding the First Generation of Digital Natives. 31st International Conference of Data Protection and Privacy Commissioners in Madrid, Future of Privacy Forum, (2009, p. 9).

[137] BEUC (The European Consumer Organisation), Making European Digital Identity as Safe as It Is Needed, p. 1 https://www.beuc.eu/sites/default/files/publications/beuc-x-2022-016_eidas_position_paper.pdf.

Due to the mass storage of official documents and biometric data of users, this system might pose certain security and privacy risks. Therefore, it is essential that the system adheres to the privacy requirements outlined in the GDPR and is adequately safeguarded from malevolent cyber-attacks and hacking attempts. For instance, security measures such as the use of robust encryption techniques for both data storage and transmission, as specified in the GDPR.[138] It is also crucial to safeguard the encryption keys effectively to prevent any breach. Implementing a multi-factor authentication mechanism for users accessing European Digital Identity services may enhance security.[139]

Undoubtedly, doing regular security audits and penetration testing is necessary for maintaining system security by identifying vulnerabilities. If a vulnerability is noticed, it should be promptly addressed and appropriately remedied. External professional third parties may offer security measures if needed.[140] Maintaining the latest security patches and upgrades for all software and systems is of utmost importance.[141] Another crucial measure is to provide users with comprehensive information on security protocols, including the need to generate robust passwords,[142] refrain from exchanging login credentials with anybody, including close acquaintances,[143] and promptly identify and report phishing attacks.[144]

Finally, in the event that an incident occurs despite all the diligent efforts and rigorous security measures, it is important to have a well-defined incident response plan that clearly delineates the necessary actions to be taken in the case of a security breach.[145]

Moreover, governments or service providers should not abuse the system by monitoring or tracking individuals' use of digital identities.[146] Age verification may present risks to data subjects in several contexts; for instance, if not utilized solely for its intended purpose, it could lead to profiling and identification of individuals. This may facilitate malicious attacks such as blackmail, harassment, bullying, or commercial targeting like personalized advertisements. They would pose a much greater danger to children due to their vulnerable nature. Consequently, innovative technologies should be employed to mitigate risks and prevent unnecessary processing beyond merely checking age for age-restricted content. For instance, given the current state

---

138 GDPR, Article 32(1)(a).

139 Dasgupta et al. (2017, p. 186).

140 GDPR, Article 32(1)(d) and for more information see: Shah and Mehtre (2015, pp. 27–49).

141 Shah and Mehtre (2015, p. 38).

142 McCrohan et al. (2010, pp. 24–27).

143 McCrohan et al. (2010, p. 26).

144 Jensen et al. (2017, p. 599).

145 Eric C. Thompson: The incident response strategy, Cybersecurity Incident Response: How to Contain, Eradicate, and Recover from Incidents (2018), 65–70.

146 BEUC, Making European Digital Identity as Safe as It Is Needed, p. 1 https://www.beuc.eu/sites/default/files/publications/beuc-x-2022-016_eidas_position_paper.pdf.

of the art, measures like unlinkability,[147] selective disclosure[148] and cryptographic protocols, such as zero-knowledge proofs[149] should be available to data subjects.[150]

The spirit of the GDPR and the COPPA clearly demonstrates that they are both founded on parental supervision and responsibility. However, given the natural flow of life, parents cannot always monitor their children. Even if they could monitor, they would be invading the children's privacy. Although parents have authority over their children's internet activity, it is important to recognise that children are separate individuals and not extensions of their parents. Besides, their need for and expectation of privacy grows with age, making teenagers' privacy demands incomparable to those of young children. In this scenario, we advocate for the implementation of a system that prevents children from accessing inappropriate content without jeopardizing their privacy.[151]

If the abovementioned security and privacy issues are mitigated and the security controls applied, we agree that the verification via European Digital Identity in a trustworthy ecosystem will result in an EU-wide recognized proof of age based on date of birth that is both privacy-friendly and secure.[152]

Meanwhile, many US states have implemented or proposed age verification and age assurance obligations, including requirements to check, verify or estimate users' ages.[153] However, numerous of these measures have faced constitutional challenges, especially on the basis of freedom of expression.[154]

In Free Speech Coalition, Inc. v. Paxton (2025), the US Supreme Court upheld a law from Texas mandating age verification for access to online adult content deemed

---

[147] EDPB Statement, Statement 1/2025 on Age Assurance Adopted on 11 February 2025, p. 1–11, at p.9: "The unlikability property implies that it is impossible to associate or correlate different data items, actions or transactions to a specific data subject."

[148] EDPB Statement, Statement 1/2025 on Age Assurance Adopted on 11 February 2025, p. 1–11, at p. 9: "Selective disclosure is a feature of tokens, credentials and attestations that allows data subjects to share only the information they want with specific parties on a case-by-case basis."

[149] EDPB Statement, Statement 1/2025 on Age Assurance Adopted on 11 February 2025, p. 1–11, at p. 9: "A zero-knowledge proof is a protocol in which one party (the prover) can demonstrate another party (the verifier) that some given statement is true, without conveying to the verifier any information beyond the mere fact of that statement's truth."

[150] EDPB Statement, Statement 1/2025 on Age Assurance Adopted on 11 February 2025, p. 1–11, at para. 16 and 34.

[151] Alkis (2021, pp. 18–19).

[152] European Commission, New European strategy for a Better Internet for Kids – Questions and Answers, 11 May 2022, 12. How will the new strategy address age verification?, https://ec.europa.eu/commission/presscorner/detail/en/QANDA_22_2826.

[153] Free Speech Coalition, Age Verification Bill Tracker (2025). https://action.freespeechcoalition.com/age-verification-bills/

[154] See e.g., Free Speech Coalition, Inc. v. Paxton, 606 U.S. (2025), Free Speech Coalition, Inc. v. Skrmetti, No. 2:24-cv-02933 (W.D. Tenn. Dec. 30, 2024), Free Speech Coalition, Inc. v. Anderson, No. 23–4104 (10th Cir. 2024), appeal from No. 2:23-cv-00287-TS (D. Utah, 2023), Free Speech Coalition, Inc. v. LeBlanc, No. 2:23-cv-02123, 2023 (E.D. La. Oct. 4, 2023), appeal docketed, No. 23–30,780 (5th Cir. 2023), Free Speech Coalition, Inc. v. Rokita, No. 1:24-cv-00980-RLY-MG (S.D. Ind. June 10, 2024) (order granting preliminary injunction June 28, 2024), Free Speech Coalition, Inc. v. Moody, No. 4:24-cv-00514 (N.D. Fla. filed Dec. 16, 2024).

obscene to children. The Court determined that such age-verification requirements fell within the states' traditional authority to protect children and impose only an incidental burden on adults' access to protected speech, comparable to the necessity of presenting ID when purchasing alcohol or tobacco in a retail store. Consequently, the law was determined to promote a significant governmental interest without excessively infringing upon free expression.[155]

Although various states have adopted or are trying to implement their own requirements, there is no consensus regarding the general implementation of the age assurance mechanism across the US. The persistent legal ambiguity highlights the necessity for a unified federal strategy that would set forth comprehensive, efficient, and privacy-conscious age verification standards. A federal framework, similar to that established by the European Commission's blueprint, could provide enhanced legal clarity and uniformity for service providers, regulators, and enforcement agencies.

References

Alkis A (2021) Investigating the usefulness of online age verification methods. Studia Iurisprudentiae Doctorandorum Miskolciensium 1:17

Alkis Tümtürk A (2022) The threshold age for children's online consent in light of the Watson/Legrand debate: is legal transplant possible in the digital era? The Journal of Comparative Law 17(1):235–243

Auxier B, Anderson M, Perrin A, Turner E (2020) Children's engagement with digital devices, screen time. Pew Research Center, pp 2–4

Bontrager P, Roy A, Togelius J, Memon N, Ross A (2018) Deepmasterprints: generating masterprints for dictionary attacks via latent variable evolution. In: 2018 IEEE 9th international conference on biometrics theory, applications and systems (BTAS). IEEE, p 2

Dasgupta D, Roy A, Nag A (2017) Multi-factor authentication: more secure approach towards authenticating individuals. In: Advances in user authentication. Springer International Publishing AG, p 186

Jensen ML, Dinger M, Wright RT, Thatcher JB (2017) Training to mitigate phishing attacks using mindfulness techniques. J Manag Inf Syst 34(2):599

McCrohan KF, Engel K, Harvey JW (2010) Influence of awareness and training on cyber security. J Internet Commerce 9(1):24–27

Milkaite I, Lievens E (2019) The GDPR child's age of consent for data processing across the EU–one year later (July 2019). Better Internet for Kids, pp 1–7

Patel DR, Cabral MD, Ho A, Merrick J (2020) A clinical primer on intellectual disability. Transl Pediatr 9(1):23–35

Polonetsky J (2009) Online age verification for our children a report on the tools and resources available for safeguarding the first generation of digital natives. In: 31st International conference of data protection and privacy commissioners in Madrid. Future of Privacy Forum, pp 3–4

Shah S, Mehtre BM (2015) An overview of vulnerability assessment and penetration testing techniques. J Comput Virol Hack Tech 11:27–49

Smahel D, Machackova H, Mascheroni G, Dedkova L, Staksrud E, Ólafsson K, Livingstone S, Hasebrink U (2020) EU kids online 2020: survey results from 19 countries. EU Kids Online, p 30

[155] Free Speech Coalition, Inc. v. Paxton, 606 U.S. (2025), https://www.supremecourt.gov/opinions/24pdf/23-1122_3e04.pdf.

Talley VAM (2019) Major flaws in minor laws: improving data privacy rights and protections for children under the GDPR. Indiana Int Comp Law Rev 30(1):145

Thierer AD (2007) Social networking and age verification: Many hard questions; no easy solutions. Prog Freedom Found Prog Point Paper 14(5):3

Thompson EC (2018) Cybersecurity incident response: how to contain, eradicate, and recover from incidents. Apress, New York, pp 65–70

Van der Maelen C (2019) The coming-of-age of technology: using emerging tech for online age verifications. Delphi 2:115

Váradi S (2021) Legal challenges of processing health data in the shadow of COVID-19 in the European Union. Forum Acta Jurid Polit 11(4):358–362

Verswijvel K, Walrave M, Hardies K, Heirman W (2019) Sharenting, is it a good or a bad thing? Understanding how adolescents think and feel about sharenting on social network sites. Child Youth Serv Rev 104:104407

Chapter 4
Main Rights of the Children and Their Parents Under the GDPR and the COPPA

Abstract In brief, under the GDPR, children have the same data protection rights as adults. However, neither the children nor their parents are given any guidance on how to exercise these rights. Unlike the GDPR, the COPPA does not explicitly grant children privacy rights; rather, it grants parental rights over their children's personal information. We acknowledge that certain rights may be too complicated for children to exercise, thus parents should be able to do so if required. Nonetheless, the right to access, ratification, and deletion may be easier for children to exercise without parental participation if they are mature enough to understand the consequences of their online actions. As we mentioned in the previous chapter, children should not lose control over their data since it might lead to detrimental consequences, such as Amanda Todd's suicide because she was unable to remove it on her own. Children shall be provided with the means to acquire knowledge regarding their rights and then engage in their exercise independently or give such responsibility to their parents. Ergo, legislation alone is insufficient in establishing a safe online environment for children. Instead, a collaborative effort involving data controllers, service providers, and parents is necessary to accomplish this goal.

This chapter will begin with evaluating the requirements concerning the data protection rights of children in accordance with the GDPR, followed by an examination of the rights afforded to parents under the COPPA. Ultimately, we will draw a conclusion by offering our recommendations for the ideal approach via a comparative analysis of the two legislations.

Children have the same rights as adults under the GDPR. They have the right to be informed, the right to access, the right to rectification, the right to erasure (including the right to be forgotten), the right to processing restriction, the right to data portability, the right to object, and the right not to be subject to a decision based solely on automated processing, including profiling.[1]

First and foremost, data subjects have the right to have easily understandable information about who is processing their data, what data is being processed, and

[1] GDPR, Article 12–23.

A. Alkış Tümtürk, *Online Privacy and Data Protection of Children in the European Union and the United States*, Ius Gentium: Comparative Perspectives on Law and Justice 141, https://doi.org/10.1007/978-3-032-27534-9_4

what is the purpose of processing.[2] Article 12 of the GDPR requires data controllers to use plain and clear language, particularly when any information relates to a child.[3]

Second, data subjects have the right to request access to any personal information about them obtained by data controllers.[4] If feasible, the data controller shall provide data subjects with remote access to a secure system where they can have direct access to their personal information.[5] For example, if a child wishes to access his/her data that is being processed by an educational children's website (e.g., Funbrain.com[6]), the privacy policies usually mention this right for EU data subjects.[7] However, the children may be unaware of the privacy policies, therefore, it would be ideal for them to create short videos or colourful vivid pictures with plain language so that the children can understand their data protection rights much better.

Third, data subjects have the right to rectification, which means they have the right to request that the data controller rectify any inaccurate information on them without undue delay.[8] Fourth, data subjects have the right to erasure, which they can exercise when the purposes for which the data controller collected their data no longer exist; if the data subjects withdraw their consent; where the data subjects object to the processing of their personal information.[9] Most importantly, the data subjects exercise this right if they give consent when they are children and are not fully aware of the consequences and risks. Even if the data subject is now an adult, he/she can still use this right.[10]

Furthermore, Article 17(2) of the GDPR refers to the right to be forgotten.[11] The "right to be forgotten" is a broader concept that originated in a European Court of Justice decision.[12] It allows individuals to request that search engines remove links to information about them, which is inaccurate, inadequate, irrelevant, or excessive for the purpose it was processed.[13] The right to erasure is limited to personal data retained by the controllers, whereas the right to be forgotten extends to publicly available information on the internet.

---

[2] GDPR, Article 12–14.

[3] GDPR, Article 12.

[4] GDPR, Article 15.

[5] GDPR, Recital 63.

[6] Fun Brain: https://www.funbrain.com/.

[7] Fun Brain, Privacy Policy: https://www.funbrain.com/privacy-policy.

[8] GDPR, Article 16.

[9] GDPR, Article 17.

[10] GDPR, Recital 65.

[11] GDPR, Article 17(2).

[12] The first time the "right to be forgotten" was used in a case decided by the European Court of Justice (ECJ) was in the case of Google Spain SL, Google Inc. v Agencia Española de Protección de Datos, Mario Costeja González, which was decided on May 13, 2014.

Case C 131/12 Google Spain SL and Google Inc. v Agencia Española de Protección de Datos (AEPD) and Mario Costeja González EU:C:2014:317.

[13] Case C 131/12 Google Spain SL and Google Inc. v Agencia Española de Protección de Datos (AEPD) and Mario Costeja González EU:C:2014:317, para 92.

In the US, for example, there is a case named Sidis v. F-R Publishing. Sidis, the child prodigy, became a public figure in the early 1900s due to his parents' desire. When he became an adult, the New Yorker published an article about him, and Sidis filed a lawsuit because he didn't want to be seen by the public. However, the court ruled against his free will because, like all other famous persons, the public is interested in learning more about them.[14] Was it, however, Sidis' decision to be in the spotlight at the beginning? Did he have a saying when his parents put him in front of the public when he was a child?

In the hypothetical scenario of this case occurring in the present day, it is worth considering that while the physical newspaper articles cannot be retroactively altered, Sidis might have potentially pursued the option of requesting the anonymisation of his personal information on the newspaper's website.[15] Consequently, this would afford him the opportunity to finally fade into obscurity in the public's perception. Thus, the GDPR's right to be forgotten is critical, particularly in cases like Sidis'.

Fifth, data subjects have the right to restrict the processing of their personal information. These limitations might include, but are not limited to, temporarily relocating their personal data to another processing system, making certain personal data inaccessible to other users, and temporarily deleting published data from the website. The processing restriction should be noted on the given system.[16] This right may be too complicated for a child to exercise, but their parents can exercise it on their behalf if necessary.

Sixth, if the personal data is obtained based on consent or the performance of a contract, and the processing of personal data is managed by automated means, data subjects have the right to transmit their data from one controller to another in order to strengthen their control over their data. If technically feasible, data subjects should be able to transmit their data directly from one controller to another.[17] As the previous right, parents can use this right to data portability on children's behalf if they feel it is necessary.

Data subjects have the right to object to processing where it is based on the performance of a task in the public interest, the exercise of official authority vested in the data controller, or the controller's legitimate interests. The controller must cease processing the personal data unless it proves compelling legitimate reasons for the processing that outweigh the data subject's interests, rights, and freedoms.[18] However, justifying the legitimate interest is hard for the data controller where the data subject is a child, because Article 6(1) states that the interests, freedom, and fundamental rights of the data subject take precedence over the interests of the data

---

[14] Case 113 F.2d 806, Sidis v. F-R Pub. Corporation (No. 400), Judgment of the Court of Appeals for the Second Circuit, New York, 22 July 1940 cited in Steinberg (2016), pp. 859–860.

[15] Hurbain v. Belgium judgment on 21 June 2021, referral to the Grand Chamber 11 October 2021, no.57292/16 para. 132 et seq. and Hurbain v. Belgium judgment (Grand Chamber) on 4 July 2023, no.57292/16 para. 255 et seq.

[16] GDPR, Recital 67.

[17] GDPR, Article 20 and Recital 68.

[18] GDPR, Article 21(1).

controller or third parties particularly when the data subject is a child.[19] In addition, data controllers shall perform a data protection impact assessment (DPIA), if the processing of children's personal data poses a high risk to the rights and freedoms of children and other vulnerable natural people, as well as to their physical, material or non-material wellbeing.[20] For example, as mentioned above if the children's data is being processed with other aggravating factors (large number of data subjects, purpose of profiling, together with biometrics etc.), it may be required by the DPA in charge.[21]

Furthermore, data subjects have the absolute right to object to the use of their personal data for direct marketing purposes. In such a case, the data controller has no exemptions or reasons for refusal. In other words, the processing of the personal data for such purposes should cease.[22] Besides, the GDPR's preamble offers additional protections for children when it comes to the use of their data for direct marketing purposes.[23] This special protection should, in our view, be interpreted so that, if a child objects to a processing for direct marketing purposes, the data controller should act immediately, without waiting for parental consent.

Eighth, data subjects have the right not to be the subject of a decision based solely on automated processing, including profiling, unless the decision:

> "is necessary for entering into, or performance of, a contract between the data subject and a data controller; is authorised by Union or Member State law to which the controller is subject and which also lays down suitable measures to safeguard the data subject's rights and freedoms and legitimate interests; or is based on the data subject's explicit consent."[24]

Although Recital (71) indicates that profiling should not be used on children, Recital (38) does not deny profiling but requires special protection for underage children.[25] Furthermore, because Article 22 does not explicitly exclude children from its content, the GDPR's spirit on child profiling is unclear. However, we strongly advocate that, given the children's relative immaturity and naïve understanding of the consequences of algorithms and personalized advertisements on websites, data controllers should not use the exceptions mentioned above, as specified in Article 22(2), to justify children profiling.[26]

---

[19] GDPR, Article 6(1)(f).

[20] GDPR, Article 35(1) and Recital 75.

[21] See the mandatory DPIA list of Hungarian DPA: Nemzeti Adatvédelmi és Információszabadság Hatóság (NAIH), GDPR 35 (4) Mandatory DPIA List, List of Processing Operations Subject to DPIA GDPR 35 (4), points (2), (19), and (20), https://www.naih.hu/data-protection/gdpr-35-4-mandatory-dpia-list.

[22] GDPR, Article 21(2) and Article 21(3).

[23] GDPR, Recital 38.

[24] GDPR, Article 22(1) and (2).

[25] GDPR, Recital 38 and 71.

[26] GDPR, Article 22(2).

Article 29 Data Protection Working Party, Guidelines on Automated individual decision-making and Profiling for the purposes of Regulation 2016/679, 17/EN WP251rev.01, last revised and adopted on 6 February 2018, pp. 1–37, 26.

The GDPR does not specify how or when children can exercise these rights although the rights outlined above apply to children. And there is no guidance as to whether parents can use these rights on behalf of their children, or how they might do so in practice. However, it may be instructive to review other countries' applications in this circumstance.[27] In Scotland, for example, there is a rebuttable assumption that a child of 12 has reached the maturity to exercise their data protection rights until shown otherwise. This assumption does not exist throughout the rest of the United Kingdom. They think that competency is determined by one's level of understanding rather than by one's age. Therefore, if the child is competent to give consent for their personal data processing, they believe it is reasonable to assume that those children are also competent to exercise their own data protection rights.[28]

According to the Data Protection Commission of Ireland, not only the child's age and maturity should be considered, but also the type of personal data being processed, the service offered by the data controller to a child and the context of processing, the type of request a child seek, whether enabling children to exercise their rights is in their best interests, and whether the child seeks parental assistance or participation to exercise their rights. For example, accessing or erasing sensitive data (e.g., medical data) on the Internet requires a different handling than accessing or erasing personal data shared on social media networks (e.g., Facebook).[29] We consider that Ireland's approach in this respect is more comprehensive, and we also endorse the idea that not only age and maturity but also the sorts of rights held by children should be examined.

To summarize, while the GDPR has not clarified it, children should have the right to exercise their data protection rights whenever it is in their best interests. It would be preferrable if children could use their rights individually, depending on the types of rights, or via parental representation if they have not reached maturity or the age of consent.[30] Additionally, it would be optimal if there were forthcoming official guidance for children and their parents to effectively exercise the aforementioned data protection rights.

We recognise that there may be some rights that are too complex for children to exercise, hence parents should have the ability to do so if necessary. However, children who are sufficiently competent to comprehend the repercussions of their

---

[27] Data Protection Commission Ireland, Children Front and Centre, Fundamentals for a Child-Oriented Approach to Data Processing-Draft Version for Public Consultation, December 2020, 33.

[28] Information Commissioner's Office (ICO), What rights do children have?, When may a child exercise these rights on their own behalf?, https://ico.org.uk/for-organisations/guide-to-data-protection/guide-to-the-general-data-protection-regulation-gdpr/children-and-the-uk-gdpr/what-rights-do-children-have/.

[29] Data Protection Commission Ireland, Children Front and Centre, Fundamentals for a Child-Oriented Approach to Data Processing-Draft Version for Public Consultation, December 2020, 34.

[30] Data Protection Commission Ireland, Children Front and Centre, Fundamentals for a Child-Oriented Approach to Data Processing-Draft Version for Public Consultation, December 2020, 34–35.

online acts may find it simpler to exercise their rights to access, ratification, and deletion without parental involvement. Besides, the exercise of these rights will not give rise to perilous circumstances for children under normal conditions.

Furthermore, the COPPA does not address the privacy rights of children, but rather focuses on outlining the "parental rights" related to the personal information of children. First and foremost, there is a parental right of notice, which requires operators to offer notice and get verifiable parental consent before collecting, using, or disclosing personal information from children.[31] Second, parents have the right to review any personal information provided online by their children. The operator should provide the parents with the option "to refuse the operator's further use or future online collection of personal information from that child at any time, and to direct the operator to delete the child's personal information."[32]

It would have been ideal, though, if the children had such rights rather than their parents having them on their behalf. Because there is no reason why children should be prevented from asserting their rights if they are mature enough to do so. If we merely provide their parents access to their data, it may not always be in the best interests of the children. Assuming, for example, that the children submitted personal information on a website and, after some time, discovered that the information is no longer relevant and decides to delete it. They should have the right to have their personal information deleted, and operators should make this process easier for children, because the information they want to delete could be more sensitive for them, and the longer the process takes, the riskier it is to keep that information online, especially if the data is open to the public.

Loss of control over one's own personal information can have tragic consequences, as can be seen in case of *Amanda Todd*, a Canadian teenager who took her own life after being exposed to long-term bullying because of a single photo she couldn't erase. In the end, Amanda had created a silent YouTube video in which she shared her story using a collection of handwritten notes before she committed suicide. Amanda says on one of the notes: "I can never get the photo back, it's out there forever…". These sorts of events may happen to anyone, due to the increasing use of social media among children and teenagers. Therefore, it is essential to broaden the COPPA's provided rights to include children.[33]

Moreover, considering the above-mentioned GDPR data subject rights, at least the right to access, ratification, deletion, and not being subject to a decision based solely on automated processing (especially profiling) could be provided to children under the COPPA as well. If the children are not mature enough to exercise these rights and have not yet reached the age when they may grant consent for their online actions, parents can exercise these potential rights on their behalf. Otherwise, the children may exercise these rights themselves.

[31] 16 CFR COPPA 312.4(a).

[32] 16 CFR COPPA 312.6(a)(2).

[33] YouTube, Thesomebodytoknow channel: My story: Struggling, bullying, suicide, self-harm, available at: https://www.youtube.com/watch?v=vOHXGNx-E7E cited in Alkis Tümtürk (2022, p. 3).

Children enjoy several rights under the United Nations Convention on the Rights of the Child (UNCRC),[34] which the US has signed but not ratified, while all EU Member States have signed and ratified. These rights include the right to freely express themselves and be heard,[35] the right to seek and receive any kind of information in any form written, orally, in the form of art, or via any other media that a child chooses,[36] and the right to engage in play and recreational activities appropriate to their age and maturity.[37] Accordingly, it is critical for parents to give these opportunities to their children and allow them to use their rights freely within the limits of what is possible.

However, the GDPR's, and particularly the COPPA's overprotective parental approach, would have a severe impact on the mentioned children's rights. Therefore, it is very important to offer a safe environment for children without depriving them of the benefits of the internet, while also attempting to protect their right to privacy and data protection from third parties without being infringed by their own parents. The GDPR and the COPPA should not disregard this, and children should be given as much control over their personal data as feasible, appropriate with their age and maturity level. This may be achievable by granting them specific rights that they can exercise independently of their parents to a reasonable extent. Finally, we suggest for the expansion and implementation of these children's privacy and data protection rights in practice.

This is not a result that can be achieved only by legislation, but rather with the active engagement of parents, the service providers, and the data controllers. On one hand, parents should provide their children with the benefits of the Internet, secure their children's personal data from malicious third parties by participating appropriately, when necessary, without jeopardizing their children's privacy, and be able to manage this balance sufficiently. On the other hand, data controllers and service providers (e.g., third party suppliers) should be able to communicate and display these rights to children using colourful and vivid pictures and simple and clear language.

In this case, children will be more aware of their rights and will be able to comprehend the limitations to which they may use their rights, as well as how much assistance they need from their parents if necessary. The main obligations imposed on data controllers will be discussed in further depth in the next chapter.

References

---

[34] UN Commission on Human Rights, Convention on the Rights of the Child, E/CN.4/RES/1990/74, 07.03.1990.

[35] UNCRC, Article 12.

[36] UNCRC, Article 13.

[37] UNCRC, Article 31.

Alkis Tümtürk A (2022) Implications of parental sharing of children's personal data online. ArsBoni Jogi Folyoirat, X. evfolyam 2022/1-2:3
Steinberg SB (2016) Sharenting: children's privacy in the age of social media. Emory Law J 66:859–860

Chapter 5
Main Obligations Imposed on Data Controllers Under the GDPR and the COPPA

Abstract Chapter 5 examines data controller's obligations under the GDPR and operator's obligations under the COPPA comparatively. We claim that the GDPR doesn't sufficiently address data controllers' obligations to process children's personal data. Accordingly, we suggest a GDPR article that includes only the data controller's child-specific obligations based on children's data protection rights. The COPPA takes a different approach and particularly addresses the obligations of operators regarding processing children's personal data. Yet, COPPA requires operators to engage with parents to protect children's personal data, rather than directly communicating with the children in question. We propose that operators provide children (when mature enough) control over their data, particularly when it comes to activities like erasing or restricting transfers to third parties/countries. We also suggest that data controllers should collaborate with supervisory authorities and always conduct data protection/privacy impact assessments via data protection/privacy officers to detect, analyse, and mitigate risks before processing children's personal data. We justify this suggestion by asserting that processing children's personal data would almost certainly pose a high risk owing to children's vulnerability.

This chapter will commence by assessing the requirements imposed by the GDPR on data controllers, with particular emphasis on the data protection and privacy rights of children. Subsequently, we will proceed to examine the aforementioned matter within the context of the COPPA. Finally, we will do an analysis that compares the data controller requirements regarding children (and their parents) within both legislations.

The GDPR defines the data controller as "[t]he natural or legal person, public authority, agency or other body which, alone or jointly with others, determines the purposes and means of the processing of personal data"[1] and the first and foremost obligation of the data controller under the GDPR is to comply with the Regulation. Article 24 of the GDPR explains it as follows:

[1] GDPR, Article 4(7).

A. Alkış Tümtürk, *Online Privacy and Data Protection of Children in the European Union and the United States*, Ius Gentium: Comparative Perspectives on Law and Justice 141, https://doi.org/10.1007/978-3-032-27534-9_5

> "Taking into account the nature, scope, context and purposes of processing as well as the risks of varying likelihood and severity for the rights and freedoms of natural persons, the controller shall implement appropriate technical and organisational measures to ensure and to be able to demonstrate that processing is performed in accordance with this Regulation. Those measures shall be reviewed and updated where necessary."[2]

This implies that the data controller should be well-versed in the GDPR's responsibilities and adhere to the personal data processing principles outlined in Article 5. These are the principles of lawfulness, fairness, and transparency, as well as accuracy, purpose limitation, data minimisation, storage limitation, integrity, confidentiality, and accountability of the controller for this compliance.[3]

Second, the following measures should be implemented by the data controller: appropriate technical measures including pseudonymisation and encryption of relevant personal data,[4] and organizational measures including risk assessment which means mitigating solutions to reduce risks[5] as well as having effective and compliant data protection policies in place.[6] Third, the data controller shall make it possible and easy for data subjects to exercise their rights.[7]

Fourth and most significantly for our research, data controllers must make all reasonable attempts to get consent for processing children's data from the holder of parental responsibility for the child if the child is underage, considering available technology.[8]

[2] GDPR, Article 24(1).

[3] GDPR, Article 5(1)(a)(b)(c)(d)(e)(f).

[4] GDPR, Article 32(1)(a).

[5] GDPR, Article 35 (Data Protection Impact Assessment).

[6] GDPR, Article 24(2).

[7] GDPR, Article 12(2).

[8] GDPR, Article 8(2).

Approved codes of conduct, as defined in Article 40 of the GDPR,[9] or approved certification mechanisms, as defined in Article 42 of the GDPR,[10] might be used to demonstrate that the data controller is appropriately implementing the obligations.[11]

Fifth obligation of the data controller is to guarantee that the concept of data protection by design and by default is followed.[12] Data protection by design involves the incorporation of data protection principles from the first stages of a project, product, or asset's development, and throughout its entire life cycle. To attain this objective, the GDPR requires data controllers to implement suitable technological or organisational measures, including the use of pseudonymisation and encryption mechanisms.[13]

The principle of data protection by default entails that data controllers exclusively handle data that is essential for the fulfilment of their processing purposes. The concept is linked to the fundamental principles of data minimization and purpose limitation. In this scenario, should there be any alterations in the personal data processing conducted by the data controller, or if the data controller opts to process more data pertaining to the data subject, it is imperative for the data controllers to obtain updated consent from the data subjects accordingly. It is important to ensure that accessibility is limited as well. For instance, it is recommended to promote the implementation of

[9] GDPR, Article 40. "Associations and other bodies representing categories of controllers or processors may prepare codes of conduct, or amend or extend such codes, for the purpose of specifying the application of this Regulation, such as with regard to: fair and transparent processing; the legitimate interests pursued by controllers in specific contexts; the collection of personal data; the pseudonymisation of personal data; the information provided to the public and to data subjects; the exercise of the rights of data subjects; the information provided to, and the protection of, children, and the manner in which the consent of the holders of parental responsibility over children is to be obtained; the measures and procedures referred to in Articles 24 and 25 and the measures to ensure security of processing referred to in Article 32; the notification of personal data breaches to supervisory authorities and the communication of such personal data breaches to data subjects; the transfer of personal data to third countries or international organisations; or out-of-court proceedings and other dispute resolution procedures for resolving disputes between controllers and data subjects with regard to processing, without prejudice to the rights of data subjects pursuant to Articles 77 and 79."

[10] GDPR, Article 42 and Recital (100): "In order to enhance transparency and compliance with this Regulation, the establishment of certification mechanisms and data protection seals and marks should be encouraged, allowing data subjects to quickly assess the level of data protection of relevant products and services."

[11] GDPR, Article 24(3).

[12] GDPR, Article 25.

[13] GDPR, Article 25(1).

European Commission, What does data protection 'by design' and 'by default' mean?, https://commission.europa.eu/law/law-topic/data-protection/reform/rules-business-and-organisations/obligations/what-does-data-protection-design-and-default-mean_en.

ICO, Data protection by design and default, at What is data protection by design?, and at What is data protection by default?, https://ico.org.uk/for-organisations/guide-to-data-protection/guide-to-the-general-data-protection-regulation-gdpr/accountability-and-governance/data-protection-by-design-and-default/#dpd3.

user profile settings on social media platforms that prioritise privacy, ensuring that they are not by default accessible to an unlimited number of individuals.[14]

Sixth, if data controllers involve someone to process personal data on their behalf, they should ensure that these processors are knowledgeable, reliable, and have adequate resources to ensure the requirement of appropriate technical and organizational measures that meet the Regulation's requirements.[15]

These processors are defined as "a natural or legal person, public authority, agency, or other body that processes personal data on behalf of the controller" under the GDPR[16] and should be governed by a legal contract that includes the following: the type of personal data that they are processing and the categories of data subjects, the purpose and scope of processing, the risk to the data subjects' rights, and their certain tasks and responsibilities regarding the relevant processing.[17] The processor's responsibility also includes returning or deleting the processed data at the end of processing, if demanded by the data controller.[18]

Seventh, each data controller and processor shall also document their processing actions and make them available to the supervisory authority if required, so that this documentation may be used to monitor such processes. This documentation should include: the name and contact details of the controller and, if available, the processor; the purpose of the processing; the type of personal data and categories of data subjects; with whom the personal data have been shared or will be shared, e.g., third parties or international organisations; documentation of the adequate safeguards if the collected personal data has been shared with third parties; the time limit for the erasure of processed data; and the description of implemented technical and organisational security measures.[19]

Eighth, data controllers and processors should collaborate with the supervisory authority to perform its tasks where required.[20] Furthermore, as a ninth obligation,

---

[14] GDPR, Article 25(2).

European Commission, What does data protection 'by design' and 'by default' mean?, https://commission.europa.eu/law/law-topic/data-protection/reform/rules-business-and-organisations/obligations/what-does-data-protection-design-and-default-mean_en.

ICO, Data protection by design and default, at What is data protection by design?, and at What is data protection by default?, https://ico.org.uk/for-organisations/guide-to-data-protection/guide-to-the-general-data-protection-regulation-gdpr/accountability-and-governance/data-protection-by-design-and-default/#dpd3.

[15] GDPR, Article 28(1) and Recital 81.

[16] GDPR, Article 4(8). For more information about the obligations of the controllers, processors and their relationships: EDPB, Guidelines 07/2020 on the concepts of controller and processor in the GDPR Version 2.1 Adopted on 07 July 2021, pp. 1–51.

[17] GDPR, Article 28(3) and Recital (81).

[18] GDPR, Article 28(3)(g).

[19] GDPR, Article 30 and Recital (82).

[20] GDPR, Article 32 and for information about the tasks of supervisory authority see Article 57: "…monitor and enforce the application of this Regulation; promote public awareness and understanding of the risks, rules, safeguards and rights in relation to processing. Activities addressed specifically to children shall receive specific attention; advise, in accordance with Member State law, the national parliament, the government, and other institutions and bodies on legislative and

as soon as the data controller gets aware of a personal data breach, they must notify the supervisory authority within seventy-two hours of being aware of it.[21] Failure to address the data breach might:

> "[r]esult in physical, material or non-material damage to natural persons such as loss of control over their personal data or limitation of their rights, discrimination, identity theft or fraud, financial loss, unauthorised reversal of pseudonymisation, damage to reputation, loss of confidentiality of personal data protected by professional secrecy or any other significant economic or social disadvantage to the natural person concerned".[22]

If the personal data in question is related to children, data controllers must proceed with greater caution, since a data breach might have far-reaching negative implications for children than for adults. For example, in September 2021, NBC News gathered and examined school files from hackers' dark web pages and discovered they were rife with children's personal data including permanent information such as birth dates and social security numbers, which can result in a lifetime of identity

---

administrative measures relating to the protection of natural persons' rights and freedoms with regard to processing; promote the awareness of controllers and processors of their obligations under this Regulation; upon request, provide information to any data subject concerning the exercise of their rights under this Regulation and, if appropriate, cooperate with the supervisory authorities in other Member States to that end; handle complaints lodged by a data subject, or by a body, organisation or association in accordance with Article 80, and investigate, to the extent appropriate, the subject matter of the complaint and inform the complainant of the progress and the outcome of the investigation within a reasonable period, in particular if further investigation or coordination with another supervisory authority is necessary; cooperate with, including sharing information and provide mutual assistance to, other supervisory authorities with a view to ensuring the consistency of application and enforcement of this Regulation; conduct investigations on the application of this Regulation, including on the basis of information received from another supervisory authority or other public authority; monitor relevant developments, insofar as they have an impact on the protection of personal data, in particular the development of information and communication technologies and commercial practices; adopt standard contractual clauses referred to in Article 28(8) and in point (d) of Article 46(2); establish and maintain a list in relation to the requirement for data protection impact assessment pursuant to Article 35(4); give advice on the processing operations referred to in Article 36(2); encourage the drawing up of codes of conduct pursuant to Article 40(1) and provide an opinion and approve such codes of conduct which provide sufficient safeguards, pursuant to Article 40(5); encourage the establishment of data protection certification mechanisms and of data protection seals and marks pursuant to Article 42(1), and approve the criteria of certification pursuant to Article 42(5); where applicable, carry out a periodic review of certifications issued in accordance with Article 42(7); draft and publish the requirements for accreditation of a body for monitoring codes of conduct pursuant to Article 41 and of a certification body pursuant to Article 43; conduct the accreditation of a body for monitoring codes of conduct pursuant to Article 41 and of a certification body pursuant to Article 43; authorise contractual clauses and provisions referred to in Article 46(3); approve binding corporate rules pursuant to Article 47; contribute to the activities of the Board; keep internal records of infringements of this Regulation and of measures taken in accordance with Article 58(2); and fulfil any other tasks related to the protection of personal data."

[21] GDPR, Article 33(1).

[22] GDPR, Recital (85).

theft because these data remain the same even when they become adults.[23] However, children are likely to be less aware of the ramifications and dangers of identity theft. Therefore, it is the obligation of data controllers to notify the supervisory authority of such data breaches without any delay.[24]

The tenth obligation states that if the data breach is likely to result in a high risk to a data subject's rights and freedoms, data controllers should notify the data subject without undue delay. This communication should be made with plain and clear language and should include at least the name and contact information of the data protection officer, a description of the potential consequences of the personal data breach, and a description of the measures taken or proposed to be taken by the controller to reduce the negative effects.[25]

Data subjects may not need to be warned in some cases. First, if the data controller has established appropriate technological and organisational protections, such as encryption, the communication is not required. Second, where the controller has taken steps to reduce the high risk to data subjects' rights and freedoms, contacting them is also unnecessary. Third, the communication shall not be required when disproportionate effort is involved. Instead, in such cases, public communication may occur to inform data subjects.[26]

If data controllers apply this personal data breach notification obligation to children's personal data, they must consider the age and maturity of the children whose personal data has been violated. In case the affected children can consent to the processing of their personal data, the data controllers consider notifying the children about the data breach. Nonetheless, it would be more reassuring if both parents and children were informed simultaneously. Yet, when the children are underage, data controllers should contact their parents and notify them of the data breach. In addition, data controllers may opt to directly notify other individuals in order to mitigate certain potential impacts on children.[27] For instance, a teacher or principal of the impacted child may be chosen if the data breach involves a student's personal details from school records (e.g., cyber attackers hacking into school databases and stealing students' personal data).

The occurrence of a data breach involving children's data with sensitive nature might lead to even more dangerous scenarios. For example, if some computers were taken from a children's health centre that collected health[28] and social welfare data

---

[23] NBC News, Hackers are leaking children's data — and there's little parents can do, 10 September 2021, by Kevin Collier, https://www.nbcnews.com/tech/security/hackers-are-leaking-childrens-data-s-little-parents-can-rcna1926.

[24] GDPR, Recital 38: "Children merit specific protection with regard to their personal data, as they may be less aware of the risks, consequences and safeguards concerned and their rights in relation to the processing of personal data." and Article 33(1).

[25] GDPR, Article 34(1) and (2).

[26] GDPR, Article 34 (3)(a)(b) and (c).

[27] Article 29 Data Protection Working Party, Opinion 03/2014 on Personal Data Breach Notification, 693/14/EN WP 213, 25 March 2014, p. 5–6.

[28] Health data falls into special category of personal data with sensitive nature under the Article 9(1) of the GDPR.

on a particular number of children, the children and their families may be put in jeopardy. Because sensitive information about those children has now fallen into the hands of unauthorized and malicious individuals, anything is possible, including blackmailing those parents and children using the gathered sensitive information or targeting parents of critically ill children to profit from their vulnerability (e.g., charlatans).[29]

Given the vulnerability of children, as well as the risks and consequences of data breaches, data controllers should not apply the aforementioned exceptions to their notification obligation for data breaches. Even if they have put in place the necessary technological and organizational safeguards, they should notify the parents and children as quickly as possible. Furthermore, they shall give guidance and advice to parents in order to help them mitigate the adverse impact of personal data breaches on their children.[30]

As per the eleventh obligation under the GDPR, in cases where new technologies are employed and a particular method of data processing is expected to pose a high risk to the rights and freedoms of individuals, data controllers shall conduct a data protection impact assessment (DPIA) before the processing occurs.[31] It is particularly applicable to large-scale processing activities that aim to process a large amount of personal data. However, if medical physicians or lawyers process the personal data of their patients or clients, a data protection impact assessment is not mandatory. Because, according to the GDPR, their personal data processing "should not be considered to be on a large scale".[32] The reason of this exception can be due to the obligation of confidentiality of these professions.

Moreover, the DPAs provide comprehensive information on DPIA methodologies, which may help data controllers in determining how to conduct DPIAs.[33] DPAs may also publish guidelines outlining the specific processes that necessitate mandatory DPIAs.[34] Besides, it should be noted that when conducting the data protection impact assessment, the data controller should ask for the advice of the data protection officer,

---

[29] Article 29 Data Protection Working Party, Opinion 03/2014 on Personal Data Breach Notification, 693/14/EN WP 213, 25 March 2014, p. 5.

[30] GDPR Recital (86) states: "The controller should communicate to the data subject a personal data breach, without undue delay, where that personal data breach is likely to result in a high risk to the rights and freedoms of the natural person in order to allow him or her to take the necessary precautions. The communication should describe the nature of the personal data breach as well as recommendations for the natural person concerned to mitigate potential adverse effects. Such communications to data subjects should be made as soon as reasonably feasible [...]". We suggest that we apply this statement even more strongly to situations of breach of personal data of children, which are significantly more sensitive and may include severe risk scenarios.

[31] GDPR, Article 35(1).

[32] GDPR, Recital (91).

[33] CNIL (French DPA), Privacy Impact Assessment (PIA) Methodology, (February 2018), https://www.cnil.fr/sites/cnil/files/atoms/files/cnil-pia-1-en-methodology.pdf.

AEPD (Spanish DPA), Risk Management and Impact Assessment in the Processing of Personal Data, (June 2021), https://www.aepd.es/es/documento/risk-management-and-impact-assessment-in-processing-personal-data.pdf.

[34] See various mandatory DPIA listings of different DPAs:

if one has been appointed.[35] The data controller or processor shall assist and provide enough resources to data protection officers in order for them to carry out their functions and obligations as outlined in Article 39[36] of the GDPR.[37]

Therefore, companies have been forming new teams for data protection and privacy operations only to assess whether personal data processing is being carried out in accordance with the GDPR and other data protection legislation.[38] There are new platforms (e.g., OneTrust,[39] the open source DPIA software by the French DPA[40]) that data protection officers may use to create, disseminate, and analyse data protection impact assessments using pre-built templates, including questions regarding the

---

Nemzeti Adatvédelmi és Információszabadság Hatóság (NAIH), GDPR 35 (4) Mandatory DPIA List, List of Processing Operations Subject to DPIA GDPR 35 (4), https://www.naih.hu/data-protection/gdpr-35-4-mandatory-dpia-list.

AEPD (Spanish DPA), List of The Types of Data Processing That Require a Data Protection Impact Assessment under Art 35.4, p. 1–3, https://www.aepd.es/sites/default/files/2019-09/listas-dpia-en-35-4.pdf.

Data Protection Commission Ireland, List of Types of Data Processing Operations which.

require a Data Protection Impact Assessment, p. 1–6, https://www.dataprotection.ie/sites/default/files/uploads/2018-11/Data-Protection-Impact-Assessment.pdf.

CNIL (French DPA), Analyse d'impact relative à la protection des données: publication d'une liste des traitements pour lesquels une analyse est requise (6 November 2018), https://www.cnil.fr/fr/analyse-dimpact-relative-la-protection-des-donnees-publication-dune-liste-des-traitements-pour.

[35] GDPR, Article 35(2).

[36] GDPR, Article 39:" The data protection officer shall have at least the following tasks:

(a) to inform and advise the controller or the processor and the employees who carry out processing of their obligations pursuant to this Regulation and to other Union or Member State data protection provisions;

(b) to monitor compliance with this Regulation, with other Union or Member State data protection provisions and with the policies of the controller or processor in relation to the protection of personal data, including the assignment of responsibilities, awareness-raising and training of staff involved in processing operations, and the related audits;

(c) to provide advice where requested as regards the data protection impact assessment and monitor its performance pursuant to Article 35;

(d) to cooperate with the supervisory authority;

(e) to act as the contact point for the supervisory authority on issues relating to processing, including the prior consultation referred to in Article 36, and to consult, where appropriate, with regard to any other matter."

[37] GDPR, Article 38(2).

[38] If we search on LinkedIn or other job search platforms, we may come across several announcements for open positions such as data protection/privacy officer, data privacy specialist, privacy operations specialist, and so on: LinkedIn, Privacy Officer jobs in Hungary, https://www.linkedin.com/jobs/search/?geoId=100288700&keywords=privacy%20officer&location=Hungary.

[39] OneTrust, PIA and DPIA Automation, Gain visibility and efficiency while minimizing risk https://www.onetrust.com/products/pia-and-dpia-automation/.

[40] CNIL, The open source PIA software helps to carry out data protection impact assessment, (30 June 2021), https://www.cnil.fr/en/open-source-pia-software-helps-carry-out-data-protection-impact-assessment. (Portable and online versions are available. CNIL provided English translations for the tool, and a few EU DPAs offered translations as well, such as Hungarian DPA and Italian DPA. In addition, other translations are given by the community, such as Spanish and Croatian.)

scope, purpose context and nature of that process for better comprehension, which helps to estimate the risk score of the new project, asset, or product.

According to the twelfth obligation, before processing personal data, the data controller shall consult the supervisory authority if the data protection impact assessments shows that data controller cannot mitigate unacceptably high residual risks. If the supervisory authority opines that the proposed data processing might breach the GDPR, they must provide written advice within eight weeks of receiving the consultation request, and this time period can be extended by up to six more weeks considering the complexity of the planned data processing.[41]

Data protection impact assessments are an essential component of data protection by design and by default. For example, data protection officers and data controllers can use data protection impact assessments to establish the technical and organizational measures to put in place to limit the risks of the proposed processing. Unlike the privacy by design principle, the data protection impact assessment is only necessary, when there is a high risk to the data subjects' rights and freedoms. However, it would be preferable if data protection impact assessments were performed in any case, just to be on the safe side.[42]

There is a long list of risks to natural persons' rights and freedoms in GDPR Recital (75), including physical, material, and non-material damage, and it is explicitly stated that the risk may result from data processing, especially where vulnerable natural persons' personal data, particularly children's personal data, is processed. As a result, while dealing with children's data, the data protection impact assessment should be carried out with extra care, because the processing is likely to be high risk in this case.[43]

Furthermore, when analysing the processing of children's data, data controllers, data processors and data protection officers should also consider the children's age, maturity, and capacities. However, their capacities are not fixed, but rather evolve as a result of their age and other environmental circumstances. As a result, while assessing the data protection impact, measurements must be revised based on children's short and long-term development.[44]

Ultimately, data controllers have an additional important responsibility under the GDPR. Personal data transfers to third countries can only occur if data controllers comply with the criteria outlined in Chapter 5 of the GDPR.[45]

---

[41] GDPR, Article 36 (1) and (2).

[42] ICO, Data protection by design and default, How does data protection by design and by default link to data protection impact assessments (DPIAs)?, https://ico.org.uk/for-organisations/guide-to-data-protection/guide-to-the-general-data-protection-regulation-gdpr/accountability-and-governance/data-protection-by-design-and-default/#:~:text=A%20DPIA%20is%20a%20tool,by%20design%20and%20by%20default.

[43] GDPR, Recital (75).

[44] United Nations Committee on the Rights on the Child (2013) General Comment No. 14 on the right of the child to have his or her best interests taken as a primary consideration (art. 3, para. 1). CRC/C/GC/14, p. 18, para. 84.

See also: Van der Hof and Lievens (2018), p. 20.

[45] GDPR, Article 44–50.

As previously indicated, the exchange of personal data between countries outside the European Union is essential for fostering the growth of international trade and cooperation.[46] In accordance with Article 45 of the GDPR, the transfer of data to a third country or international organisation is allowed only if the European Commission determines that said third country or international organisation offers an adequate level of data protection, as mandated by the Regulation. In the event that the European Commission ascertains that the third country or international organisation in question offers a sufficient level of protection, there is no need for any additional measures to be taken by the data controller in facilitating the transfer.[47]

In the absence of an adequacy decision, it remains feasible to transfer personal data from the EU to a third country in accordance with the GDPR. This can be achieved by implementing appropriate safeguards by the data controller or processor and ensuring that data subjects possess enforceable rights and effective legal remedies.[48] Therefore, it is important to thoroughly assess every single case for both data importers and exporters. In the absence of adequacy decisions, data controllers bear a substantial burden.

According to Article 46 of the GDPR, suitable measures for ensuring data protection may involve various safeguards such as binding corporate rules (BCRs), standard contractual clauses (SCCs), certification mechanisms, and codes of conduct.[49] The BCRs and SCCs were established specifically targeting controllers and processors (data exporters) who transfer personal data from the EU to third countries. On the other hand, the certification system and codes of conduct were developed for controllers and processors located in third countries that fall outside the scope of the GDPR. Certification and codes of conduct mechanisms can be sought and obtained by the data importer established in a third country.[50]

Furthermore, in the absence of an adequacy decision or appropriate safeguards, the transfer of personal data to a third country or international organisation may be allowed if one of the exceptions enumerated in Article 49 of the GDPR is applicable.[51]

These exceptions include the following: the data subject has expressly consented to the transfer after being informed of the possible risks and consequences of such a transfer; there is a contract between the data subject and the controller; the transfer

---

[46] GDPR, Article 101.

[47] GDPR, Article 45(1).

For the list showing the countries who have been determined as possessing an adequate level of data protection by the European Commission see: European Commission, Adequacy decisions: How the EU determines if a non-EU country has an adequate level of data protection' (13 January 2018) https://ec.europa.eu/info/law/law-topic/data-protection/international-dimension-data-protection/adequacy-decisions_en.

[48] GDPR, Article 46(1).

[49] GDPR, Article 46(2)(a-f).

[50] For more information about the certification mechanism: EDPB, Guidelines 07/2022 on certification as a tool for transfers, version 2.0, 14 February 2023, pp. 1–19, For more information about the codes of conducts: EDPB, Guidelines 04/2021 on codes of conduct as tools for transfers, 22 February 2022, pp. 1–16.

[51] GDPR, Article 49.

is necessary for reasons of public interest; or the transfer is necessary to protect the vital interests of the data subject, or another person, when the data subject cannot consent to the transfer.[52]

However, the derogations stated in Article 49 cannot be utilised in any way that would involve the transfer of data in a repeated manner. These exceptional data transfers will only be accepted in specific circumstances, on an occasional basis, where absolutely necessary for a certain purpose.[53] Accordingly, the transfer of personal data even the personal data with sensitive nature must be legal if, for example, an EU data subject is unconscious and in need of urgent medical care while travelling outside of the EU, and only a data exporter (for example, his regular doctor) based in a member state of the EU can offer some information regarding his/her health conditions. In this scenario, the transfer of these data would be legal. The reason for this is that the rule presupposes that the risk of possible harm to the data subject should be greater than the concerns for data protection.[54]

The GDPR does not specifically include provisions regarding the transfer of data pertaining to children. Nevertheless, it is our contention that children need to possess a certain degree of agency in managing their data transfers, particularly in low-risk scenarios such as the cessation of those transfers. We suggest that if a child demonstrates sufficient maturity to request, for example, the termination of the transfer of their personal data to third countries, it should be incumbent upon data controllers to fulfil this request, even in the absence of parental consent.

Moreover, it is possible to observe instances from real-life scenarios. Due to the requirements set forth by the GDPR, children who are underage are not permitted to exercise control over the transfer of their personal data. Consequently, the services listed below do not offer the option for underage children to grant consent for a prohibition or termination of such data transfers without the involvement of their parents.

In terms of children data policy, Google has a comparatively improved application called Family Link, with which parents may control the Google accounts of their underage children.[55] Google clarifies that they can share children's data with parental consent that their external processor can process children's data on their behalf according to their instructions, and that they can also process them for legal reasons (e.g., to comply with any applicable law, to prevent/detect/address fraud or security issues).[56]

---

[52] GDPR, Article 49(1) (a-g).

[53] GDRP, Recital 111 and Guidelines 2/2018 of the European Data Protection Board (EDPB) on derogations of Article 49 under Regulation 2016/679 7 (May 25, 2018), pp. 4–5.

[54] Guidelines 2/2018 of the European Data Protection Board (EDPB) on derogations of Article 49 under Regulation 2016/679 7 (May 25, 2018), p. 12.

[55] Google Family Link https://families.google/familylink/.

[56] Google Family Link, Privacy Notice for Google Accounts and Profiles Managed with Family Link, for Children under 13 (or applicable age in your country) ("Privacy Notice"): Information Google Shares https://families.google.com/familylink/privacy/child-policy/.

YouTube Kids is a new and relatively safer platform for children, and its privacy standards are identical to those of Google.[57] It means that they share children's data under the following conditions: if parental consent is obtained, if their trusted processors process children's data on their behalf in accordance with their instructions, and if they process children's data for legal reasons (for example, to protect Google's, its users', or the public's rights and safety as permitted or required by law).[58]

The sole statement Johnson & Johnson made in their privacy policy addressing children's data was that they do not offer services to individuals under the age of 16 and request that these individuals do not provide them with personal information. If parents discover that their children have provided them with personal information, they ensure that they may contact them to get the information removed.[59] However, they make no mention of the processing or transfer of their data, since they claim that they do not provide services for children. This does not, however, imply that children will be excluded from these services in reality. According to the recent news, Johnson & Johnson is undertaking study on children to determine the efficacy of COVID-19 vaccinations in various age ranges. It implies that they should collect the personal data of children in the vaccinated group and the control group in order to perform a comparison for research purposes.[60] The news claims that the Centers for Disease Control and Prevention (CDC) will collect data from vaccine recipients, which raises privacy concerns, because the CDC may share these data with sensitive nature with third parties or there could be a cyber-attack and disclosure of these sensitive information even without the CDC's knowledge.[61] Johnson & Johnson is also based in the US; consequently, according to these latest updates, the data protection and privacy rights of Johnson & Johnson vaccine study participants, who are children, are at risk of being violated.[62]

The current privacy policies of Facebook and Instagram do not provide any specific information on the transfer of children's data from the EU to third countries.[63] The

---

[57] YouTube Kids: An application specially designed for children https://www.youtube.com/kids/.

[58] YouTube Kids Privacy Notice: Information we share https://kids.youtube.com/t/privacynotice.

[59] Johnson & Johnson, Privacy Policy: Use by Minors https://www.jnj.com/corporate/privacy-policy.

[60] Carrie MacMillan: COVID-19 Vaccine Authorized For Kids Ages 5 to 11: What Parents Need to Know, Yale Medicine, 20 May 2022, https://www.yalemedicine.org/news/covid-vaccine-for-ages-5-to-11.

CHOC (Children's Hospital of Orange County): The COVID-19 vaccine for kids under 12: What parents should know, last updated 11 November 2022, https://health.choc.org/the-covid-19-vaccine-for-kids-under-12-what-parents-should-know/.

[61] Rachel Sandler: CDC Will Collect Personal Data On Vaccine Recipients, Raising Privacy Concerns, Forbes, 8 December 2020, https://www.forbes.com/sites/rachelsandler/2020/12/08/cdc-will-collect-personal-data-on-vaccine-recipients-raising-privacy-concerns/?sh=2ac8021d50ec.

[62] "Johnson & Johnson Services, Inc., located at One Johnson & Johnson Plaza New Brunswick, New Jersey 08,933, is the company responsible for collection, use, and disclosure of personal information under this Privacy Policy." Johnson & Johnson, Privacy Policy: Contacting us https://www.jnj.com/corporate/privacy-policy.

[63] Facebook, Privacy Policy: How do we transfer information?, https://www.facebook.com/privacy/policy?section_id=9-HowDoWeTransfer.

utilisation of social media platforms by children is evident based on news reports, research studies, and statistical data, as will be further explored in Chapter 6 of research. However, the privacy policies of Facebook and Instagram neglect this aspect of the matter.

Chapter 5 of the GDPR does not apply to the transfers of personal data within the EU. It is important to note that there are no restrictions in place concerning the free movement of personal data within the Union.[64] Nevertheless, another issue arises when the transfer of personal data is conducted between different Member States. The age restrictions for processing personal data based on consent among children in EU Member States differ, as indicated in Subchapter 3.3 of this research.[65]

The first Commission report on the assessment and review of the GDPR, particularly regarding the implementation and functioning of the regulations on the transfer of personal data to third countries and the rules on cooperation and consistency,[66] raises some concerns about this matter. According to this report, the GDPR offers a unified approach to data protection throughout the EU, but facultative specification clauses cause fragmentation. It is claimed that varying age of consent for information society services across Member States generates uncertainty and difficulties for cross-border commerce.[67]

The Commission Staff Working Paper accompanying the first report notes that distinguishing ages for offering online services to children by Member State is contradictory to the GDPR's core purpose of ensuring equal protection for individuals and business opportunities in all Member States. Moreover, the Commission also

Instagram, Privacy Policy, How do we transfer information?, https://privacycenter.instagram.com/policy/?section_id=9-HowDoWeTransfer.

64 "The free movement of personal data within the Union shall be neither restricted nor prohibited for reasons connected with the protection of natural persons with regard to the processing of personal data."

GDPR, Article1(3).

65 EU Member States' digital platform-related consent ages for children: Austria (14), Belgium (13), Bulgaria (14), Croatia (16), Cyprus (14), Czech Republic (15), Denmark (13), Estonia (13), Finland (13), France (15), Germany (16), Hungary (16), Greece (15), Ireland (16), Italy (14), Latvia (13), Lithuania (14), Luxembourg (16), Malta (13), the Netherlands (16), Poland (16), Portugal (13), Romania (16), Slovakia (16), Slovenia (15), Spain (14), and Sweden (13).

See the Table 5.1 of this research under the Subchapter 3.3.

66 Article 97 of the GDPR mandates that the Commission examine and assess the Regulation beginning with the first report after two years and continuing every four years.

See the report: European Commission, Communication from the Commission to the European Parliament and the Council Data protection as a pillar of citizens' empowerment and the EU's approach to the digital transition - two years of application of the General Data Protection Regulation, Brussels, 24.6.2020, COM (2020) 264 final, pp. 1–18.

67 European Commission, Communication from the Commission to the European Parliament and the Council Data protection as a pillar of citizens' empowerment and the EU's approach to the digital transition - two years of application of the General Data Protection Regulation, Brussels, 24.6.2020, COM (2020) 264 final, p. 7.

concerns about national divergences' costs. National differences in legislation implementation and data protection authorities' interpretation raise EU legal compliance costs.[68]

Notwithstanding these concerns raised in the first report and accompanying Commission Staff Working Document, no improvements have been implemented addressing the harmonisation of the varying age of online consent across Member States. This gap should be filled, in our opinion, by making the age requirement uniform throughout all EU Member States.

In Chapter 6 of this research, we will propose an age of digital consent that would be applicable to all Member States. This proposal will be predicated upon the influence of age disparities on the comprehension of online data protection and privacy among children and teenagers.

The GDPR lacks a particular provision that addresses the specific obligations of data controllers in relation to the processing of personal data belonging to children. Yet, the COPPA specifically addresses the responsibilities of operators with respect to the processing of children's personal information. Further, we will examine how COPPA's approach differs from that of the GDPR. This will enable us to compare the two pieces of legislation and offer suggestions in accordance with our findings.

The term "operator" is used instead of "data controller" in the COPPA. The operator is defined as:

> "....any person who operates a Web site located on the Internet or an online service and who collects or maintains personal information from or about the users of or visitors to such Web site or online service, or on whose behalf such information is collected or maintained, or offers products or services for sale through that Web site or online service, where such Web site or online service is operated for commercial purposes involving commerce among the several States or with 1 or more foreign nations; in any territory of the United States or in the District of Columbia, or between any such territory and another such territory or any State or foreign nation; or between the District of Columbia and any State, territory, or foreign nation."[69]

The term "processor" does not appear in the COPPA, but they are defined as "an agent or service provider of the operator" who collects or maintains personal information on behalf of the operators.[70]

The first obligation of operators under the COPPA is to provide notice on their websites outlining their practices with children's personal information collected online. The description should go into detail regarding how they will use and disclose this information.[71] The regulation does not specify a way for doing so.

---

68 European Commission, Commission Staff Working Document, Accompanying the document Communication from the Commission to the European Parliament and the Council Data protection as a pillar of citizens' empowerment and the EU's approach to the digital transition - two years of application of the General Data Protection Regulation, Brussels, 24.6.2020, SWD(2020) 115 final, pp. 1–52, p. 17.

69 16 CFR COPPA 312.2 "Operator".

70 16 CFR COPPA 312.2 "Operator" (1) and (2).

71 16 CFR COPPA 312.3(a).

In our opinion, it would be ideal if the privacy policy included some vivid graphics that a child could comprehend and be attracted to read. There may be videos for younger children that explain collection procedures and their consequences so that the children may also have a comprehension of the operators' process.

Second, before collecting information from children, operators should provide direct notification to parents and get verifiable parental consent from them.[72] There are, however, several exceptions to these prior parental consent requirements. For example, if the operator's sole purpose for collecting a child's or parent's information is to alert the parents about the collection, the operator does not need to get parental consent beforehand. They should erase this contact information if they do not get parental consent within a reasonable time.[73] However, the duration in this phrase is vague, because everyone has a different understanding of what "reasonable" duration means. Other examples would be the collecting of a child's e-mail address in order to respond to a child's request[74] or for the child's safety.[75] If the operator believes that the child's safety is in jeopardy, they should use all reasonable efforts to reach out to the parents and inform them about the risks.[76]

Nonetheless, reasonable efforts are likewise a vague phrase in this context, as it is in Article 8 of the GDPR.[77] For instance, some website administrators could understand "reasonable efforts" as the act of looking for parents on social networking platforms and discontinuing the search if their account cannot be found.

Third, the operator shall provide parents the choice of giving consent for the collection of their children's data without giving consent for the disclosure of such data to third parties.[78] Fourth, the operator guarantees that parents have access to their children's personal data in order to review and/or delete it.[79]

Fifth, operators should provide parents with the option to restrict future use or collection of their children's personal information.[80] It is beneficial for the children that their parents have this level of control over their personal information. However, one question remains unanswered: Wouldn't it be better if children had also control over their data, if they have the capability and maturity to do so?

Undoubtedly, an online service provider cannot measure a child's capability or maturity. However, if a child requests erasure of his or her personal data, prohibits future use of his or her data, or prohibits disclosure of his or her personal data, providers may assume that the child should have the capacity to manage their data.

---

[72] 16 CFR COPPA 312.4(a)(b).

[73] 16 CFR COPPA 312.5(c)(1).

[74] 16 CFR COPPA 312.5(c)(3).

[75] 16 CFR COPPA 312.5(c)(5).

[76] 16 CFR COPPA 312.5(c)(5).

[77] GDPR, Article 8(2): "The controller shall make *reasonable efforts* to verify in such cases that consent is given or authorised by the holder of parental responsibility over the child, taking into consideration available technology."

[78] 16 CFR COPPA 312.5(a)(2).

[79] 16 CFR COPPA 312.6(a).

[80] 16 CFR COPPA 312.3(c).

In this instance, we argue that the online service provider should erase the data immediately without waiting for the parents' reaction. It is because, in the usual course of events, deletion, restriction of usage, or restriction of disclosure should not be harmful to children.

Sixth, the operators should keep the information they gather from children confidential, secure, and intact. This requirement includes disclosing the children's collected information to parties they trust with the same level of confidentiality and security.[81] Nevertheless, it should be critical to obtain parental consent before disclosing information. Even if the third party whom the operator trusted and released the information is trustworthy for the operator, they might not be trustworthy for the parents. Thus, in our point of view, it is critical to notify the parents ahead of time and obtain their consent before releasing the child's personal data.

The seventh obligation of operators under the COPPA is consistent with the GDPR's purpose limitation.[82] The operator shall only keep the obtained information for as long as it is required for the purpose for which it was collected in the first place.[83]

Finally, the eighth obligation of operators under the COPPA is consistent with the GDPR's data minimisation principle.[84] It is prohibited for operators to condition children's participation in a game or other online activities on disclosing more information about the children than is required to engage in such activity.[85] For example, if the game simply requires a nickname to join, the operators cannot ask for further information such as the children's full name, e-mail address, or any other identifying information.

The following Table 5.1 presents the obligations and responsibilities of data controllers under the GDPR and operators under the COPPA, aiming to facilitate comprehension prior to comparing the approaches of these two legislations.

Comparing the two approaches, it is evident that the GDPR is more comprehensive and detailed in terms of data controller obligations since data controllers shall protect the personal data of data subjects by making it possible and easy for data subjects to exercise their rights, cooperating with supervisory authorities when necessary, and conducting data protection impact assessments to reduce the risks of processing. However, the GDPR lags behind in terms of data controllers' obligation for children's data protection.

The GDPR makes some distinctions between data subjects as adults and data subjects as children (e.g., data controllers should conduct a data protection impact assessment with additional care when processing children's data and shall make all reasonable efforts to get parental consent before processing the personal data of children); yet children require more special protection since they fall into a more vulnerable category of data subjects.

---

[81] 16 CFR COPPA 312.8.

[82] GDPR Article 5(1)(b).

[83] 16 CFR COPPA 312.10.

[84] GDPR Article 5(1)(c).

[85] 16 CFR COPPA 312.7.

Table 5.1 The obligations of data controllers under the GDPR and operators under the COPPA

Obligations of data controllers under the GDPR	Obligations of operators under the COPPA
Adhering to the personal data processing principles outlined in Article 5 (Lawfulness, fairness, and transparency, accuracy, purpose limitation, data minimisation, storage limitation, integrity, confidentiality, and accountability)	Providing detailed notice on their websites outlining their practices with children's personal information collected online
Implying appropriate technical measures (e.g., pseudonymisation and encryption of personal data), and organizational measures (e.g., risk assessment which means mitigating solutions to reduce risks) as well as having effective and compliant data protection policies in place	Providing direct notification to parents and getting verifiable parental consent from them prior to collecting information from children
Enabling data subjects to exercise their rights efficiently and easily	Granting parents the option to provide consent for the collecting of their children's data while withholding consent for the disclosure of this data to third parties
Making reasonable efforts, considering current technology, to get consent for processing children's data from the holder of parental responsibility for the child if the child is underage	Ensuring that parents have access to their children's personal data in order to review and/ or delete it
Ensuring adherence to the concept of data protection by design and by default is being followed	Offering parents the opportunity to restrict future use or collection of their children's personal information
Choosing processors who are knowledgeable, reliable, and having adequate resources to ensure the requirement of appropriate technical and organizational measures	Keeping the information, they gather from children confidential, secure, and intact
Documenting their processing actions and making them available to the supervisory authority if required	Keeping the obtained information for as long as it is required for the purpose for which it was collected in the first place (analogous to GDPR's purpose limitation principle)
Cooperating with the supervisory authority to perform its tasks	Avoiding from making children's involvement in a game or other online activities contingent upon the disclosure of excessive personal information beyond what is necessary for participation (analogous to GDPR's data minimisation principle)
Notifying the supervisory authority within seventy-two hours of being aware of a personal data breach	
Notifying data subjects without undue delay if the data breach is likely to result in a high risk to a data subject's rights and freedoms	

(continued)

Table 5.1 (continued)

Obligations of data controllers under the GDPR	Obligations of operators under the COPPA
Conducting a DPIA prior to processing in cases where new technologies are employed, and a particular method of data processing is expected to pose a high risk to the rights and freedoms of individuals	
Consulting the supervisory authority before processing personal data if the data protection impact assessments shows that data controller cannot mitigate unacceptably high residual risks	
Facilitating the transfer of personal data from the EU to third countries (via adequacy decisions/appropriate safeguards/derogations for specific situations)	

Hence, it would be ideal to have a dedicated GDPR article that lists solely the data controller's child-specific obligations based on the children's data protection rights and provides data controllers with guidance on how and when to interact children directly. As indicated previously, if a child is mature enough to request the deletion of his/her data, the data controllers may assume that they can directly communicate to the child instead of the parents. Accordingly, this approach is feasible for all online child activities with low risk. For instance, children may request the termination of the transfer of their data to third countries without the consent of their parents as discussed above.

It is crucial to acknowledge the significance of children's opinions and preferences and how these relate to their overall well-being.[86] For riskier actions, such as sharing content on publicly available websites or transferring data, data controllers may still seek parental consent.[87]

In light of the preceding discussions in Chapter 4 and 5, it is possible to suggest an article for the GDPR that focuses on the specific obligation of data controllers with regard to children. The article would be presented as follows:

> "1. Children may lack awareness regarding privacy policies and their rights pertaining to privacy and data protection. In accordance with best practises, data controllers shall employ simple video presentations or visually engaging images accompanied by easily comprehensible language to enhance children's understanding of their data protection rights, particularly with regard to the right to be informed and the right to access their personal data.
>
> 2. The use of the rights to ratification, erasure and prohibition or termination of data transfers shall be allowed in cases when children possess the necessary level of maturity to independently request such actions, hence eliminating the requirement for parental consent.

[86] Macenaite (2017), p. 775.

[87] Data Protection Commission Ireland, Children Front and Centre, Fundamentals for a Child-Oriented Approach to Data Processing-Draft Version for Public Consultation, December 2020, pp. 33–35.

3. The practise of profiling may be subject to prohibition unless there exists a compelling or public interest that may outweigh the interests of the child in question. However, in the event that such a situation arises, it shall be still possible for a child to object to this profiling. In this scenario, it is imperative for the data controller to take prompt action, without delay, even in the absence of parental consent.

4. In the event of data breaches, data controllers are required to inform parents and children concurrently, even if the children are at an age where they can provide consent, as a precautionary measure. In addition, it is essential that they provide parents with information and assistance to assist them in mitigating the negative consequences of personal data breaches on their children. The exemptions specified in Article 34(3) shall not be applicable in cases where the individual whose data is being processed is a child.

5. The Regulation shall reserve all other responsibilities of data controllers and all other rights of children."[88]

Unlike the GDPR, all the obligations of the operators under the COPPA are related to the protection of children's privacy and how the operators should ensure parental control over their children's personal data. It is obviously advantageous when the children are young and unable to make decisions or comprehend the consequences of personal data processing. Nonetheless, we assert that the children should be allowed to undertake less risky activities such as removing data from a website, unsubscribing, or prohibiting the transfer of personal data to third parties without parental consent if they have the capacity and willingness to do so.[89]

Furthermore, we propose that the COPPA should oblige operators to collaborate with supervisory authorities and impose data protection or privacy impact assessments for the processing of children's personal data, as the GDPR does. Given the potential high risk involved in processing children's personal data, it would be advantageous for operators to work together with supervisory authorities and carry out data protection/privacy impact assessments with the help of specialised data protection/privacy officers. This would allow for the identification, evaluation, and mitigation of risks prior to processing the children's personal data, ultimately benefiting them.

In conclusion, it is essential for operators regulated by COPPA and data controllers regulated by GDPR to ensure that children have access to data protection and privacy rights, enabling them to have control over their data and make informed choices about their online activities with mitigated risks.

References

Macenaite M (2017) From universal towards child-specific protection of the right to privacy online: dilemmas in the EU general data protection regulation. New Media Soc 19(5):765–779

---

[88] The sample draft article created by the author.

[89] Data Protection Commission Ireland, Children Front and Centre, Fundamentals for a Child-Oriented Approach to Data Processing-Draft Version for Public Consultation, December 2020, pp. 33–35.

Van der Hof S, Lievens E (2018) The importance of privacy by design and data protection impact assessments in strengthening protection of children's personal data under the GDPR. Commun Law 23(1):20

Chapter 6
Examples from the Practice - Social Networking Services, Privacy Policies, Child Influencers and Parental Sharing

Abstract This chapter examines the privacy policies and practices of Facebook, Instagram, and YouTube concerning children's data protection and privacy to illustrate the discrepancies between law in text and law in practice. Statistics, surveys, and studies corroborate our conclusions. We contend that it is imprudent for parents to disseminate their children's private moments without any limitations imposed by the GDPR and COPPA, as numerous parents possess inadequate digital literacy and may be unaware of the ramifications of sharing their children's information online. This chapter also illustrates the content restrictions imposed by social media networks concerning children's personal data. Despite their privacy policies and terms and conditions, real-world instances in this chapter demonstrate that social media networks can harbor restricted information. We advised the implementation of a human-reviewed AI and ML system to identify potentially harmful content before to its dissemination by parents or other adults, so preventing its exposure to the Internet and malicious individuals. We advocate for amendments to the GDPR and COPPA to restrict parental sharing of children's information lawfully, accompanied by suitable proportional sanctions for parents who fail to comply with the law. We ultimately propose a more sustainable and successful solution: educating children and parents in digital literacy.

The sociology and culture of memory sharing have been modified by social networking sites. Once upon a time, our family vacations, birthday parties, and graduation ceremonies were preserved solely in photo albums that were presented to visiting relatives. The most private aspects of children's lives and experiences were only disclosed over the phone or at family gatherings with family members and close friends. Child actors, models, and musicians were the only children whose photos and videos were available to the public. Nevertheless, those family photo albums are now accessible to the whole Internet community via social media; hence, every child has the potential to become a minor celebrity or child influencer with relative ease. Prior to the emergence of social networking sites such as Facebook, Instagram, and

A. Alkış Tümtürk, *Online Privacy and Data Protection of Children in the European Union and the United States*, Ius Gentium: Comparative Perspectives on Law and Justice 141, https://doi.org/10.1007/978-3-032-27534-9_6

YouTube, children's privacy and data protection were not as significant concerns as they are currently.[1]

As Facebook, YouTube, and Instagram are the most popular social networks in the world,[2] we will explore their data policies and practises concerning the privacy of children in this chapter. Since the Federal Trade Commission (FTC) considers children under the age of 13 to be vulnerable,[3] and the COPPA rule defines a child as an individual under the age of 13,[4] the majority of US-based social media platforms, including Facebook, Instagram, and YouTube, do not allow children under the age of 13 to have accounts.[5]

However, parents who post their children's material, images, and/or videos online suffer no consequences under the COPPA and the GDPR. Furthermore, these parents are not bound by any legal restrictions imposed by the COPPA or the GDPR.[6] Even so, it is important to note that parents may encounter some repercussions under the civil laws of EU Member States and the US.[7] Given the scope of our research,

---

[1] Sorensen (2016, pp. 156–157).

[2] Statista: Most popular social networks worldwide as of January 2023, ranked by number of monthly active users (in millions), https://www.statista.com/statistics/272014/global-social-networks-ranked-by-number-of-users/.

[3] "In enacting the Children's Online Privacy Protection Act, Congress determined to apply the statute's protections only to children under 13, recognizing that younger children are particularly vulnerable to overreaching by marketers and may not understand the safety and privacy issues created by the online collection of personal information." Federal Trade Commission: Complying with COPPA: Frequently Asked Questions, Why does COPPA apply only to children under 13? What about protecting the online privacy of teens? https://www.ftc.gov/business-guidance/resources/complying-coppa-frequently-asked-questions.

[4] 16 CFR COPPA 312.2 "Child": "means an individual under the age of 13."

[5] Facebook Help Center, How to Report Things, How do I report a child under the age of 13 on Facebook?: https://www.facebook.com/help/157793540954833/?helpref=uf_share.

Instagram, Help Centre, Tips for Parents: Report a child under 13 on Instagram, https://help.instagram.com/517920941588885/?helpref=uf_share.

YouTube, Terms of Service, General Terms and Conditions: Who can use the service?, Age requirements https://kids.youtube.com/t/terms.

[6] Alkis Tümtürk (2022, p. 3).

[7] For example, according to Hungarian civil law, parents might potentially face loss of parental custody if they engage in the act of disclosing their child's personal data on the internet, provided that this action causes serious harm or violation of the child's interests.

"Section 4:191 [Judicial termination of parental custody] (1) The court shall terminate parental custody if a) the parent is at fault in seriously harming or jeopardising the interests of the child, in particular the physical well-being, mental or moral development of the child [...]"

"Section 4:193 [Eligibility for bringing an action for the termination and restoration of parental custody rights; defendants in the action] (1) An action for the termination of parental custody shall be brought by the other parent; and for its restoration by either parent. The child, the guardianship authority and the prosecutor shall also be eligible to bring an action in both cases. [...]"

Act V of 2013 on the Civil Code (2013. évi V. törvény a Polgári Törvénykönyvről) (1 July 2021), Section 4:191(1)(a) and Section 4:193(1) [Translated by Nemzeti Jogszabálytár], https://njt.hu/jogszabaly/en/2013-5-00-00.

Other such instances may exist within the civil legislation of various countries.

which focuses on data protection and privacy legislations, we shall not delve into the provisions of civil laws in this context.

It is an improvement that both the GDPR and the COPPA require parents to be accountable for their children's data protection and privacy. In other words, it is better than disregarding the presence of children in the online world. However, this is not always a wise idea, because some parents lack digital literacy skills or technology understanding and do not know what is best for their children. On the other side, there are those parents who are either oblivious to what is best for their children or are malicious. Consequently, they might share their children's digital footprints without understanding or ignoring the long-term consequences for their children's futures.[8]

Children's self-confidence, personal growth, and future academic and professional opportunities might all be damaged as a result of adults revealing an excessive amount of personal information and embarrassing anecdotes, images, and videos about the children in their lives. These kinds of posts also have the potential to lead to identity theft, cyberbullying, or bullying among peers or adults in the physical world (e.g., at the school or family gatherings).[9]

In earlier chapters on the data protection and privacy rights of children, we discussed the tragic case of Amanda Todd, a Canadian girl who committed suicide after losing control over her personal data. We stated that she was subjected to long-term bullying because of a single photograph that she was unable to delete. Before her suicide, Amanda had prepared a YouTube video in which she told her tale through a series of handwritten letters. Amanda conveys her conviction that she will never be able to get her photo from the Internet back in one of her notes. These kinds of occurrences are possible for any youngster who endures long-term, severe bullying and blackmail.[10]

As with Amanda Todd, such occurrences may be caused by parental neglect. Nonetheless, we should also highlight that in Amanda's situation, not only her parents but also law enforcement officers were incompetent. The officers of the Royal Canadian Mounted Police (RCMP) suggested the deletion of Amanda Todd's Facebook account as a measure aimed at protecting her from the adverse outcomes associated with bullying and blackmail. Nevertheless, this proposition remains a cosmetic solution that neglects to address the underlying issue.[11] Indeed, the parents of Amanda strongly encouraged her to deactivate her Facebook account, a course of action she undertook for a duration of a couple of months, but without yielding

[8] Alkis Tümtürk (2022, p. 3).

[9] Keltie (2020, p. 1006).

[10] YouTube, Thesomebodytoknow channel: My story: Struggling, bullying, suicide, self-harm, available at: https://www.youtube.com/watch?v=vOHXGNx-E7E cited in Bunn (2019, p. 41).

[11] CBC News: Parents, Dutch police investigator testify in trial of man accused of cyberbullying Amanda Todd, (11 June 2022) https://www.cbc.ca/news/canada/british-columbia/amanda-todd-week-one-1.6485200.

any favourable outcomes.[12] Amanda's response to the police officer's query about why she communicates with so many strangers online was heart-breaking as she expressed her loneliness as the reason.[13]

Aydin Coban has been found guilty of engaging in child luring, child pornography, extortion, and harassment in relation to Amanda Todd. For a duration of three years, Coban engaged in persistent online harassment towards the girl, using a total of 22 different fake social media profiles. The individual employed coercion by issuing a threat to Amanda, wherein he asserted his intention to disseminate sexual visual content featuring her to her friends, family members, and school staff unless she consented to perform a so-called "show" for him in front of a webcam.[14]

During the period in question, Coban concealed his IP address and managed to evade arrest due to either insufficient technological capabilities or the negligence of law enforcement agencies.[15] A decade had elapsed following Amanda's tragic suicide, culminating in Coban being sentenced to a jail term of 13 years for his involvement in activities such as child luring, child pornography, extortion, and harassment. However, no formal charges were brought against him in connection with Amanda's death.[16]

The "right to be forgotten" provisions of the GDPR have been investigated in previous chapters; nevertheless, they only serve to erase the revealed material from the Internet and usually from search engines' results. However, after the information has been downloaded to the computer of the malevolent person, the right to be forgotten is no longer functional.[17] There may be potential ramifications within the fields of civil law or criminal law. However, as our research does not centre around these specific areas, we shall refrain from delving into the discussion of this matter within the framework of criminal and civil law.[18] Hence, ensuring the right to be

---

[12] CBC News: Amanda Todd's parents recall teenager's anguish at recurring social media torment (7 June 2022) https://www.cbc.ca/news/canada/british-columbia/todd-sextortion-trial-coban-1.6480477.

[13] Global News: Exclusive: Mountie who worked Amanda Todd case speaks for first time (10 August 2022) https://globalnews.ca/news/9050914/amanda-todd-officer-speaks/

[14] BBC News: Amanda Todd: Dutchman sentenced for fatal cyber-stalking (15 October 2022) https://www.bbc.com/news/world-us-canada-63218797.

[15] Global News: Exclusive: Mountie who worked Amanda Todd case speaks for first time (10 August 2022) https://globalnews.ca/news/9050914/amanda-todd-officer-speaks/.

[16] BBC News: Amanda Todd: Dutchman sentenced for fatal cyber-stalking (15 October 2022) https://www.bbc.com/news/world-us-canada-63218797.

[17] Alkis Tümtürk (2022, p. 3).

[18] For example, the Hungarian Criminal Code has provisions for the imposition of penalties on those who possess pornographic recordings of individuals who are under the age of 18. The severity of the sentence would be heightened in cases when the child's age is below 12 years. Moreover, the imposition of sanctions is more severe than mere possession of the record, particularly if that individual distributes it to others, makes it accessible to a wider audience, or profits from its dissemination.

Act C of 2012 on the Criminal Code (Magyar Büntető Törvénykönyvről szóló 2012. évi C. törvény) (1 January 2023) Section 204(1)(a,b,c) and (2)(a) [Translated by Nemzeti Jogszabálytár], https://njt.hu/jogszabaly/en/2012-100-00-00.

forgotten remains crucial in enabling children to regain control over their personal data within the framework of our research.

In today's digital age, it may not be reasonable to expect parents to share no information or to prohibit their children from sharing one at all, but there should be a balance between online sharing activities and freedom of expression and children's right to a private life.[19] Accordingly, in this chapter, we will offer examples of child influencers and evaluate the consequences and potential risks of parental sharing on these social media sites while addressing the balanced-rights approach, including the protection of children's privacy rights and the freedom of online expression for parents. In conclusion, we will attempt to offer suggestions for improving practises and privacy policies, as well as mitigating the risks associated with online sharing.

6.1 How Aware Are Children and Parents of the Risks to Privacy and Data Protection Posed by the Internet?

Given the prevalence of computers and electronic devices in the lives of the current generation of children, it could be possible to suggest that they might possess a higher level of proficiency in utilising such technologies compared to their parents. They have been early adopters of several forms of technology, beginning use of computers, tablets, and smartphones. In recent years, it is possible that children have exceeded their parents' proficiency in operating these technological devices, but they still lack an understanding for the need of privacy and data protection, the potential consequences of their online actions, or the inevitable unpredictability of the Internet.[20]

A study conducted in the UK involving 29 children under the age of 11 demonstrated that these children recognized and expressed concerns regarding risks such as oversharing personal information, exposure to inappropriate content, and the dangers posed by strangers. For instance, they refrained from utilizing actual names online and disclosed passwords solely to trusted individuals. Nevertheless, the children encountered difficulties in comprehending intricate, implicit risks such as data tracking and personalized online advertisements. They frequently misconstrued terms such as "hacking", employing it to refer to ambiguous threats, including pop-ups or unfamiliar features.

Numerous individuals did not associate online promotions, autoplay videos, or well-known applications with privacy threats, placing their trust in familiar platforms or YouTubers while disregarding the associated risks. They made decisions based on their own or their peers' experiences, presuming safety in the absence of immediate harm.[21]

---

[19] Steinberg (2017, pp. 876–877).

[20] Donovan (2020, p. 43).

[21] Zhao et al. (2019, pp. 6–9).

A US study of 26 children (aged 4–10) found that younger children see data as stored locally (on devices or apps) and static, with little awareness of backend systems, data flow, or cloud storage. They believe apps collect data to improve user experience, like saving progress or personalizing content. Older children (aged 8–10) sometimes recognize commercial motives, like companies benefiting from user engagement, but their understanding is limited. Children link data-driven conclusions to their inputs or in-app actions, with few older ones grasping advanced mechanisms like aggregation or profiling. Most understand that content recommendations stem from past behavior but only visible activities (e.g., videos watched). Younger children view tracking as interpersonal, imagining developers monitoring them through cameras. Older children occasionally recognize automated processes but still focus on individual observation over large-scale analytics. Ads are seen as irrelevant or random, with limited understanding of targeting based on tracked behavior. Privacy risks are largely viewed as interpersonal, such as hackers or strangers, rather than institutional threats from companies. Younger children focus on physical risks (e.g., kidnapping), while older ones (aged 8–10) start to worry about data breaches and misuse. Younger children rely on parental guidance and avoid sharing personal information. Older children employ strategies like fake identities, adjusting privacy settings, and deleting apps. However, children, overall, are still unaware of long-term implications of corporate data collection or profiling.[22]

According to a Pew Research Center study, the majority of teenagers (60%) feel they have little control over the data collected by social media companies. Nonetheless, they are not much concerned about it. Only 21% of respondents said that they are very or extremely concerned about the information these social media sites have on them. However, 44% of them have little to no concern regarding the amount of information that these businesses may possess. As seen, even relatively older children seem unconcerned, and it is reasonable to claim that younger children are much more oblivious to the repercussions of social media companies knowing a great deal about them and their personal life.[23]

While the focus of the survey is on how companies may access children's personal information, the results indicate that teenagers are more concerned with keeping their information protected from people than from companies. Hence, their notion of online privacy relates to other individuals using these social media platforms rather than social media service providers or advertising companies, as evidenced by the responses of anonymous teenagers within the scope of this study.[24]

Some teenagers answer that they have not given much thought to how companies may utilise their personal information. However, several are aware that social

[22] Sun et al. (2021, pp. 5–12).

[23] Pew Research Center, Connection, Creativity and Drama: Teen Life on Social Media in 2022, p. 1 (16 November 2022) https://www.pewresearch.org/internet/2022/11/16/connection-creativity-and-drama-teen-life-on-social-media-in-2022/.

[24] Pew Research Center, Connection, Creativity and Drama: Teen Life on Social Media in 2022: Teens have a range of definitions for digital privacy, p. 4 (16 November 2022) https://www.pewresearch.org/internet/2022/11/16/connection-creativity-and-drama-teen-life-on-social-media-in-2022/.

networking sites are monitoring them. Some of them even express their awareness that companies are selling their data and using it for personalised marketing.[25]

Teens are vaguely aware of the tracking of social media sites, but they are unconcerned about it since they do not fully understand the effects of profiling and behavioural marketing. An EU study on the impact of marketing through social media, online games, and mobile applications on children's behaviour found that marketing practises of companies have clear and sometimes subliminal effects on children's consuming habits, meaning that they influence children's behaviour without their knowledge.[26]

Accordingly, empirical studies over past two decades has revealed a significant link between the usage of social media among teenagers and the development of negative body views. A study was conducted utilising a sample of 103 adolescent female students, ranging in age from 12 to 18 years (with a mean age of 15.4), who were selected from a public middle/high school located in the state of New York. This research investigated the association between body image and the online activity of adolescent girls on the social media platform Facebook.[27]

The findings of the study reveal a positive correlation between the duration of time spent on Facebook participating in activities related to photos and increased levels of internalisation of the thin-ideal, self-objectification,[28] dissatisfaction with weight, and aspiration for thinness.[29] Besides, another study conducted on female teenagers aged 10–19 in the US revealed a noteworthy association between self-objectification, disordered eating, and body shame.[30]

The eating disorders and phenomenon of body shaming might be linked to the culture of dieting and bodybuilding that is popular on various social media platforms. A study was undertaken to examine the influence of body shame on adolescents' use of social networking sites and their controlling of body image in the photographs they upload on these platforms. The study involved the participation of 693 Italian teenagers, with 45% of them being male. The average age of the participants was 16 years, with an age range spanning from 13 to 19 years. The findings of this research demonstrate a noteworthy correlation between feelings of body shame and the act of altering and manipulating photographs on social media platforms. Consequently, this relationship indirectly contributes to the development of problematic patterns of social media engagement among adolescent individuals, irrespective of

[25] Pew Research Center, Teens' views about social media: In their own words: Teens explain what they think social media companies do with their data, p. 3 (16 November 2022) https://www.pewresearch.org/internet/2022/11/16/2-teens-views-about-social-media/.

[26] European Commission, Study on the impact of marketing through social media, online games and mobile applications on children's behaviour (1 March 2016) https://commission.europa.eu/publications/study-impact-marketing-through-social-media-online-games-and-mobile-applications-childrens-behaviour_en.

[27] Meier and Gray (2014, p. 200).

[28] For more information about self-objectification see: Fredrickson and Roberts (1997, pp. 179–180) and Meier and Gray (2014, p. 202).

[29] Meier and Gray (2014, p. 202).

[30] Harrison and Fredrickson (2003, p. 228).

their gender. In conclusion, while the correlation between body shame and problematic social media usage is more pronounced among female teenagers, the presence of similar patterns among male adolescents implies a growing involvement in self-objectification experiences.[31]

Furthermore, one Instagram user reported seeing 33 Instagram stories from accounts she follows in addition to 14 advertisements, many of which focused on physical looks, within 2 min of watching Instagram stories.[32] Furthermore, in March of 2020, Instagram researchers posted on an internal message board that their survey data showed that 1/3 of the teenage girls who reported having body image issues felt worse after using Instagram.[33]

The aforementioned findings together suggest that children possess limited awareness of the consequences associated with relinquishing control over their personal data when utilising the Internet. They may also have a limited understanding of the level to which they can be used and manipulated by social media platforms, as well as by others who employ harmful practices on these platforms, whether intentionally or unintentionally. Furthermore, many lack awareness of the various possible dangers that the Internet may provide, encompassing both mental and physical risks, which will be examined in greater detail. Consequently, it is imperative to provide children with adequate supervision and assistance in order to ensure their safe utilisation of the advantages offered by the online realm, while mitigating the risks associated with online manipulations.

It has been determined that children may exhibit a deficiency in comprehending the significance of their privacy and protecting of their personal data on the Internet. What happens if the parents also lack digital literacy, and they are not aware of the need of privacy and hazards of Internet?

According to the same EU study referenced above, the majority of parents do not perceive online marketing directed at their children as problematic and believe their children are not influenced. Despite the significant responsibilities imposed by the COPPA and the GDPR, many parents lack the necessary preparedness to protect their children's online privacy. The study reveals that parental strategies for regulating their children's internet use differ across countries. In France, for instance, parents intervene less with their children's internet use, but Swedish parents are more involved and restricting with their children's online activities.[34]

Besides, the findings of the same study indicate that two protective measures for online advertisements were favoured above others: namely, parental pre-approval

[31] Gioia et al. (2020, pp. 773, 776 and 781).

[32] The Wall Street Journal, Facebook Knows Instagram Is Toxic for Teen Girls, Company Documents Show (14 September 2021) https://www.wsj.com/articles/facebook-knows-instagram-is-toxic-for-teen-girls-company-documents-show-11631620739?mod=hp_lead_pos7.

[33] Meta Newsroom: What Our Research Really Says About Teen Well-Being and Instagram (26 September 2021) https://about.fb.com/news/2021/09/research-teen-well-being-and-instagram/.

[34] European Commission, Study on the impact of marketing through social media, online games and mobile applications on children's behaviour (1 March 2016) https://commission.europa.eu/publications/study-impact-marketing-through-social-media-online-games-and-mobile-applications-childrens-behaviour_en.

and school instruction for children about online advertising. There are variances across the countries regarding the effectiveness of different approaches. For example, German parents seeing parental pre-approval as the most efficacious, whereas Spanish, Swedish, and Dutch parents regarded school teaching on advertising for their children as the most effective.[35]

There is a related legal case involving online ads targeted at children. YouTube generates millions of dollars by employing identifiers, often known as cookies, to serve tailored advertisements to users of these channels. Even without a YouTube account, you can see the video, and your cookies may be used to provide targeted advertisements to users. This would allow minors to watch content without having to sign in (since children under the age of 13 cannot sign in). The Federal Trade Commission (FTC) and the New York Attorney General claimed that YouTube violated the COPPA by collecting personal information from children under the age of 13 without parental consent. This data, acquired using persistent identifiers (cookies), was used to provide targeted ads to children on YouTube's child-directed channels, in violation of COPPA standards. The U.S. District Court for the District of Columbia ordered Google and YouTube to pay $170 million to settle the allegations in 2019.[36]

Currently, YouTube requests consent for data processing through a privacy notice that appears as soon as the platform is launched. This notice clarifies the implications of selecting the "accept all" or "reject all" buttons regarding the display of personalized ads and the generation of contextual video recommendations. Users will have the choice to either opt in or opt out. However, since the platform does not require creating an account to watch videos, it cannot distinguish between adult and child users and allows children to access the content as freely as adults, without needing parental consent.

YouTube could resolve this issue by requiring users to create an account in order to view the content. Accordingly, children may access the videos solely with parental consent, ideally via the YouTube Kids platform. YouTube should operate in a manner akin to Instagram and Facebook, necessitating account creation for using the service.

Targeted advertisements may pose greater risks regarding extensive, systemic privacy infringements and psychological manipulation, impacting millions of children concurrently. Parental sharing, however, is often profoundly personal and may expose children to distinct, concrete risks, including online predators, bullying, or enduring reputational harm.

Besides, in numerous jurisdictions, advertisements directed at children are governed by legislation such as COPPA and GDPR.[37] Platforms must comply with more stringent regulations regarding the collection of data on children, thereby

---

[35] European Commission, Study on the impact of marketing through social media, online games and mobile applications on children's behaviour, Final Report, p. 126 (March 2016) https://commission.europa.eu/document/download/100b9546-87eb-4f4f-a33b-1d897eae09b7_en?filename=online_marketing_children_final_report_en.pdf.

[36] Fed. Trade Comm'n v. Google LLC, No. 1:19-cv-2642 (D.D.C. 2019) and Fed. Trade Comm'n v. Google LLC, No. 1:19-cv-02642, Stipulated Order for Permanent Injunction and Civil Penalty Judgment (D.D.C. 2019).

[37] GDPR, Recital 38 and 71 and 16 CFR COPPA 312.4–312.5.

providing certain safeguards. Conversely, parents frequently encounter minimal, if any, legal limitations regarding the online sharing of information about their children.

What occurs regardless of whether parents are aware of the hazards of parental sharing and are reluctant to forego the advantages of posting updates on their children on social media platforms? What might be the advantages of parents revealing their children's most private moments? It might be feeling less alone and receiving support from other parents who are experiencing the same difficulties. Sharing the videos/ photos of their children with relatives and friends who liked and commented on the shared postings enabled them to feel close and connected. Additionally, these shared experiences offer them with the approval they require when parenting. Parents want to be seen as good parents and Facebook, Instagram and YouTube posts assist them to fulfil the expectations of parents and offer them a positive online image of parenting. Earning money to save for their children's future or to provide them with a higher quality of living might be another motive for parents, given that collaborations with brand owners and advertising their products would generate a substantial amount of money.[38]

However, can it be said that these benefits outweigh the children's right to data protection and privacy? Posting children's data online poses risks such as cyberbullying, exposure to child pornography, and the dissemination of dangerous content on paedophilia blogs and forums. A number of additional risks may be enumerated inside this subchapter.

First, there is always a possibility of kidnapping or violent crimes against children whose comprehensive personal information was disclosed on social media by their parents or themselves. Not just strangers, but even certain ill-intentioned relatives or acquaintances using the same social media platforms may use the information provided to persuade or deceive children to follow them, which can lead to kidnapping and the demand for ransom to release the children. Concerns about non-strangers are understandable given the FBI research, which found that relatives or acquaintances were responsible for 76% of kidnappings and 90% of all violent crimes against children.[39]

Second, it is possible that children may become victims of the organ black market, leading to the potential loss of crucial organs and posing a significant threat to their well-being.

Third, releasing this information on the Internet may have long-term consequences, as the digital footprint remains. Due to the fact that the principle of equal opportunity has not yet been adopted by all organizations throughout the world, sensitive information about children's race, gender, or health may have a detrimental impact on their school/college life or career path.[40]

Fourth risk may be that data brokers create profiles of individuals and sell them to advertisers, spammers, virus distributors, job agencies, and college admissions offices. The commercial market for new-borns and children in the US alone is worth

---

[38] Ouvrein and Verswijvel (2019, p. 320).

[39] Minkus et al. (2015, p. 777).

[40] Steinberg (2017, p. 849).

hundreds of billions of dollars. As a result, it is not surprising that data brokers are attempting to gather as many profiles as they can sell. They merely need to collect the information submitted on the children by the parents or children themselves. Furthermore, the data brokers' mini profiles may be improved over time when children engage in further Internet activities, particularly through the use of social media sites.[41]

As a fifth risk, aside from the threats posed by other individuals or businesses, there is also the possibility of governmental surveillance for children whose personal information is exposed in the Internet environment. By parental sharing or the children's own online activities, the children's likeness and identifying information are exposed to monitoring, such as that of intelligent services. When the children grow up, it will be extremely difficult for them to reduce their digital footprint.[42] If we consider individuals over 30 years old, their internet presence only extends back 10 to 15 years at most, but when it comes to today's babies and children, their existence begins even before they are a foetus, due to the shared ultrasound images.[43] According to one research, approximately 80% of children in developed Western countries have a digital footprint by the age of 2, owing to their parents' online sharing habits.[44]

The potential dangers of surveillance could be blackmailing, discrimination, and persuasion. Because possessing personal information provides the tracer a lot of power, if the government is monitoring the individual, it gains a significant amount of power over people whose personal information is posted on the Internet in some manner. Instances of humiliating incidents or disgraceful offenses, specifically, might serve as key elements in the act of blackmail. The information obtained through tracking people's online behaviour provides the government with a huge chance to influence, persuade, or even control people's choices, decisions, and subsequent actions. Furthermore, surveillance may be utilised as a technique for sorting and discriminating. For example, during World War II, census information provided an idea for locating Japanese internment camps in North America and concentration camps in Europe.[45]

Yet, the practises and the findings below indicate that parents are not very worried about the online data they disclose about their children via social media sites. Roughly eight in ten parents say they share information about their children on social networking sites, and majority (84%) of them stated they seldom or never

---

[41] Minkus et al. (2015, p. 777).

[42] Minkus et al. (2015, p. 777).

[43] Steinberg (2017, pp. 849–850).

[44] United Nations, Office of the United Nations High Commissioner for Human Rights (OHCHR): Children's right to privacy in the digital age must be improved (15 July 2021) https://www.ohchr.org/en/stories/2021/07/childrens-right-privacy-digital-age-must-be-improved.

[45] Richards (2013, pp. 1952–1958).

fear that their children may be upset in the future about the photos, videos and other information they shared about them.[46]

We have explored how difficult it would be for children and adolescents to comprehend the importance of online privacy and its possible implications and risks in the event of violence. Therefore, parents should take responsibility for their children's online privacy and data protection rights, as required by the GDPR, the COPPA, and social networking platforms. However, what happens when parents do not realize the future ramifications and dangers of disclosing their children's private lives online, as shown in the findings mentioned above? In this scenario, we suggest that the laws should restrict the parents' ability to share private moments with their children.

We assert that both the age and the content may be used as restrictions. For instance, if the parents choose to share anything including their children's sensitive information, private moments, or anything that might affect their dignity, honour or reputation either now or in the future, this content should be restricted.[47]

Indeed, social networking platforms have made some progress in restricting some content pertaining to children, and they have already taken steps to remove some restricted content relating to children (we will examine those solutions in detail in the Subchapters 6.3 and 6.4). We assume that if the COPPA and the GDPR restrict parental sharing, social media companies would be more compelled to prohibit certain content, particularly involving nudity, sexual exploitation, and violent content, but they should restrict even more.[48]

Only appropriate family portraits (e.g., a typical photo of family members celebrating Christmas/New Year) or content that does not disclose any personal or sensitive information about children, such as their age, race, address, health conditions, religious or political beliefs (if applicable), biometric data, or any identifying data, should be shared. Additionally, some photos taken from behind, blurred images, or

---

[46] Pew Research Center, Parenting Children in the Age of Screens: Parents' attitudes – and experiences – related to digital technology, p. 5 (28 July 2020) https://www.pewresearch.org/internet/2020/07/28/parents-attitudes-and-experiences-related-to-digital-technology/.

[47] The basis for this can be found in the Article 16 of the UNCRC: "1. No child shall be subjected to arbitrary or unlawful interference with his or her privacy, family, home or correspondence, nor to unlawful attacks on his or her honour and reputation. 2. The child has the right to the protection of the law against such interference or attacks."

UNCRC, Article 16(1) and (2).

[48] The Digital Services Act imposes restrictions on some types of information pertaining to children, including targeting materials associated with child sexual abuse and child pornography. However, in our perspective, these restrictions are not enough and should be more extensive. Social media platforms impose restrictions on various types of content beyond child sexual abuse, which we will discuss in Chapter 6 of research. In our point of view, lawmakers should adopt a proactive approach rather than falling behind social media platforms. Lawmakers should take the initiative to assert a greater influence over these platforms by implementing stricter enforcement measures.

Regulation (EU) 2022/2065 of the European Parliament and of the Council of 19 October 2022 on a Single Market for Digital Services and amending Directive 2000/31/EC (Digital Services Act) OJ L 277, 27.10.2022, pp. 1–102, Recitals 12, 61, 64, 80 and 119.

the insertion of emojis to the children's faces might potentially serve as a mild kind of censorship.[49]

If parents fail to implement the legally mandated limits, they should face legal sanctions and fines. As shown in Subchapter 6.4, platforms such as social media may enforce temporary suspensions or permanent termination of parental accounts that violate privacy standards. Instances from practical applications will be shown in the pertinent Sub-chapter.

Additionally, fines should be imposed by the GDPR and the COPPA on parents who violate privacy rules by disclosing children's information or photographs without agreement, particularly for commercial interests. Increased penalties for recurrent infractions should be imposed, particularly when the infringement pertains to sensitive data, including health records, sexual orientation, ethnic background, religious beliefs, or images that may jeopardize a child's safety (e.g., nudity).

Should the parent's actions harm a child's reputation or violate their privacy rights, the child (or their representative) may pursue civil litigation for damages, and this should be mandated by the civil laws of the respective countries.

Repeated violations of privacy regulations by one parent may prompt the court to reevaluate custody arrangements. This may entail diminished decision-making authority for the child's internet presence. Custody may be revoked if the court deems the infractions to be substantial in exceptional situations. An actual case concerning custody loss will be presented in the forthcoming Subchapter 6.3.

The children of today who suffer/will suffer from their parents' and data controllers' online activities may not yet be mature enough to comprehend the risks and consequences of excessive online sharing of their personal information and private lives. Consequently, Internet-victimized children now may lack the maturity to take legal actions against their parents and/or the relevant data controllers. In the near future, however, we expect legal cases from today's children regarding violations of their privacy and data protection rights.[50]

6.2 Children's Right to Self-Determination and the Conflict Between Parental Freedom of Speech and the Right of Children to Privacy and Data Protection

Parents have several opportunities to share their children's family time and important events with the world through social media. They may justify their online sharing activities by invoking their right to freedom of expression. Indeed, everyone has the right to freedom of speech, as stated in Article 11 of the CFR, which includes the

[49] Alkis Tümtürk (2022, p. 9).

[50] See supporting supervisory authority guidance: CNIL, Sharing photos and videos of your child on social networks: what risks (28 November 2025), https://www.cnil.fr/en/sharing-photos-and-videos-your-child-social-networks-what-risks.

noting that children may take action against their parents for privacy violations.

freedom to hold opinions as well as the freedom to receive and share information and ideas.[51] Regarding the US, the freedom of speech is guaranteed by the first amendment of the US Constitution.[52]

However, as stated by the ECHR, freedom of expression should be limited so that it does not harm the reputation of others.[53] The US government also restricts freedom of expression in certain categories, such as privacy invasion and the visual representation of children engaging in a variety of sexual activities or genital exposures in films or photographs.[54] The sharing of naked photographs and the most intimate moments of children by millions of families is extremely likely to harm the children's self-esteem and dignity as well as their privacy, considering toilet training and the first bath as examples.

Sidis v. F-R Publishing is an example of an earlier case from the US that supports this viewpoint as it was also discussed in the chapter regarding the main rights of the children and their parents under the GDPR and the COPPA. As a child prodigy in the early 1900s, Sidis rose to prominence in the public eye, but as he reached adulthood, he decided he did not want to continue to be in the spotlight. However, without his desire, *The New Yorker* published an article on him, and as a result, he decided to sue the publication. The judge concluded that Sidis, just like any other public person, was unable to hide from the scrutiny of the public. The court recognised that a person had the right to privacy and that they had an interest in maintaining their private; yet

[51] Charter of Fundamental Rights of The European Union, OJ C 364, 18.12.2000, pp. 1–22, Article 11: "1. Everyone has the right to freedom of expression. This right shall include freedom to hold opinions and to receive and impart information and ideas without interference by public authority and regardless of frontiers. 2. The freedom and pluralism of the media shall be respected."

[52] U.S. Const. amend. I: "Congress shall make no law respecting an establishment of religion, or prohibiting the free exercise thereof; or abridging the freedom of speech, or of the press; or the right of the people peaceably to assemble, and to petition the government for a redress of grievances."

[53] Council of Europe, European Convention for the Protection of Human Rights and Fundamental Freedoms, as amended by Protocols Nos. 11 and 14, 04.11.1950, ETS 5, Article 10: "1. Everyone has the right to freedom of expression. This right shall include freedom to hold opinions and to receive and impart information and ideas without interference by public authority and regardless of frontiers. This Article shall not prevent States from requiring the licensing of broadcasting, television or cinema enterprises. 2. The exercise of these freedoms, since it carries with it duties and responsibilities, may be subject to such formalities, conditions, restrictions or penalties as are prescribed by law and are necessary in a democratic society, in the interests of national security, territorial integrity or public safety, for the prevention of disorder or crime, for the protection of health or morals, for the protection of the reputation or rights of others, for preventing the disclosure of information received in confidence, or for maintaining the authority and impartiality of the judiciary."

[54] The US government restricts the following categories of speech content: "Seditious Speech and Seditious Libel, Fighting Words and Other Threats to the Peace, Threats of Violence Against Individuals, Group Libel, Hate Speech, Defamation, False Statements, Invasion of Privacy, Emotional Distress Tort Actions, "Right of Publicity" Tort Actions, Publication of Legally Confidential Information, Obscenity, Child Pornography, Non-obscene But Sexually Explicit and Indecent Expression." U.S. Government Publishing Office (GPO): The Constitution of the United States of America Analysis and Interpretation Centennial Edition Interim Edition: Analysis of Cases Decided by the Supreme Court of the United States to June 27, 2016, 112th Congress 2nd Session, Document No: 112–9, pp. 1–2835, 1285 et seq.

they also accepted that the public had an interest in gaining knowledge about his life.[55]

Is it realistic to ask someone like Sidis, whose parents made a decision that thrust them into the public eye, to give up their right to privacy as a result of that decision? What if today's child influencers grow up to be adults who are unable to exercise the right to have their privacy respected simply because they have already been elevated to the status of public figures without their consent or knowledge? In our opinion, it would not be fair to draw conclusions about an adult's request based on the actions or behaviours of their parents in the past. This opinion is justified by the right to informational self-determination, which gives individuals control over their data by enabling them to choose when and for what purposes their personal information may be used and shared with third parties.[56]

In Europe, the German Federal Constitutional Court was the first to enunciate the concept of informational self-determination.[57] Afterwards, it became one of the foundational pillars of Article 8 of the CFR's right to protection of personal data.[58] Finally, it is consistent with the spirit of the GDPR, which offers people more control over their data,[59] for example by assuring the rights to access, rectify, delete, and object. In addition, the duties imposed by the GDPR on data controllers, such as notifying the subject and obtaining consent, would be also based on the right to informational self-determination.[60]

At this point, we should argue whether or not children have the right to informational self-determination. When we examine Article 8 of the GDPR and the COPPA, we can generally assert that parents have the right to informational self-determination on their children's behalf. Parents may exercise this right by consenting to the processing of their children's personal data and by accessing, requesting rectification or deletion, and, if necessary, objecting to the processing.[61] Obviously, this right is not absolute; as children attain maturity, they may gain control over their data. This maturity is represented by the age of digital consent, which is 13 under the

---

[55] Case 113 F.2d 806, Sidis v. F-R Pub. Corporation (No. 400), Judgment of the Court of Appeals for the Second Circuit, New York, 22 July 1940 cited in Steinberg (2016, pp. 859–860).

[56] Schwartz (2011, p. 368) cited in Thouvenin (2021, p. 248).

[57] BVerfG, Order of the First Senate of 15 December 1983 - 1 BvR 209/83 -, paras. 1–214, BVerfGE 65, 1 - 71 Volkszählung.

[58] Thouvenin (2021, p. 248).

CFR Article 8 provides the individuals control over their data with this paragraph: "Such data must be processed fairly for specified purposes and on the basis of the consent of the person concerned or some other legitimate basis laid down by law. Everyone has the right of access to data which has been collected concerning him or her, and the right to have it rectified."

Charter of Fundamental Rights of the European Union, OJ C 326, 26.12.2012, p. 391–407, Article 8(2).

[59] GDPR, Recital 7: "[...] Natural persons should have control of their own personal data. [...]".

[60] Thouvenin (2021, pp. 250–252).

[61] For more information about the data protection and privacy rights of children and their parents see the Chapter 4.

COPPA and from 13 to 16 under the GDPR.[62] The content may also limit a parent's ability to exercise this right. If parents choose to post anything that might potentially compromise their children's privacy or future self-image, such as photos or videos of them engaging in activities that could be considered humiliating, then disclosing such content should be restricted.[63]

In general, children have minimal or no influence on their parents' decisions to publicly display them on social media. As already mentioned in the previous chapter regarding parental consent, a study conducted with 817 teenagers revealed that they are uncomfortable with their parents' social media posts about them and find them pointless and embarrassing.[64] If children (even if they are underage) would like to delete their shared data, this should indicate that the children are able to/mature enough to exercise their right to informational self-determination. As mentioned in the previous chapters, some less risky or risk-free online activities should be enabled by data controllers without parental consent.

Article 17 of the GDPR states that "the data subject shall have the right to obtain from the controller, without undue delay, the erasure of personal data concerning him or her where legal grounds apply."[65] Moreover, the Recital (65) stipulates as follows:

> "[...]That right is relevant in particular where the data subject has given his or her consent as a child and is not fully aware of the risks involved by the processing, and later wants to remove such personal data, especially on the internet. The data subject should be able to exercise that right notwithstanding the fact that he or she is no longer a child. [...]"[66]

Moreover, Article 17(2) of the GDPR refers to the right to be forgotten as follows:

> "Where the controller has made the personal data public and is obliged pursuant to paragraph 1 to erase the personal data, the controller, taking account of available technology and the cost of implementation, shall take reasonable steps, including technical measures, to inform controllers which are processing the personal data that the data subject has requested the erasure by such controllers of any links to, or copy or replication of, those personal data."

As discussed before in Chapter 4, the right to erasure allows individuals to request the deletion of their personal data, but the right to be forgotten is a broader concept that refers to the right of individuals to have specific information about them removed

---

[62] GDPR, Article 8 and 16 CFR COPPA 312.2 "Child".

[63] The reason behind this restriction may be Preamble of the UNCRC as follows:

"Considering that the child should be fully prepared to live an individual life in society, and brought up in the spirit of the ideals proclaimed in the Charter of the United Nations, and in particular in the spirit of peace, dignity, tolerance, freedom, equality and solidarity, [...]" and the Article 16 of the UNCRC as follows: "No child shall be subjected to arbitrary or unlawful interference with his or her privacy, family, home or correspondence, nor to unlawful attacks on his or her honour and reputation."

UNCRC, Article 16 and the Preamble.

[64] Verswijvel et al. (2019, p. 104,407).

[65] GDPR, Article 17(1).

[66] GDPR, Recital 65.

from the Internet (usually from the search engine results). Therefore, the right to be forgotten is a key aspect of the right to erasure in the GDPR.

Although freedom of speech is an exemption to the right to erasure and right to be forgotten under Article 17,[67] where the data subject is a child, freedom of expression must be construed far more narrowly, as shown by *the Murray v. Express Newspapers Ltd (CA)* decision. The image of *J.K. Rowling*'s son was shot by a photographer and published by a newspaper without his parents' consent. J.K. Rowling and her husband challenged this invasion of their son's privacy to court.[68] The trial court ruled that publisher newspaper has the right to publish or acquire the publishing of the image in accordance with Article 10 of the European Convention on Human Rights.[69] After this decision, J.K. Rowling and her husband filed an appeal, which the Court of Appeal allowed it on the grounds that:

> "The claimant's status as a child strongly enhances his claim to invoke the protection of article 8 of the Convention for the Protection of Human Rights and Fundamental Freedoms. In common with any other child, and regardless of who his mother is, the claimant has a reasonable expectation of privacy that he should be entitled to grow up and be brought up by his parents free from unwanted intrusion and interference by the media and, in particular, the paparazzi."[70]

Accordingly, in the end, the Court of Appeal concluded that the balance between Article 8 (right to privacy) and Article 10 (right to freedom of speech) of the European Convention on Human Rights should favour the child's right to privacy.[71] In light of this example, and in our point of view, the Article 17 exemption referring to "exercising the right to freedom of speech and information" should not be invoked as a justification where the data subject is a child.[72]

As a result, we may infer that the right to be forgotten can strike a balance between the freedom of expression of parents and other adults and the right to a child's private life in favour of the child, and that it allows a child to regain control over his or her data. The non-absolute nature of this right is evident when considering that, if a user downloads child-related material, no one else has the authority to erase this information until the user chooses to remove it from their own device. However, the right to be forgotten remains a crucial right in terms of eliminating harmful material from the Internet, such as search engines (e.g., Google, Yandex etc.). This is the bare minimum that data controllers such as Google can do to assist children, and legislation and the government should also encourage data controllers to make it easier for

---

[67] GDPR, Article 17(3)(a).

[68] Case EWCA Civ446, Murray v Express Newspapers plc and another, Judgment of the Court of Appeal, England and Wales, 7 May 2008, 481.

[69] Case EWCA Civ446, Murray v Express Newspapers plc and another, Judgment of the Court of Appeal, England and Wales, 7 May 2008, 512, para 62.

[70] Case EWCA Civ446, Murray v Express Newspapers plc and another, Judgment of the Court of Appeal, England and Wales, 7 May 2008, 485.

[71] Case EWCA Civ446, Murray v Express Newspapers plc and another, Judgment of the Court of Appeal, England and Wales, 7 May 2008, 512, para 62.

[72] Alkis Tümtürk (2022, p. 11).

children to exercise their right to be forgotten. Otherwise, terrible circumstances like the one with Amanda Todd might occur.[73]

Similar to the right to be forgotten, California implemented what is commonly known as the "Online Eraser Button Law", which allows children to remove or de-identify online material they uploaded.[74] However, the COPPA does not provide children with the right to be forgotten at the federal level. Instead, it gives parents the right to request the removal of content belonging to their children and to refuse to permit further collection or use of their children's data by data controllers.[75] It would have been better to offer this right not just to parents, but also to children, as indicated by the GDPR, and even to individuals who are no longer children, as suggested by Recital 65.[76]

6.3 Manifestation of Parental Sharing Restrictions on Social Media in Practise

The COPPA and the GDPR do not place a general restriction on what parents may share regarding their children, which could be associated with their freedom of expression. However, the DSA introduces platform-design and systemic risk obligations that complement the GDPR's emphasis on data protection. The DSA requires online platforms to reconfigure their systems to eliminate manipulative design[77] and provide a high standard of privacy, security, and safety for children.[78] Targeted advertising directed to children based on profiling is prohibited.[79] The DSA also stipulates additional standards for very large online platforms, such as YouTube, Facebook, and Instagram, as well as for very large online search engines, like Google.[80] For instance, systemic risk assessments (e.g., risks relating to the dissemination of illegal

---

[73] Alkis Tümtürk (2022, pp. 11–12).

[74] Lee (2015, p. 1203).

For further information see the Online Eraser Button Law: S.B. 568, 2013 LEG. 2013–14 SESS. (Cal. 2013), https://leginfo.legislature.ca.gov/faces/billNavClient.xhtml?bill_id=201320140SB568.

[75] 16 CFR COPPA Part 312.4(d)(3).

[76] GDPR, Recital (65): "That right is relevant in particular where the data subject has given his or her consent as a child and is not fully aware of the risks involved by the processing, and later wants to remove such personal data, especially on the internet. The data subject should be able to exercise that right notwithstanding the fact that he or she is no longer a child."

[77] Regulation (EU) 2022/2065 of the European Parliament and of the Council of 19 October 2022 on a Single Market for Digital Services and amending Directive 2000/31/EC (Digital Services Act) OJ L 277, 27.10.2022, pp. 1–102, Article 25.

[78] DSA, Article 28(1).

[79] DSA, Article 28(2).

[80] European Commission, Digital Services Act: Commission designates first set of Very Large Online Platforms and Search Engines (25 April 2023) https://ec.europa.eu/commission/presscorner/detail/en/ip_23_2413.

content; adverse effects on fundamental rights, including children's rights; and negative impacts on public health as well as individuals' physical and mental well-being, particularly in relation to children) must be carried out and documented and made available to the European Commission four months after designation as a very large online platform and at least annually thereafter.[81] Very large online platforms and search engines must implement mitigation measures to handle such risks, which may involve redesigning their services, adapting their terms and conditions, online interfaces, and algorithmic systems as required.[82]

Accordingly, social media platforms have implemented privacy policies that restrict adults from sharing specific content pertaining to children. We will start our discussion by examining the YouTube restriction policies regarding to content that is targeted toward children. These include sexualisation of children, harmful or dangerous acts involving children, such as pranks, content that could cause children participants or viewers emotional distress, such as violence or simulating parental abuse, misleading family content that targets young people and involves drugs, sex, alcohol, death, etc., cyberbullying and harassment involving children, such as sharing a content that encourages others to bully or harass a child. This list is neither complete nor exhaustive. It can be improved.[83]

In addition, YouTube's policy includes "do not" recommendations such as filming children in private spaces (e.g., bedrooms and bathrooms), disclosing personal information about a child, and sharing content involving children's body twists or contortions that could attract unwanted attention from malicious individuals.[84] YouTube's enforcement team may initially provide a warning; if the behaviour persists, they may issue a strike; if 3 strikes are issued, they may terminate the channel; and if they believe a child is in danger based on reported content, they will assist law enforcement in investigating the content.[85]

We do not consider that the policy and its sanctions are very stringent, as there are still several videos on YouTube that include restricted content. For instance, you may find a barber pranking a child by pretending to chop off his ear, and at 37th second in this video, it is stated that the boy's parents provided consent for the prank. You may

---

[81] DSA, Article 34.

[82] DSA, Article 35.

[83] YouTube Help, YouTube Policies: Child Safety Policy, https://support.google.com/youtube/answer/2801999?hl=en&ref_topic=9282679#zippy=%2Ckorhat%C3%A1ros-tartalom%2Ckiskor%C3%BAakat-megc%C3%A9lz%C3%B3-tartalom.

[84] YouTube Help, YouTube Policies, Child Safety Policy: Content Featuring Minors, Don't post content on YouTube that features minors and meets one or more of the following, https://support.google.com/youtube/answer/2801999?hl=en&ref_topic=9282679#zippy=%2Ckorhat%C3%A1ros-tartalom%2Ckiskor%C3%BAakat-megc%C3%A9lz%C3%B3-tartalom%2Ccontent-featuring-minors.

[85] YouTube Help, YouTube Policies, Child Safety Policy: What happens if content violates this policy, https://support.google.com/youtube/answer/2801999?hl=en&ref_topic=9282679#zippy=%2Ckorhat%C3%A1ros-tartalom%2Ckiskor%C3%BAakat-megc%C3%A9lz%C3%B3-tartalom%2Ccontent-featuring-minors.

observe his distress and pain in his eyes, body language, and facial expressions.[86] When the child reaches adolescence, they are likely to find this video humiliating and may take action to have such inappropriate content removed.

Can we presume that parents are solely accountable for allowing the barber to share this information with the whole Internet community? Is the barber not responsible if he violates the child's privacy, body, and mind? YouTube is unable to effectively restrict such content to be published. Is YouTube not liable? Considering they are all liable, where is the regulation governing the child's data protection and privacy rights that applies? In actual fact, the GDPR and the COPPA were created with the intention of giving parents more authority over the data protection and privacy rights of their children. What results from a situation in which the parents have lost control? Who, then, has the authority to act against those parents' privacy decisions in relation to their children, and on what basis could such actions be made?

The *Martins* couple was sentenced to five years of probation for child abuse after releasing YouTube prank videos in which they shouted at and destroyed their children's toys. According to the prosecution, the Martins' pranks including yelling and causing to move their children to tears resulted in severe impairments of their mental or psychological well-beings. As a result, the Martins lost custody of their children after the recordings went viral on the Internet and sparked widespread criticism. Due to their probationary status, the Martins were not allowed to have contact with their children unless the court grants permission.[87] Law enforcement is effective if there is a significant public response, as in the instance of Martins, but it is far less effective if there is no public backlash, as in the case of the barber chopping off the ear of the child.

Children's privacy can also be violated without the use of nasty jokes or upsetting events. It may also be a peaceful video showing the daily routines of children with their parents. For instance, a video by a well-known influencer mother has more than one million views on YouTube, and its content is her three children's bedtime ritual. The majority of the video takes place in the bathroom and bedroom, which is against YouTube policy.[88] Although the children in the video seem happy, they are probably unaware that these special memories are being shared with millions of strangers. Even if they were aware of this situation, they would be unable to comprehend the implications of this sharing practice.

When a social media user shares intimate moment with the world, he/she must also understand that there will be many remarks on their personal life. For instance, there are comments under this video regarding the children's hair that must be shaved and the D vitamins that they take, the ages of the children, the baby boy's new teeth,

---

[86] YouTube, Newsnercom channel: Barber Pranks Kid By Pretending He's Cut His Ear Off, https://www.youtube.com/watch?v=0TSNKp4Xs0U.

[87] The Guardian: Couple who screamed at their kids in YouTube 'prank' sentenced to probation (12 September 2017) https://www.theguardian.com/us-news/2017/sep/12/youtube-parents-children-heather-mike-martin.

[88] YouTube, Simply Allie Channel: Night Time Routine of a Mom 2021 // Mom Of 3 // Preschooler, Toddler and Infant, https://www.youtube.com/watch?v=Dx7Ty0Yg2-k.

the breastfeeding machine, and everything else shown on the video.[89] What would these children feel when they get older and are able to read these comments and realise that many strangers have opinions on their private moments? How would they feel if they realized that their parents allow strangers to invade their personal space?

Furthermore, there are several videos of children practising yoga on YouTube. Unfortunately, these yoga sessions also feature children performing yoga positions, which may attract unwanted attention from ill-intentioned (e.g., paedophilic) YouTube users and be published to their forums, social media groups, and websites. Since the instructors are adults, it is unnecessary for children to participate in such videos. Instead of showing children's bodies, adult instructors would be clothed in a variety of vividly coloured apparel and the walls behind them would be covered with cartoon/anime characters to attract the interest of children. As previously described in this chapter, this is another sort of video that violates YouTube's terms of service, because it contains twists and/or contortions that might draw the attention of malicious users. However, we do not see any practical consequences of uploading such content, as a video containing a twenty-five minutes of yoga session for children with an adult instructor and two children following her has apparently been accessible on YouTube for more than 7 years without any restrictions and has received 16 million views.[90]

Not only YouTube, but also Instagram, serves as a platform for parents to share their children's daily routines or special moments, and it has been a huge trend over the past few years for parents to create Instagram accounts on their children's behalf, even creating a personality and posting as if they were the children themselves.

A lady justified her choice to establish a secondary account using her child's name for the purpose of disseminating his pictures and videos in the following manner: She wants the ability to post her son's images throughout the day while still retaining her profile and preserving her own identity apart from her role as a mother.[91]

Another lady, who has secured employment through social media marketing for other companies, challenges the aforementioned statement. She expresses contentment with her social media profile and its positive impact on her professional trajectory. However, she believes that her son should have the autonomy to decide whether to have a social media profile in the future and to shape that profile according to

---

[89] YouTube, Simply Allie Channel: Night Time Routine of a Mom 2021 // Mom Of 3 // Preschooler, Toddler and Infant, https://www.youtube.com/watch?v=Dx7Ty0Yg2-k.

[90] YouTube, Storyhive Channel: Yoga for Kids! https://www.youtube.com/watch?v=X655B4ISakg.

[91] Today, Have a social media account for your baby? 40 percent of millennial moms do (18 October 2014) https://www.today.com/parents/have-social-media-account-your-baby-40-percent-millennial-moms-%201D80224937 cited in Shannon Sorensen: Protecting Children's Right to Privacy in the Digital Age: Parents as Trustees of Children's Rights, Children's Legal Rights Journal 36, no. 3 (2016), 160.

his preferences. She believes that it is not within a parent's purview to make such choices on behalf of their children.[92]

We agree with the second mother that no parent should create an account on behalf of their child. What may a child think of a parent-created account that so-called belongs to him/her when the child reaches age of maturity? Parents should understand the close connection between privacy, dignity, and individuality.[93] Hence, they should be concerned about their children's future self-image and reputation, as well as keeping them from being bullied or humiliated, as these are potential outcomes of loss of privacy.[94]

Furthermore, the Instagram Community Guidelines explicitly prohibit, for instance, the sharing of nudity.[95] In reality, though, some parents share images of their children that are nearly nude with the internet community. For instance, there are parents who share potty training images, videos of their children online,[96] and once a mom acknowledged on her blog that she found her baby's naked potty-training photos on paedophilic websites and warned other parents on Twitter parent not to make the same mistake she made.[97]

Another example is that the parents of a very famous child influencer are sharing their daughter's bikini photos with total strangers, and she has almost three hundred and fifty inappropriate comments under the photo, such as stating that "she is hot", "very sexy", and "only if someone catches her", and other comments that will likely make her very disturbed and disgusted when she will be able to check those views and read the comments.[98]

Due to the fact that they are both owned by the same parent company called Meta, Facebook's and Instagram's policies are similar. In Facebook's Community Guidelines, they also claim that they do not tolerate child sexual exploitation or anything that endangers children.[99] Besides, in accordance with current law,[100] they

---

[92] Today, Have a social media account for your baby? 40 percent of millennial moms do (18 October 2014) https://www.today.com/parents/have-social-media-account-your-baby-40-percent-millennial-moms-%201D80224937 cited in Sorensen (2016, p. 160).

[93] Lukács (2016, p. 259).

[94] Sorensen (2016, p. 160).

[95] Instagram, Help Centre, Community Guidelines, Post photos and videos that are appropriate for a diverse audience, https://help.instagram.com/477434105621119/?helpref=uf_share.

[96] For an example see: YouTube, Gabriela Terese Channel: 3 DAY POTTY TRAINING METHOD 101 | How I Successfully Potty Trained My 1 Year Old in 3 Days!, https://www.youtube.com/watch?v=PXFcSSeG2_g.

[97] Twitter, BlogHer: "So I Posted Photos of My Kid Online and This is Where They Ended Up http://ow.ly/2uSjRn" (14 February 2013) https://twitter.com/blogher/status/302079107901046784 cited in Steinberg, p. 847.

[98] Instagram, Kids Diana Show (image posted on 21 August 2021) https://www.instagram.com/p/CSeZgdHjkVF/?hl=tr.

[99] Meta, Facebook Community Standards, Child sexual exploitation, abuse and nudity, Policy rationale, https://transparency.fb.com/en-gb/policies/community-standards/child-sexual-exploitation-abuse-nudity/.

[100] 18 U.S.C. 2258A (2011) (Reporting requirements of electronic communication service providers and remote computing service providers) (a).

report instances of child sexual exploitation to the National Center for Missing and Exploited Children (NCMEC).[101]

The suggestions provided by Facebook about prohibited content pertain to instances of child sexual exploitation and the solicitation of sexual material, encompassing both actual and fictitious children, including the sharing of nude photos. Moreover, the aforementioned suggestions may involve information pertaining to non-sexual abuse of children. In addition to instances of physical abuse, it is important to acknowledge that this may cover emotional and psychological forms of abuse. Engagement in inappropriate interactions with children is likewise prohibited. This form of online communication could consist of obtaining sexual material from children through private chat, as well as arranging in-person meetings for the purpose of forcing children into sexual acts. The act of sextortion and the dissemination of exploitative personal photos are also forbidden. This sort of online conduct includes the act of pressuring children into offering monetary resources, favours, or intimate material using threats to reveal intimate images or associated private data belonging to the children in question.[102]

While implementing a complete ban on parental sharing may not be a feasible approach, it is imperative to consider the implementation of some legislative restrictions, as previously indicated. In this manner, social media platforms would possess a basis and structure upon which to enhance their privacy policies. To emphasise again briefly, allowing only modest family images that do not reveal any personal information to others, posting photos of children fully from behind, concealing their facial features, or placing emojis on their faces may be acceptable.[103]

In alignment with our recommendations in this research, it is important to highlight a notable recent example. Ruby Franke, the proprietor of the 8 Passengers YouTube channel, frequently documented her family's daily routines, milestones, and private moments, including herself and her six children. Ruby's utilization of parental sharing garnered substantial criticism due to its intrusive and contentious parenting strategies, which encompassed publicly disciplining her children and disclosing intimate details of their lives. Eventually, the channel was removed, and Ruby Franke was subjected to legal repercussions as a result of allegations of child abuse. These allegations included neglect, excessive punishments, and a failure to provide adequate care. The case garnered substantial attention when one of Ruby's children escaped to a neighbor's residence in search of help. This incident resulted in the identification of

---

[101] Meta, Facebook Community Standards, Child sexual exploitation, abuse and nudity, Policy rationale, https://transparency.fb.com/en-gb/policies/community-standards/child-sexual-exploitation-abuse-nudity/.

[102] Meta, Facebook Community Standards, Child sexual exploitation, abuse and nudity, Do not post, https://transparency.fb.com/en-gb/policies/community-standards/child-sexual-exploitation-abuse-nudity/.

[103] Alkis Tümtürk (2022, p. 10).

alarming circumstances and Ruby was sentenced to four consecutive prison terms of one to 15 years each.[104]

In October 2024, Shari Franke, the eldest daughter of convicted influencer Ruby Franke, testified before Utah legislators to advocate for protections for child influencers. Drawing from her personal experiences, she highlighted several pivotal issues[105]:

Shari described family vlogging as a full-time endeavor wherein children serve as primary content creators without adequate consent and compensation. She emphasized that children, from infancy to adulthood, are often perceived as employees in these enterprises.

She underlined the absence of legislation ensuring that children featured in monetized online content receive fair compensation. Shari noted that the payments she received often masqueraded as bribes for her participation in particularly humiliating incidents. Legal safeguards akin to the *Coogan Law*,[106] which requires parents to designate 15% of a minor's income into a trust for child performers, ought to be instituted in this context as well. This research does not primarily concentrate on this issue; however, we examined it in one of our previous study regarding Youtuber Kids and their unpaid labor and exploitation.[107]

Shari recounted instances when her personal challenges and private experiences were revealed publicly, leading to lasting emotional distress. She asserted that continuous filming compromised her privacy, negatively impacting her social interactions as friends were reluctant to be filmed.

She urged legislators to address these issues proactively, promoting regulations that protect children from exploitation in family vlogging. Shari expressed her wish for a ban on family vlogging, emphasizing that no monetary benefit could justify the violation of a child's privacy and innocence. She expressed a preference for having an empty bank account over having her childhood publicly displayed on the Internet.

Shari's speech, summarising the issues we have emphasized thus far, is particularly compelling as it reflects insights derived from the personal experiences of a child influencer. Her testimony underscores the potential risks of parental sharing without restrictions and emphasizes the need for legal regulations and safeguards for child influencers.

---

[104] The Washington Post, YouTuber Ruby Franke sentenced to prison for child abuse (20 February 2024) https://www.washingtonpost.com/nation/2024/02/20/ruby-franke-sentence-youtube-8-passengers/.

[105] YouTube, KUTV2News Salt Lake City Channel (17 October 2024) Ruby Franke's oldest daughter, Shari, speaks to Utah legislative committee about child influencers, https://www.youtube.com/watch?v=yDtYlTYeLSk.

[106] California Family Code, §§ 6750–6753 (1939), commonly known as *Coogan's Law*.

[107] Alkis (2020, pp. 357–367).

6.4 Social Media Solutions Against Threats to Children's Privacy and Protection of Personal Data in Light of Current Technology

Children's internet safety should be handled differently than adults' since they are more vulnerable and lack discernment. They may experience threats that adults are unlikely to encounter. Even in such situations, adults have the ability to stand up for their rights. Children, on the other hand, lack the necessary tools to combat difficulties, particularly at younger ages. For example, if an adult encounters a predator and discovers that his/her naked images are being disseminated, they may contact the police and sue the individual immediately. They may also be cognitively more prepared to deal with the emotional consequences of such violations.

However, if children are being exploited online by predators, they may not even be aware of such violations or the repercussions of such malevolent behaviours, let alone claim their rights to privacy and data protection. Thus, it is critical that violations are avoided before they occur.

Given that the GDPR and COPPA do not include instructions or restrictions requiring data controllers to develop solutions specifically for children's online safety, other relevant regulations should be considered when designing platforms. For example, as mentioned in the previous subchapter, the DSA establishes child-specific requirements for the online platforms and search engines that go beyond the GDPR framework. Most importantly, it restricts targeted advertising to children and requires platforms to identify and address potential risks to minors that could be posed by recommender systems, interface design, and engagement-driven features.[108] This strategy is supplemented by the Digital Markets Act (DMA), which operates on a separate but related scale. While the DMA does not include child-specific regulations, it does target data-driven business models that enable large-scale profiling and cross-service data aggregation. By limiting data combination across services and constraining dominant gatekeeper behavior, the DMA indirectly limits incentives for widespread tracking and behavioral exploitation.[109] Additionally, legal cases and enforcement actions may also be considered as guidance for platform architecture. If existing legislation or pertinent legal precedents do not provide solutions, data controllers can develop their own privacy-enhancing technical and design measures. This subchapter will cover some of the current technological solutions used by social media providers.

At this point, it is important to highlight the leading example enforcement action against Meta Platforms Ireland Ltd. Following the EDPB's binding decision, Irish

---

[108] Regulation (EU) 2022/2065 of the European Parliament and of the Council of 19 October 2022 on a Single Market for Digital Services and amending Directive 2000/31/EC (Digital Services Act) OJ L 277, 27.10.2022, pp. 1–102, Recital 71, 81, 83, 89, 102, Article 28.

[109] Regulation (EU) 2022/1925 of the European Parliament and of the Council of 14 September 2022 on contestable and fair markets in the digital sector and amending Directives (EU) 2019/1937 and (EU) 2020/1828 (Digital Markets Act), OJ L 265, 12.10.2022, pp. 1–66, Recitals 1—7, Article 5.

data protection authority announced a €405 million administrative fine for violation relating to default public settings on children's accounts on Instagram.[110] Following this action, the platform implemented new privacy defaults for teenager users, making their accounts private by default. In addition to financial consequences, enforcement have been resulted in real improvements in platform architecture.[111] The automated selection of a safer alternative for teenagers is advantageous due to the correlation between the level of accessibility of an account and the increased likelihood of encountering hate speech, bullying, condemnation, and severe criticism.

Similary, the Irish Data Protection Commission, following a binding decision of the European Data Protection Board, imposed a €345 million fine against TikTok for violating the GDPR relating to the processing of children's personal data. The decision addressed, in particular, TikTok's use of public-by-default account settings for children and its failure to present privacy information transparently in a clear and age-appropriate manner.[112] As with Instagram, the enforcement did not remain confined to financial sanctions. TikTok subsequently adjusted its platform design, including introducing private-by-default settings for users under 18 and modifying certain interface choices (certain features were not available for users younger than 18).[113] This demonstrates again that GDPR enforcement in the context of children's data protection can function as a mechanism for structural change, encouraging platforms to adopt safer default configurations that reduce children's exposure to online harms such as harassment and unwanted contact.

Moreover, on Instagram, advertisers may only target users under 18 based on their location, gender, and age. They will eliminate the opportunity to opt-in to more personalised advertisements and apply these ad targeting restrictions internationally to all young Instagram users.[114] It would be ideal, in our view, not to even allow the marketers to target their location, age, or gender, as these are still forms of personal data and may still influence teens' purchasing habits and mentality more effectively than most adults'. Due to their lack of information and life experiences, children may

---

[110] European Data Protection Board, Decision 2/2022 on the dispute arisen on the draft decision of the Irish Supervisory Authority regarding Meta Platforms Ireland Limited (Instagram) under Article 65(1)(a) GDPR, adopted 28 July 2022.; followed by.

Data Protection Commission, Decision on the inquiry into Meta Platforms Ireland Limited, formerly Facebook Ireland Limited, regarding the processing of children's personal data on the "Instagram" social media network, DPC Inquiry Reference IN-20–7-4, adopted 2 September 2022.

[111] A Parent and Carer's Guide to Instagram, Manage Privacy, pp. 15–16 https://www.internetmatters.org/wp-content/uploads/2021/11/UK_Instagram_-parent_and_carer_guide_to_instagram.pdf.

[112] European Data Protection Board, Decision 2/2023 on the dispute arisen on the draft decision of the Irish Supervisory Authority regarding TikTok Technology Limited under Article 65(1)(a) GDPR, adopted 2 August 2023; followed by.

Data Protection Commission, Decision on the inquiry into TikTok Technology Limited regarding the processing of children's personal data, DPC Inquiry Reference IN-21–9-1, adopted 8 September 2023.

[113] TikTok, Teen privacy and safety settings, https://support.tiktok.com/en/account-and-privacy/account-privacy-settings/privacy-and-safety-settings-for-users-under-age-18.

[114] A Parent and Carer's Guide to Instagram, Manage Privacy, p. 24 https://www.internetmatters.org/wp-content/uploads/2021/11/UK_Instagram_-parent_and_carer_guide_to_instagram.pdf.

be more prone to manipulation. In accordance with our viewpoint, the DSA prohibits online service providers from displaying targeted advertising on their platform using profiling techniques if they have reasonable assurance that the recipient is a minor.[115]

In compliance with recent legal requirements in the European region,[116] Instagram currently refrains from displaying advertisements to individuals under the age of 18. Consequently, advertisers are unable to target users under 18 with their products and services on the platform.[117] This change, specific to the EU, underscores the importance of stricter regulations on the operational practices of online service providers.

Research on children's comprehension of advertising indicates that children between the ages of 3 and 7 possess the ability to differentiate between advertisements and content. As an illustration, a child may assert that the advertisements are shorter compared to the relevant content. However, they lack the understanding that the primary purpose of these commercials is to encourage the acquisition of a product or service. Children between the ages of 7 and 11, with the assistance of their families and educational institutions, begin to develop an awareness of bias and deception within advertisements, while also gaining an understanding of the persuasive nature inherent in advertising. Nevertheless, there is a deficiency in their understanding of the fundamental principles behind advertising, including its nature and operational mechanisms, as well as the many approaches and strategies employed in advertising campaigns. Teenagers aged 12 and above shown the ability to recognise advertisements, discern the underlying intentions of advertisers to influence behaviour, and recognise particular advertising methods and appeals. Nevertheless, even while teenagers aged 12 and older may acknowledge the presence of persuasive intentions, it does not imply that they are impervious to marketing tactics, particularly when very enticing items are involved.[118]

The findings of this study pertain specifically to conventional advertising methods, such as television advertisements, and do not encompass emerging marketing strategies like influencer marketing and sponsored content on social media platforms.

---

[115] DSA, Article 28(2).

[116] Facebook, Help Center, What is the European Region?, https://www.facebook.com/help/681634310058367?helpref=faq_content.

"If you live in a country or territory listed below (the "European region", which includes countries in the European Union), your services are provided by Meta Platforms Ireland Limited, which is also the controller of your data and responsible for your information when you use our services:

Andorra, Austria, Azores, Belgium, Bulgaria, Canary Islands, Channel Islands, Croatia, Czech Republic, Denmark, Estonia, Finland, France, French Guiana, Germany, Gibraltar, Greece, Guadeloupe, Hungary, Iceland, Ireland, Isle of Man, Italy, Latvia, Liechtenstein, Lithuania, Luxembourg, Madeira, Malta, Martinique, Mayotte, Monaco, Netherlands, Norway, Poland, Portugal, Republic of Cyprus, Réunion, Romania, San Marino, Saint-Martin, Slovakia, Slovenia, Spain, Sweden, Switzerland, United Kingdom sovereign bases in Cyprus (Akrotiri and Dhekelia) and Vatican City.

If you don't live in one of the countries or territories listed above, your services are provided by Meta Platforms Inc."

[117] Instagram, Help Center, How ads are shown to teens, https://help.instagram.com/1079023176238541/?helpref=related_articles.

[118] John (1999, pp. 183–213).

For instance, the utilisation of widely popular unpacking and toy-play videos,[119] along with influencers providing reviews or demonstrations of sponsored items, might be more efficacious in comparison to traditional television commercials.[120] This phenomenon may be attributed to the facilitation of direct contact through social media platforms, wherein influencers have the ability to immediately respond to comments from their followers. Consequently, this interaction fosters the development of a one-sided relationship in which a follower invests time, energy, and interest in influencers who remain oblivious to their presence.[121] This phenomenon leads individuals to perceive influencers as peers or friends rather than just promoters of things. In this manner, individuals, including both children and parents, have the chance to cultivate trust and establish the reliability of influencers, operating under the assumption that influencers would only promote a product if they genuinely had a favourable opinion of it.[122]

According to Instagram's policies, once individuals begin following influencer accounts and engaging with related information, the algorithms employed by social media platforms ensure that such content continues to appear in their newsfeeds. For instance, Instagram provides suggestions to its users in order to facilitate their exploration of new communities and content. Instagram has the capability to suggest content and profiles that users do not already follow. The process of personalising content for Instagram users involves the generation of individualised recommendations for each person, utilising artificial intelligence (AI) and machine learning (ML) techniques. For instance, when toddlers engage with toy-play videos on Instagram, the platform may then suggest material related to toy reviews, unboxing videos, and similar genres.[123]

Besides to these aforementioned findings, Instagram has also addressed the issue of varying age requirements among EU Member States. Since it varies from country to country, Instagram has increased the minimum age for restricting personalised advertisements and creating private accounts by default to under 18.[124] This change is intended to provide a more inclusive approach in the absence of a standardised age of digital consent among Member States. Thus, we should emphasize our prior

[119] Some examples are presented below:

YouTube, Ryan's World Channel: Christmas Morning 2016 Opening Presents with Ryan ToysReview, https://www.youtube.com/watch?v=WyOkjW5FqBU.

YouTube, Vlad and Niki's Channel: Vlad and Nikita play with Toy Cars - Collection video for kids, https://www.youtube.com/watch?v=NtzftGb0EcM.

[120] Radesky et al. (2020, p. 2).

[121] Evans (2020, p. 1).

[122] Evans (2020, pp. 1–2).

[123] Instagram Help Centre, Recommendations on Instagram, https://help.instagram.com/313829416281232/?helpref=uf_share.

Meta, Instagram Feed Recommendations AI system (25 June 2024) https://transparency.meta.com/features/explaining-ranking/ig-feed-recommendations/?referrer=1.

[124] A Parent and Carer's Guide to Instagram: Manage Privacy, 24 https://www.internetmatters.org/wp-content/uploads/2021/11/UK_Instagram_-parent_and_carer_guide_to_instagram.pdf.

recommendation that the EU should adopt a uniform age threshold requirement within the GDPR, rather than leaving this decision to the Member States.

As mentioned earlier, the regulatory frameworks governing Facebook and Instagram demonstrate similarities as they are both under the umbrella of Meta. As stated by the Meta Safety Centre, the platform places clear emphasis on proactively avoiding damage from occurring in the first place. This is achieved by the implementation of zero-tolerance rules and the state-of-the-art preventive measures. The company makes a commitment to promptly remove any nude images of children, regardless of the initial intent for their sharing. This proactive approach is motivated by the recognition that such images possess the potential to be exploited or misused by others.[125]

In one of our published papers, we recommended that AI and ML technologies be utilised by social media platforms to detect and eliminate nudity and other hazardous content related to children. We have emphasised that Facebook once deployed a facial recognition technique for tagging individuals, which might also be applied for detecting children's faces when parents would like to publish images. This method, along with a pertinent disclaimer pop-up, would inform parents of the possible hazards of sharing and provides the option to obscure their children's faces if they still choose to share the pictures of the children.[126]

Indeed, Facebook and Instagram has begun employing these technologies to detect and remove shared harmful data in a manner similar to our earlier recommendation.[127] However, it would have been ideal if they employed these tools to notify and even prevent parents and other adults before they share the content. Because removing them later is a good solution, but it might be insufficient, as once the photograph or video is uploaded on the Internet, it is not possible to predict who would have access to it and for what purpose they will use such content. Therefore, it would be ideal to employ AI and ML to identify inappropriate data and prohibit its sharing before it reaches other users.

From 2018 through 2025, the total amount of relevant content deleted by Facebook due to their association with child nudity and sexual exploitation has been displayed by a Statista chart.[128] During the second quarter of 2021, Facebook saw a significant increase in the volume of material pertaining to child exploitation that was removed, which may be attributed to the implementation of a modified detection system.[129]

Besides, it is visible that there was a decline in the removal of Facebook material related to child sexual exploitation, child nudity, and physical abuse during the first

---

[125] Meta, Safety Centre, Online Child Protection, https://about.meta.com/actions/safety/onlinechildprotection.

[126] Alkis Tümtürk (2022, p. 10).

[127] Meta, Online Child Protection: Tools and Technology https://about.meta.com/actions/safety/onlinechildprotection.

[128] Statista, Global number of child nudity and sexual exploitation-related content items removed by Facebook from 3rd quarter 2018 to 3rd quarter 2025 (in millions), https://www.statista.com/statistics/1013776/facebook-child-exploitation-removal-quarter/.

[129] Meta, Community Standards Enforcement Report, Second Quarter 2021 (18 August 2021), https://about.fb.com/news/2021/08/community-standards-enforcement-report-q2-2021/.

quarter of 2023. The downward trend persisted throughout the second quarter of 2023. Currently, the average number of removals seems to have returned to pre-system change levels seen before to the implementation of the system modification in the second quarter of 2021. The results reveal that 9.7 million pieces of content related to child sexual abuse were removed, along with 922,000 pieces of content involving child nudity and physical abuse.[130]

There might be underlying factors contributing to the notable increase seen after the change of tracking the relevant consent in the second quarter of 2021, as well as the following decrease observed from the first quarter of 2023. It is reasonable to assume that the improved ability of Facebook to identify and eliminate such data, together with the notable rise in the quantity of erased data, stems from the progressions achieved in its own technology and tools. Facebook's proactive strategy, which involves taking action without relying only on user reports to address improper content, represents a notable advancement.

However, the use of AI solutions by Facebook may lead to mistakes and excessive identification of innocent material, including situations when parents share private content of their children for their best interests. Later in this subchapter, we will discuss relevant and specific real-life examples to illustrate this point. The primary cause of this issue may be due to the limitations of existing AI technologies. The significant decline seen in 2023 might be attributed to the heightened vigilance of reviewer teams of Facebook after becoming aware of instances when AI systems produced excessive false alarms due to the limitations of current detection methods.

Google also combats child sexual abuse via the use of technical solutions. (The YouTube platform is subject to the same requirements since it is a product of Google.[131]) Google utilises two primary solutions: hash matching and AI. Hash matching involves the process of assigning distinct digital signatures, referred to as "hashes," to photos and videos. These hashes are then compared to a pre-existing database of recognised signatures. When the two items are identical or exhibit significant resemblance, the content is said to be equivalent or nearly analogous. The hashes are acquired from reputable entities such as the Internet Watch Foundation (IWF) and the National Centre for Missing and Exploited Children (NCMEC). Hash matching is a technique used to identify pre-existing instances of child sexual abuse material. In conjunction with this, AI is utilised to detect novel content exhibiting striking resemblances to established patterns of proven child sexual abuse material. A group of skilled individuals is assigned to examine and assess every newly identified picture, ensuring its classification as child sexual abuse material before it is reported. As mandated by US legislation, following this review, the team notifies NCMEC of any images designated as containing sexually abusive material involving children.[132] The

---

[130] Statista, Global number of child nudity and sexual exploitation-related content items removed by Facebook from 3rd quarter 2018 to 3rd quarter 2025 (in millions), https://www.statista.com/statistics/1013776/facebook-child-exploitation-removal-quarter/.

[131] See the list of products owned by Google:
Google, Products, https://about.google/products/.

[132] 18 U.S.C. 2258A (2011) (Reporting requirements of electronic communication service providers and remote computing service providers) (a).

National Centre for Missing and Exploited Children (NCMEC) thereafter assesses the submitted report and may choose to direct the matter to an appropriate law enforcement entity.[133]

However, as this technology is new and not flawless, controls should be in place. In some circumstances, mistaken assumptions may cause major issues when attempting to safeguard children. For example, a father recently took images of his child's groin since the child had a medical concern and wanted to submit these photos to the doctor on the advice of their healthcare provider. The doctor detected the problem using the images and recommended antibiotics, which rapidly resolved the medical condition. However, Mark, the father who would like to be called only by his first name, encountered serious troubles following the detection of hazardous content concerning child sexual abuse and exploitation by an AI tool of Google.[134]

By the time Mark comprehended the underlying cause, all of his Google accounts involving Google cloud, Gmail, Google Calendar, and Google Fi had already been disabled. The San Francisco Police Department already begun an investigation after Google's review team detected a video he shot with his son and unclothed wife in their bed. Mark received a letter from the San Francisco Police Department in December 2021. It included a letter notifying him that he was being investigated, as well as copies of the search warrants executed on Google and his internet service provider.[135]

Nicholas Hillard, the investigator, declared in the report that the incident did not satisfy the criteria for a crime and that no crime had taken place. Despite the fact that law enforcement acquitted Mark, he was still unable to access his account or material on Google accounts since a Google spokesperson stated that they stick to their decision due to the zero-tolerance policy against this content.[136]

On the one hand, we believe that Google's cooperation with law enforcement may be critical and beneficial to children's online safety. One the other hand, if the review teams of technology companies or investigators are not cautious, it may cause some major challenges, and in the worst circumstances, some parents may lose custody. In the present conditions, it is inevitable that human involvement is necessary. Nevertheless, it is crucial that companies shall be highly finicky in their decisions when they are assigning experts to such reviewing teams. Hence, in such

---

[133] Google, Safety and Security, How we detect, remove and report child sexual abuse material, Susan Jasper (28 October 2022), https://blog.google/technology/safety-security/how-we-detect-remove-and-report-child-sexual-abuse-material/.

[134] The New York Times, A Dad Took Photos of His Naked Toddler for the Doctor. Google Flagged Him as a Criminal, Published 21 August 2022, Updated 21 June 2023, https://www.nytimes.com/2022/08/21/technology/google-surveillance-toddler-photo.html.

[135] The New York Times, A Dad Took Photos of His Naked Toddler for the Doctor. Google Flagged Him as a Criminal, Published 21 August 2022, Updated 21 June 2023, https://www.nytimes.com/2022/08/21/technology/google-surveillance-toddler-photo.html.

[136] The New York Times, A Dad Took Photos of His Naked Toddler for the Doctor. Google Flagged Him as a Criminal, Published 21 August 2022, Updated 21 June 2023, https://www.nytimes.com/2022/08/21/technology/google-surveillance-toddler-photo.html.

delicate issues, service providers should make the process simple for data subjects to challenge even the final decisions of review teams.[137]

Carissa Byrne Hessick, a law professor at the University of North Carolina who is specialised in child pornography crimes, has remarked that it is critical that technology firms provide information to law authorities in order to combat child sexual abuse. She does, however, say that there should be an opportunity for corrections.[138]

After all, Mark's is not the only example. Similar incidents exist, such as the one that occurred in Texas. Cassio, who also likes to be named only by his first name, photographed his son's infected intimates at his paediatrician's request. He then sent them to his wife using Google's chat service. Google photos was also used to preserve the images. His Gmail account was similarly disabled, and he was in the midst of purchasing a home at the time. His mortgage broker was sceptical when Cassio suddenly wanted to alter his mailing address until the real estate agency vouched for him.[139]

There might be countless additional cases like this all throughout the world. Obviously, not all naked children's images are child pornography. However, parents should exercise extreme caution since once it is collected and stored in the cloud, it may be accessed on the Internet by malevolent individuals. Sharing those images for health reasons, in our view, is also not very prudent, although in exceptional circumstances, such as pandemic periods, it may be acceptable.

As AI and ML improve, there may be certain modifications and a reduced need for humans to participate in assessing shared information. Nonetheless, given the current circumstances, it is evident that the AI may make mistakes, and well selected review teams and investigators may be of great assistance, particularly in situations involving law enforcement. Furthermore, as the GDPR currently grants data subjects the right not to be subject to a decision based only on automated processing, compliance with the Regulation's requirements in its current version would necessitate human intervention and simple mechanisms to object their final decisions.[140]

---

137 GDPR, Article 22 and Recital 71.

138 The New York Times, A Dad Took Photos of His Naked Toddler for the Doctor. Google Flagged Him as a Criminal, Published 21 August 2022, Updated 21 June 2023, https://www.nytimes.com/2022/08/21/technology/google-surveillance-toddler-photo.html.

139 The New York Times, A Dad Took Photos of His Naked Toddler for the Doctor. Google Flagged Him as a Criminal, Published 21 August 2022, Updated 21 June 2023, https://www.nytimes.com/2022/08/21/technology/google-surveillance-toddler-photo.html.

140 GDPR, Article 22(1).

6.5 Long-Term Solutions for Protecting Children's Privacy and Data Protection in Practice

In addition to the legal and technological remedies and restrictions stated above, there is a more essential alternative that will be more difficult to adopt but more effective in the long-term: education in digital literacy for children and their parents. Digital literacy encompasses the ability to use digital devices or software safely, to generate meaningful content for the digital world and communities, and to be a conscious and responsible digital consumer.[141]

When addressing data and privacy literacy, it is important to consider three distinct aspects of privacy: interpersonal privacy, which involves an individual's digital footprint; institutional privacy, which concerns the collection of information by governments or public authorities; and commercial privacy, which relates to how businesses utilise personal information for marketing purposes.[142]

Furthermore, children and their parents should be aware of three types of data: the data given, which means that individuals have contributed this information about themselves, or others have contributed about those individuals; the data traces, which individuals have left behind, usually unknowingly, and which are captured using data-tracking technologies; and the inferred data, also known as profiling, which is the result of analysing the data given and data traces and posing a conclusion about individuals.[143]

The study conducted by Livingstone et al. (2020) on data and privacy online of children growing up in the digital age revealed that children aged 5–7, 8–11, and 12–17 have different understandings about the typology of privacy. However, all of their understandings are usually related to interpersonal privacy rather than commercial or institutional ones. It indicates that they responded to issues and queries regarding commercial and institutional processes in the context of interpersonal terms. This might be due to the children's familiarity with offline interpersonal situations. Nonetheless, online privacy does not operate like this, especially when it comes to data economy. As children are less conscious of the activities of institutions and commerce, they may expose information about them without being aware of potential data breaches or exploitative commercial operations.[144]

According to the study, children aged 5–7 are cultivating a sense of independence regarding interpersonal privacy, learning to maintain secrets and comprehend rules without fully grasping their consequences. They utilise devices with certain limitations and perceive adult supervision as beneficial. Their comprehension of institutional and commercial privacy is inadequate, and they remain oblivious to the

---

141 Nascimbeni and Vosloo (2019, p. 10).

142 Livingstone et al. (2020, p. 415).

143 Van der Hof (2016, pp. 412–414) cited in Livingstone et al. (2020, p. 415).

144 Livingstone et al. (2020, p. 416).

associated hazards. They possess a few strategies for managing risk situations, such as contacting parents or terminating the application.[145]

Regarding interpersonal privacy, children aged 8–11 are beginning to comprehend the hazards, however they often remain unguarded. Privacy management is seen as adherence to regulations rather than the internalisation of behaviours. They lack awareness of dangers and are unable to distinguish between offline and online risk disparities. Parental surveillance remains beneficial for ensuring their safety. Concerning institutional and commercial privacy, there are deficiencies in comprehending online privacy terms and conditions; nonetheless, they exhibit enhanced responsiveness to interactive learning, and their awareness improves with experience.[146]

Children aged 12–17 comprehend the significance of privacy and the notion of privacy hazards. However, they remain oblivious to the long-term consequences and often make decisions about online behaviours solely on immediate advantages. They established extensive confidence in parental and school restrictions, although expressed worry over parental surveillance. In terms of institutional and commercial privacy, they recognise device monitoring and online targeting, although they are less cognisant of the potential future ramifications. Media literacy is most successful for the teenagers who want to use their knowledge to make informed choices in practice.[147]

Even more confusing is the fact that interpersonal and commercial activities are no longer truly distinct, as they once were. For instance, when a child shares a photo with a friend via Instagram, the photo is shared with Instagram simultaneously and, depending on the settings of the Instagram account, with Facebook as well.[148] Dual-meaning online interactions are not only perplexing for children, but also for the parents who should be guiding their children.[149]

The study also reveals children's perspectives on the management of their online data and privacy. The responses indicate that children of all ages are concerned about who collects their personal data, how the data is gathered, and why the data is collected. It has been observed that children of different ages approach types of data differently. The younger children regard personal information as data given, such as phone numbers, but the older children are aware of data taken and inferred as well (e.g., via face recognition technology), along with the various types of data, including sensitive, biometric, and profiled data. Some of the older ones had a strong grasp of how data profiling is performed and the data economy which profiling is one of the components. This understanding stems from their prior experiences of doing searches and then receiving targeted adverts. Some teenagers are also asked about advanced privacy issues, such as data transfers, data retention periods, and age

[145] Livingstone et al. (2020, p. 417).

[146] Livingstone et al. (2020, p. 417).

[147] Livingstone et al. (2020, p. 417).

[148] Instagram Help Centre, Sharing to other social networks, https://help.instagram.com/169948159813228.

[149] Livingstone et al. (2020, p. 419).

verification methods. At the end, when they learned about the extensive collecting of their personal data from the research's authors, they were angered and confused; nevertheless, this is paradoxically the business model of social networking sites and advertising firms.[150]

This study demonstrates that data and privacy education should be tailored to the age of children, beginning with interpersonal privacy and data given for comparatively younger children and proceeding to institutional and commercial privacy and data taken and inferred (i.e., profiling) as children grow and develop.

The results illustrate that children aged 15 to 16 posed very insightful queries about the storage, sharing, and transfer of data. They enquired if the sensitive data was also disseminated to other parties. They were curious about the onward data transfers. They expressed significant recommendations regarding corporate practices, including the enhancement of age restrictions, the disclosure of information pertaining to data subjects, the secure storage of sensitive data, the limitation of data retention periods, the assurance of data subjects' access rights, the augmentation of scrutiny over age verification systems, and the adherence to the principle of data minimisation.[151]

Accordingly, we consider the age of 16 adopted by the GDPR as the uniform age for digital consent across the EU is appropriate, since studies show that children at this age are capable of comprehending the consequences of their online behaviour. If these children are sufficiently taught media literacy at the age of 16, they will gain even more knowledge to the point where they may be considered fully competent. Furthermore, the age of 16 would be consistent with the consent ages indicated in Subchapter 3.3 for other legal disciplines and situations, such as medical treatment or sexual activity.

However, in order to avoid the existing lack of consistency across EU Member States regarding the age of digital consent, we believe that the clause in Article 8 of the GDPR stating that Member States may provide through legislation for a lower age not less than 13 years should be removed. Even further, considering the aforementioned findings, it would be ideal for the COPPA to increase the age requirement from 13 to 16. The mentioned change would provide an enhanced level of protection for teenagers and promote the harmonisation between the EU and the US.

The results of this study also suggest that parents generally possess little knowledge about privacy and the digital realm, as seen by their remarks when queried about online experiences and Internet dangers. The remarks indicate that parents are uninformed about the possible risks of the Internet. One of the fathers stated that schools should educate children about digital skills, since he is unfamiliar with concepts such as profiling.[152]

Parents, who are unfamiliar with the internet world, expect the school and instructors to teach their children about it. Whereas teachers believe that parents should take greater responsibility in raising their children to be aware of potential dangers

---

150 Livingstone et al. (2020, p. 417–419).

151 Livingstone et al. (2020, p. 418).

152 Livingstone et al. (2020, p. 421).

of Internet and be careful with their online presence and activities. Teachers also believe that the curriculum does not teach students the necessary digital literacy abilities, and that the digital literacy skills taught in schools are not transferrable into practise.[153]

According to considerations mentioned above, it is not unexpected that people, especially parents and teachers, believe they are falling behind in adoption and utilisation of emerging technologies.[154] The overall findings indicate that both parents and children often lack a comprehensive understanding of the significance of privacy and data protection, as well as the potential hazards associated with relinquishing control over children's data. Moreover, individuals lack a comprehensive understanding of how to effectively exercise their rights pertaining to privacy and data protection.

Therefore, governments and other stakeholders must take responsibility and make more investments to help parents and teachers improve their digital skills. This would enable them to effectively facilitate children's educational development and progress within the context of the digital age.[155]

References

Alkis A (2020) Protection of YouTuber kids against child labour and exploitation. In: Ristivojević Branislav R (ed) Harmonizacija srpskog i mađarskog prava sa pravom Evropske unije = A szerb és a magyar jog harmonizációja az Európai Unió jogával = Harmonisation of Serbian and Hungarian Law with the European Union Law Нови Сад. Faculty of Law of the University of Novi Sad, Újvidék, pp 357–367

Alkis Tümtürk A (2022) Implications of parental sharing of children's personal data online. ArsBoni Jogi Folyoirat, X. evfolyam 2022/1–2:3

Bunn A (2019) Children and the 'right to be forgotten': what the right to erasure means for European children, and why Australian children should be afforded a similar right. Media Int Aust 170(1):41

Donovan S (2020) 'Sharenting': the forgotten children of the GDPR. Peace Human Rights Govern 4(1):43

Evans YN (2020) One-sided social media relationships and the impact of advertising on children. Pediatrics 146(5):1

Fredrickson BL, Roberts TA (1997) Objectification theory: toward understanding women's lived experiences and mental health risks. Psychol Women Q 21(2):179–180

Gioia F, Griffiths MD, Boursier V (2020) Adolescents' body shame and social networking sites: the mediating effect of body image control in photos. Sex Roles 83:773, 776, 781.

Harrison K, Fredrickson BL (2003) Women's sports media, self-objectification, and mental health in black and white adolescent females. J Commun 53(2):228

John DR (1999) Consumer socialization of children: a retrospective look at twenty-five years of research. J Consum Res 26(3):183–213

Keltie H (2020) Sharenting and the (potential) right to be forgotten. Ind Law J 95(3):1006

Lee J (2015) SB 568: does California's online eraser button protect the privacy of minors. U.C. Davis Law Rev 48(3):1203

[153] Livingstone et al. (2020, p. 422).

[154] Livingstone et al. (2019, p. 35).

[155] Livingstone and Byrne (2015, pp. 26–29).

Livingstone S, Byrne J (2015) Challenges of parental responsibility in a global perspective. In: Gasser U (ed) Digitally connected: global perspectives on youth and digital media. Berkman Center Research Publication, pp 26–29
Livingstone S, Stoilova M, Nandagiri R (2019) Children's data and privacy online: growing up in a digital age. An evidence review. London School of Economics and Political Science, London, p 35
Livingstone S, Stoilova M, Nandagiri R (2020) Data and privacy literacy: the role of the school in educating children in a datafied society. In: The handbook of media education research, p 415
Lukács A (2016) What is privacy? The history and definition of privacy. In: Gábor Keresztes (ed) Tavaszi Szél 2016 Tanulmánykötet I., Budapest, Doktoranduszok Országos Szövetsége, p 259
Meier EP, Gray J (2014) Facebook photo activity associated with body image disturbance in adolescent girls. Cyberpsychol Behav Soc Netw 17(4):200, 202
Minkus T, Liu K, Ross KW (2015) Children seen but not heard: when parents compromise children's online privacy. In: Proceedings of the 24th international conference on World Wide Web, p 777
Nascimbeni F, Vosloo S (2019) Digital literacy for children: exploring definitions and frameworks. UNICEF Office of Global Insight and Policy, Scoping Paper 1:10
Ouvrein G, Verswijvel K (2019) Sharenting: parental adoration or public humiliation? A focus group study on adolescents' experiences with sharenting against the background of their own impression management. Child Youth Serv Rev 99:320
Radesky J, Chassiakos YLR, Ameenuddin N, Navsaria D (2020) Digital advertising to children. Pediatrics 146(1):2
Richards NM (2013) The dangers of surveillance. Harv Law Rev 126(7):1952–1958
Schwartz PM (2011) Regulating governmental data mining in the United States and Germany: constitutional courts, the state, and new technology. William and Mary Law Rev 53(2):368
Sorensen S (2016) Protecting children's right to privacy in the digital age: parents as trustees of children's rights. Child Legal Rights J 36(3):160
Steinberg SB (2017) Sharenting: children's privacy in the age of social media. Emory Law J 66(4):876–877
Sun K, Sugatan C, Afnan T, Simon H, Gelman SA, Radesky J, Schaub F (2021) "They see you're a girl if you pick a pink robot with a skirt": a qualitative study of how children conceptualize data processing and digital privacy risks. In: Proceedings of the 2021 CHI conference on human factors in computing systems, pp 5–12
Thouvenin F (2021) Informational self-determination: a convincing rationale for data protection law? J Intellect Prop Inf Technol Electron Commerce Law 12(4):248
Van der Hof S (2016) I agree, or do I: a rights-based analysis of the law on children's consent in the digital world. Wis Int Law J 34:412–414
Verswijvel K, Walrave M, Hardies K, Heirman W (2019) Sharenting, is it a good or a bad thing? Understanding how adolescents think and feel about sharenting on social network sites. Child Youth Services Rev 104:104407
Zhao J, Wang G, Dally C, Slovak P, Edbrooke-Childs J, Van Kleek M, Shadbolt N (2019) 'I make up a silly name': understanding children's perception of privacy risks online. In: CHI conference on human factors in computing systems proceedings, pp 6–9

Chapter 7
Conclusions

Abstract Although regulatory and doctrinal differences remain, both GDPR and COPPA allocate primary responsibility for children's online privacy and data protection to parents, relying heavily on parental consent as a central protective mechanism. Accordingly, parental sharing as a concept and the necessity of legal restrictions and consequences associated with it are absent from the two legislations. Indeed, the role of parents is crucial for the protection of children online; however, they should not be held entirely responsible, particularly in the context of recent developments in data-driven technologies including AI. Furthermore, regulators and industry have emphasised the importance of age assurance for online service providers when it comes to providing safer online environment to children. Nevertheless, we believe that age assurance alone is insufficient to assure meaningful and sustainable protection of children's privacy without a system design that matches their developmental capacity and a sufficient level of digital literacy. COPPA should explicitly grant children data protection and privacy rights, rather than requiring parents to exercise these rights on their behalf in all situations. We recommend that both legislations include specific provisions that specify the rights of children that they may exercise and the responsibility of data controllers to facilitate the exercise of those rights. Recent legislation (including unenacted ones), real-world cases, legal proceedings, industry practices, and organizational guidelines to protect children online demonstrate the shift toward privacy and security-focused design and system architecture. We also underline the need for stricter AI-driven technology regulations especially for processing children's data. Although technological advances require new regulations, requirements, and research, this monograph's key message remains: all stakeholders, including service providers, operators, lawmakers, judicial bodies, law enforcers, educators, and parents, should work together to protect children's online data and privacy.

A. Alkış Tümtürk, *Online Privacy and Data Protection of Children in the European Union and the United States*, Ius Gentium: Comparative Perspectives on Law and Justice 141, https://doi.org/10.1007/978-3-032-27534-9_7

7.1 Summary of Findings and Comparative Assessment

This research examines children's online data protection and privacy from various perspectives, seeking to determine the efficiency of the parental consent mechanism. We analyzed the challenges on both sides of the Atlantic, proposing solutions based on comparative legislative critique and empirical evidence gathered from literature reviews and real-world examples sourced online.

Initially, we commenced the research by examining the historical context of privacy and data protection, focusing on their emergence and evolution. We then discussed how children's internet usage prompted jurisdictions to establish specific laws for their protection, leading to the emergence of the COPPA in the US, followed by the GDPR in the EU adopting similar concepts such as the parental consent mechanism and age thresholds for consent.

In the subsequent chapter concerning consent and age thresholds for obtaining consent, we examined whether the chosen age thresholds are adequately justified. An examination of the age of consent in relation to other fields, alongside an analysis of survey findings regarding children's challenges and troubles at different ages, suggests that age thresholds lack sound legal and developmental justification. Besides, inconsistencies between the age of digital consent and other forms of consent, such as for medical care or employment, create confusion and undermine the rationale of existing regulations. According to the studies presented, we propose that teenagers aged 15-16 possess a superior comprehension of privacy and data protection compared to their younger counterparts, enabling them to make more informed decisions. Consequently, we recommend that the age of consent be established at 16 in both jurisdictions, while also advocating for a sufficiently flexible, risk-based approach that considers the maturity of the child.

Compared with traditional age-verification methods, age assurance based on digital identities in the EU is widely regarded as a more reliable approach, largely because it is built around data minimisation and selective disclosure. As reflected in the European Commission's blueprint, the effectiveness of such systems increases when they are deployed within secure and trustworthy ecosystems that are designed to preserve privacy by default. In practical terms, this involves the integration of privacy-enhancing technologies such as double-blind verification schemes, technical measures that preserve anonymity and avoid linkability, and the use of zero-knowledge proofs, which are examined in greater detail in Chapter 3.4. Similarly, introducing a harmonised and efficient age-verification mechanism at the federal level in the US could provide greater legal clarity and help address the limitations of the current state-by-state approach. However, we maintain that merely altering the age threshold does not substantially influence children's online behaviors or safety. Promoting digital literacy, providing developmentally appropriate guidance, and designing and managing online platforms and services in a way that is compatible with children's developmental capacities are more effective approaches to risk mitigation.

We have examined the rights afforded to children under the GDPR and concluded that if data controllers fail to communicate these rights and lawmakers do not clarify how children can exercise them, it will not be possible to discuss empowered rights, thereby preventing children from fully enjoying them as intended. Consequently, we proposed solutions such as explicit guidelines and interactive educational tools, including video-recorded privacy notices, to facilitate children's comprehension of their rights and their ability to exercise them. We asserted that data controllers should possess a distinct article within the GDPR specifically addressing their obligations regarding protecting children's personal data, as the current GDPR lacks practical mechanisms for this purpose. We recommend that, under the COPPA, rights be granted directly to children rather than to their parents.

For both jurisdictions, we contended that certain rights may be overly complex for children to independently exercise; therefore, it would be preferable for parents to act on their behalf when necessary. Other rights, such as access, rectification, and deletion, may be more readily exercised by children without parental consent if they possess sufficient maturity to comprehend the consequences of their online behavior.

Neither the GDPR nor the COPPA expressly regulates parental sharing of children's personal data online as a standalone concept. Nevertheless, following the enhanced platform accountability obligations introduced under the DSA, online service providers started imposing some restrictions on their terms of service and privacy notices. Accordingly, we examined the operating procedures of three popular social media platforms (YouTube, Instagram, Facebook) and their effects on the sharing behavior of parents towards their children. Due to the widespread occurrence of detrimental parental sharing practices, legislative frameworks should establish strict requirements on these behaviors, enforceable through graduated sanctions, ranging from fines to custody interventions in severe instances. We also discussed AI-driven innovative solutions provided by data controllers like Google and Facebook, examining their capabilities and limitations. Further investigation would be advantageous in examining the implications of emerging technologies (e.g., data-driven technologies including AI, ML, blockchain) on the protection of children's data.

Furthermore, we underscored the significance of digital literacy for parents and teachers, as well as age-appropriate education for children. Extensive government-funded initiatives, incorporated into educational curricula and outreach to the community, can close this gap, promoting informed and responsible online conduct among all stakeholders.

We propose that the effective safeguarding of children's data requires collaborative endeavors among governments, parents, educational institutions, and data controllers. Legislative precision and collaboration among all stakeholders can foster a safer online environment without imposing excessive burdens on any single party. Judicial bodies must also interpret privacy and data protection legislation with an emphasis on the best interests of children, establishing precedents that may inspire reforms in other jurisdictions.

In conclusion, we established that protecting children's privacy in the digital age requires a comprehensive approach that integrates legislative enhancements, the application of technology advancements for the benefit of children, and the allocation of resources for digital literacy. Although parental consent could be essential, excessive dependence on this mechanism is neither pragmatic nor adequate. By addressing the deficiencies identified in this research, policymakers can create a comprehensive framework that respects children's individuality, reduces risks, and enables all parties involved to collaboratively protect children's rights in the online environment.

7.2 Emerging Challenges and Recent Developments

As technological advancements progress more rapidly than regulatory frameworks, there is a necessity to supplement regulations on both sides of the Atlantic. The broader EU regulatory framework is progressively complementing the GDPR with measures that are more focused on safeguarding children's online safety. As noted in Chapter 6, the Digital Services Act (DSA), which has recently come into effect, establishes child-specific obligations that extend beyond the general data protection framework. Specifically, it limits targeted advertising directed at children and mandates that platforms identify and address risks to minors arising from recommender systems, interface design, and engagement-based features.

These obligations are supported, at a structural level, by the Digital Markets Act (DMA). Although the DMA lacks explicit provisions on child protection, its restrictions on cross-service data integration and gatekeeper dominance indirectly limit large-scale profiling and behavioural exploitation, including practices that impact individuals including children.

As also noted in Chapter 3, the DSA additionally cites age verification as a risk mitigation measure alongside parental control tools. The age assurance mechanisms discussed in detail in the relevant subchapter above, however, what we would like to add as a future consideration is that it remains unclear whether age verification mechanisms utilizing digital IDs will be effective or not. As we have not yet determined whether the security measures and privacy-enhancing technologies previously mentioned will be implemented appropriately. There is a potential risk that it may be employed in a manner that infringes upon individuals' rights to privacy by tracking their identities in a more intrusive manner, without respecting their fundamental rights and freedoms.

On a personal level, tracking or profiling resulting from age verification mechanisms could lead to manipulation, reputational damage, emotional distress, fraud, harassment, and bullying, contingent upon who accesses the excessive data and information. At the organizational level, specifically regarding the age assurance ecosystem providers, hacking attempts would result in financial losses due to reputational damage, diminished public trust in the industry, and potential administrative regulatory penalties. Furthermore, there are societal harms; for instance, the extensive storage of data via EUDI wallets may lead to identity data breaches, which could erode public trust in institutions, jeopardize public safety, and undermine democratic processes.

Although the US is currently engaging in discussions regarding many of the same issues underlying the DSA and DMA, it has not yet established a federal regulatory framework that aligns with their comprehensive, proactive, and systemic approach to platform governance and market dominance. Age-assurance regulation has predominantly been maintained at the state level and has faced legal challenges. At the federal level, a comprehensive solution has not yet been established, although policy discussions and legislative deliberations on the matter continue. The FTC also signalled in the Disney case, which will be elaborated upon below, that age assurance mechanisms will be broadened, implying that technological improvements may serve as age verification instead of self-declaration.[1]

Nevertheless, the COPPA rule amendments, which came into effect in April 2025, includes some signs of convergence towards the EU model. For instance, platforms are required to obtain separate opt-in consent from parents for onward transfers of children's information to other third-party companies such as related to targeted advertising.[2] Data retention is restricted to the duration that is reasonably necessary to fulfil the purpose and cannot be indefinitely extended.[3] Personal information is defined more broadly,[4] and additional factors are available to determine whether a service is "directed to" children.[5]

Furthermore, there are improvements that are being considered at the federal level, such as the COPPA 2.0 and Kids Online Safety Act (KOSA) proposals, which have not yet been implemented as law. The primary objective of COPPA 2.0 is to transition to a more comprehensive and modernized privacy approach for the protection of children's online safety. For instance, the proposal encompasses teenagers aged 13–17,[6] expands the definition of personal information even broader with the term "information reasonably linkable to a child or teen",[7] acknowledges the data subject rights of teenagers rather than restricting them to their parents,[8] and introduces or

[1] FTC, Court Approves Order Requiring Disney to Pay $10 Million to Settle FTC Allegations the Firm Enabled the Unlawful Collection of Children's Personal Data (31 December 2025) https://www.ftc.gov/news-events/news/press-releases/2025/12/court-approves-order-requiring-disney-pay-10-million-settle-ftc-allegations-firm-enabled-unlawful.

[2] 16 CFR COPPA 312.5(a)(2).

[3] 16 CFR COPPA 312.10.

[4] 16 CFR COPPA 312.2 "Personal information".

[5] 16 CFR COPPA 312.2 "Website or online service directed to children", "Mixed audience website or online service".

[6] S.836 - 119th Congress (2025–2026): Children and Teens' Online Privacy Protection Act. Congress.gov, Library of Congress, 27 January 2026, https://www.congress.gov/bill/119th-congress/senate-bill/836, Sect. 2(a)(17).

[7] S.836 - 119th Congress (2025–2026): Children and Teens' Online Privacy Protection Act. Congress.gov, Library of Congress, 27 January 2026, https://www.congress.gov/bill/119th-congress/senate-bill/836, Sect. 2(a)(3)(A)(xi): "information linked or reasonably linkable to a child or teen or the parents of that child or teen (including any unique identifier) that an operator collects online from the child or teen and combines with an identifier described in this subparagraph."

[8] S.836 - 119th Congress (2025–2026): Children and Teens' Online Privacy Protection Act. Congress.gov, Library of Congress, 27 January 2026, https://www.congress.gov/bill/119th-congress/senate-bill/836, Sect. 2(b)(3)(A)(i)(II)(dd).

expands modern and relevant concepts, including biometric identifiers,[9] geolocation data,[10] connected devices,[11] as well as individual-specific advertisements.[12]

Meanwhile, KOSA exhibits a transition that is comparable to the DSA approach, which acknowledges the operators' responsibility for risk management and platform accountability. It demonstrates a distinct transition to safety-by-design, rather than solely relying on parental consent and oversight mechanisms to ensure their safety online.[13]

It would be optimal for the US to adopt such preventive, structured, privacy-conscious, and secure approaches at the federal level in conjunction with technological advancements; however, it is also crucial to observe how the relevant EU regulations are implemented in practice. Their practicality is also significant, and we will observe these developments in the near future.

Nevertheless, it is beneficial to provide guidance to the industry and observe the operational changes along the path. There is invariably room for improvement, but it cannot be identified prior to attempting. Therefore, there is a significant shared responsibility on the part of lawmakers and the industry to establish a secure online environment without jeopardizing the rights and freedoms of individuals, particularly children.

Ultimately, enforcement actions and developing case law may also serve as supplementary sources of guidance for the industry in instances where legislative provisions are ambiguous or incomplete. Both the EU and the US have enacted stricter and substantial fines and penalties, signifying that safeguarding children's personal data and privacy is no longer solely an ethical or ideal consideration but has evolved into a matter of risk mitigation and regulatory compliance in the view of these jurisdictions. We have observed this trend in several significant cases involving Meta, TikTok, Epic, Google-YouTube above, among others. Additionally, recent cases in both jurisdictions are worth mentioning here briefly.

Following the Ireland Data Protection Commission (DPC)'s ruling on the investigation into TikTok concerning the handling of children's personal data, primarily addressing the management of such data under default public account settings, transparency, and data protection by design, TikTok recently incurred an additional fine

---

[9] S.836 - 119th Congress (2025–2026): Children and Teens' Online Privacy Protection Act. Congress.gov, Library of Congress, 27 January 2026, https://www.congress.gov/bill/119th-congress/senate-bill/836, Sect. 2(a)(3)(A)(x).

[10] S.836 - 119th Congress (2025–2026): Children and Teens' Online Privacy Protection Act. Congress.gov, Library of Congress, 27 January 2026, https://www.congress.gov/bill/119th-congress/senate-bill/836, Sect. 2(a)(16).

[11] S.836 - 119th Congress (2025–2026): Children and Teens' Online Privacy Protection Act. Congress.gov, Library of Congress, 27 January 2026, https://www.congress.gov/bill/119th-congress/senate-bill/836, Sect. 2(a)(13).

[12] S.836 - 119th Congress (2025–2026): Children and Teens' Online Privacy Protection Act. Congress.gov, Library of Congress, 27 January 2026, https://www.congress.gov/bill/119th-congress/senate-bill/836, Sect. 2(a)(18).

[13] S.1748 - 119th Congress (2025–2026): Kids Online Safety Act. Congress.gov, Library of Congress, 14 May 2025, https://www.congress.gov/bill/119th-congress/senate-bill/1748.

from the DPC for another major issue. DPC imposed a total fine of €530 million for violations concerning international data transfers and associated transparency mandates of the GDPR.[14] From a child-focused perspective, this case is significant because, although it is not solely concerned with children's data, TikTok's extensive user base of children generates a substantial amount of children's information, including identifiers, preferences, social interactions, and behavioural data.[15]

In December 2025, Disney was required to pay a civil penalty in order to address allegations that it had violated the COPPA. Disney did not indicate that the videos were intended for children when they uploaded them to YouTube. YouTube was unable to implement additional safeguards as a consequence of the absence of labelling. Parental consent must have been obtained before data of children under the age of 13 is processed. As a result, Disney was required to pay a civil penalty of $10 million and must ensure that it follows the verifiable parental consent procedures and provides the appropriate notices when acquiring children's information in the future. Unless YouTube discontinues creator based "Made for Kids" labelling or determines the ages or age categories reliably through the age assurance mechanisms, it is essential to establish a compliance program to adequately designate the content provided with "Made for Kids."[16] This provides a sense of anticipation and perspective that the age assurance technologies will undergo a gradual expansion and adoption, as noted above.[17]

Similar regulatory concerns regarding systemic deficiencies in the design and governance of digital services used by children are illustrated by recent FTC enforcement actions against services beyond dominant technology platforms, including Iconic Hearts Holdings, the operator of the Sendit app,[18] Apitor Technology, a manufacturer of connected children's toys,[19] and Cognosphere, the developer of the video

[14] Data Protection Commission, Decision on the inquiry into TikTok Technology Limited regarding transfers of personal data to China and related transparency obligations under the GDPR, DPC Inquiry Reference IN-21–9-2, adopted 30 April 2025.

[15] Data Protection Commission, Decision on the inquiry into TikTok Technology Limited regarding the processing of children's personal data, DPC Inquiry Reference IN-21–9-1, adopted 8 September 2023, at paras 101 and 338 (the decision confirms that TikTok is used by a large number of children, even though the precise figures are redacted.)

[16] United States of America (on behalf of the Federal Trade Commission) v. Disney Worldwide Services, Inc. and Disney Entertainment Operations LLC, Case No. 2:25-cv-08223 (U.S. District Court for the Central District of California).

[17] FTC, Court Approves Order Requiring Disney to Pay $10 Million to Settle FTC Allegations the Firm Enabled the Unlawful Collection of Children's Personal Data (31 December 2025) https://www.ftc.gov/news-events/news/press-releases/2025/12/court-approves-order-requiring-disney-pay-10-million-settle-ftc-allegations-firm-enabled-unlawful.

[18] United States of America (on behalf of the Federal Trade Commission) v. Iconic Hearts Holdings, Inc. and Hunter Rice, Case No. 2:25-cv-09310 (U.S. District Court for the Central District of California).

[19] United States of America (on behalf of the Federal Trade Commission) v. Apitor Technology Co., Ltd., Case No. 3:25-cv-07363 (U.S. District Court for the Northern District of California).

game Genshin Impact.[20,21] In these cases, the alleged violations arose from a range of practices, including the use of deceptive engagement and subscription mechanisms, the collection of children's geolocation data without verifiable parental consent, and the deployment of in-game monetisation systems that misrepresented costs and probabilities while enabling purchases by child users without appropriate safeguards.

Although parental consent remains a relevant component of the regulatory analysis, these enforcement actions, considered alongside the cases discussed in earlier chapters, extend beyond isolated consent failures and instead focus on unfair or deceptive practices and structural shortcomings in service design and governance. As such, they point toward a practical shift away from an exclusive reliance on parental consent to expectations of shared responsibility among developers, platform operators, and service providers, coupled with the proactive incorporation of child-appropriate safeguards through privacy-by-design across digital architectures and data flows.

Within the broader enforcement landscape, the 2025 activities of the Global Privacy Enforcement Network (GPEN)[22] further demonstrate how the regulators' focus has shifted from the limited question of formal parental consent seeking to systemic risk and design-level accountability of the service providers and data controllers. Regulators will assess whether the websites transparently inform users about their privacy practices, implement age assurance mechanisms, and maintain appropriate privacy safeguards to limit the collection of children's personal data, irrespective of parental consent.[23]

This is because GPEN serves as a signalling mechanism for both regulators and industry, emphasizing that child data protection expectations are now framed around governance, accountability, and privacy-by-design as baseline obligations throughout the digital ecosystem, rather than as exceptions that are only triggered at the point of parental consent. This direction is anticipated to be further elaborated upon in the upcoming GPEN report. Additionally, the GPEN will facilitate coordination and may contribute to the reduction of fragmentation in enforcement approaches by bringing

---

[20] United States of America (on behalf of the Federal Trade Commission) v. Cognosphere, LLC and Cognosphere Pte. Ltd., Case No. 2:25-cv-447 (U.S. District Court for the Central District of California).

[21] Regardless of their procedural posture or ultimate outcome, the enforcement actions discussed in this sentence are examined as indicative of the Federal Trade Commission's enforcement practice and its approach to addressing systemic risks to children's privacy.

[22] The Global Privacy Enforcement Network (GPEN) is an informal network of privacy enforcement authorities, established following the OECD's 2007 Recommendation on Cross-border Cooperation in the Enforcement of Privacy Laws, to facilitate information sharing, coordination, and joint initiatives in cross-border privacy enforcement.

Global Privacy Enforcement Network, Our mission, (https://www.privacyenforcement.net/content/our-mission.

[23] Global Privacy Enforcement Network, 2025 Global Privacy Enforcement Network sweep focuses on the protection of children's privacy (3 November 2025) https://www.privacyenforcement.net/content/2025-global-privacy-enforcement-network-sweep-focuses-protection-childrens-privacy.

together a variety of actors from various jurisdictions involving but not limited to multiple EU Member States' DPAs and FTC.[24]

Meanwhile, AI is reshaping children's online safety by recognizing their ages, regulating the information they see (for example, through recommendation systems, algorithm mechanisms), and determining which controls and safeguards will apply. This is a new trend in automated governance over children's online activities, raising questions and concerns about responsibility, accountability, and oversight.

Major platforms have begun to formalize the use of AI in this area. YouTube, for example, has officially declared on their blog that they will implement an AI-driven age estimation tool to ascertain whether users are under 18. If the estimation is inaccurate, the individual will have the opportunity to validate their age such as with a government-issued ID.[25] Digital wellbeing tools will be activated, and personal advertising will be disabled if a user is identified as a child. Additionally, safeguards will be implemented for recommendation algorithms, including restrictions on repetitive exposure to specific content that idealizes specific body types and physical features, promotes aggression, or disseminates unrealistic or detrimental financial advice.[26] Similarly, Meta has announced the deployment of AI age prediction technologies to improve safeguards for teenagers and restrict their access to adult features.[27]

The GDPR and COPPA were both developed in response to technological paradigms that relatively linear data flows, predefined purposes, and determined consent mechanisms. However, the efficacy of children's data protection is now more reliant on adaptive interpretation, regulatory guidance, and supplementary instruments than on static statutory rules alone, particularly in light of the recent technological advancements, such as AI systems, recommender engines, and immersive platforms that operate through continuous data extraction, inference, and repurposing.

On one hand, the responsibility should continue to be shared among data controllers, regulators, and parents, but it should not be equally distributed or assigned interchangeably. Considering data controllers deploy and design AI systems, determine interaction modalities (including persistence, intimacy, and persona), control training, refining, and updates, and possess superior risk knowledge and measurement, it is incumbent upon them to assume the primary role in mitigating risks to children. Parental oversight or controls are incapable of replacing this accountability in the context of AI systems.

---

[24] Global Privacy Enforcement Network, Authorities Listings, https://www.privacyenforcement.net/authorities-listings.

[25] YouTube Official Blog, Extending our built-in protections to more teens on YouTube, (29 July 2025) https://blog.youtube/news-and-events/extending-our-built-in-protections-to-more-teens-on-youtube/

[26] YouTube, Building content recommendations to meet the unique needs of teens and pre-teens, https://services.google.com/fh/files/misc/vibe-expansion-gtm-casestudy.pdf.

[27] Meta, How Meta uses AI to better understand people's ages on our platforms (22 June 2022) https://tech.facebook.com/artificial-intelligence/2022/6/adult-classifier/

On the other hand, setting minimum safety standards for children, requiring risk assessments and audits, and enforcing compliance through sanctions are responsibilities that properly lie with regulators. This role is essential because individual parents cannot realistically negotiate with large platforms, market incentives do not reliably account for child-safety risks, and many harms only become visible at the population level. Parents, by contrast, should not bear primary liability. Their role should be a supportive one: establishing household norms, exercising informed choice, and having meaningful visibility into their children's use of AI systems.

In addition to asserting that it maintains a substantial level of platform responsibility, Facebook also designates parents as secondary risk managers for the residual risk of children being exposed to the potentially harmful conversations, suggestions, and directions of AI characters. Teenagers' access to one-on-one conversations with AI characters and their ongoing exposure to tools such as time limits and insights into the topics they are discussing will be regulated by their parents.[28] This could potentially lead to a diminution in the obligation of data administrators and system operators, as well as a false sense of security. Although an increasing number of individuals are becoming aware of the existence of AI, this does not necessarily imply that the average parent could comprehend its operation.

The design of the AI conversations has the potential to influence the children's thinking and easily manipulate them into engaging in detrimental activities by promoting additivity, thereby promoting dependency and increasing utilization. Furthermore, there is a possibility that the safety evaluations may be circumvented by the system. This type of design failure or inadequately designed system can also affect adults; however, children may be more susceptible to the hazards due to their more vulnerable nature. AI has the ability to perceive the individual's needs and their weak and sensitive points, if they are communicated by the users. Accordingly, several lawsuits have been reported in which parents have accused AI chatbot providers, alleging that their adult or adolescent children committed suicide as a result of interactions with AI tools.[29]

OpenAI has recently announced the retirement of several GPT versions, including GPT-4.0, which exhibited the most human-like interactions.[30] The reason for the retirement of earlier versions is disputable, particularly regarding its potential connection to legal cases concerning suicides. It may not be appropriate to place entire

[28] Meta, Empowering Parents, Protecting Teens: Meta's Approach to AI Safety (17 October 2025, updated on 23 January 2026), https://about.fb.com/news/2025/10/teen-ai-safety-approach/

[29] See, e.g., BBC, Parents of teenager who took his own life sue OpenAI, Published 27 August 2025, https://bbc.com/news/articles/cgerwp7rdlvo.

The Guardian, Google and AI startup to settle lawsuits alleging chatbots led to teen suicide, Published 8 January 2026, https://www.theguardian.com/technology/2026/jan/08/google-character-ai-settlement-teen-suicide.

CNN, 'You're not rushing. You're just ready:' Parents say ChatGPT encouraged son to kill himself, Published 25 July 2025, Updated 20 November 2025, https://edition.cnn.com/2025/11/06/us/openai-chatgpt-suicide-lawsuit-invs-vis.

[30] OpenAI, Our approach to advertising and expanding access to ChatGPT (16 January 2026) https://openai.com/index/our-approach-to-advertising-and-expanding-access/

responsibility on AI chatbots for those suicide-related situations. However, it is fair and ethical to expect that AI systems immediately direct users to suicide helplines and qualified human support when interactions indicate mental or emotional distress, anxiety, anger, or potential self-harm risk. In such sensitive circumstances, AI should avoid reinforcing or praising harmful ideas or behaviours and instead prioritize safety by encouraging users to seek real-world assistance and professional care.

The EU enacted a broad regulatory -EU AI Act- to regulate the AI systems in a risk-based approach focusing on ethical considerations and transparency.[31] Unlike the EU approach, the US has not adopted a comprehensive horizontal regulatory framework for AI; instead, it relies on a decentralized, sectoral governance model combining agency enforcement, existing statutory regimes, and emerging state-level initiatives.[32]

The EU AI Act is likely to generate some concerns considering prohibited and high-risk AI solutions, as it has the potential to impede the industry and slow down the essential competitive innovation. While promoting transparency, fairness, and privacy, it is also crucial for the EU to capitalize on the innovative climate in the US, which is conducive to technological advancements and encourages the industry.

At present, the EU is lagging behind in global BigTech industry and is at a disadvantage in terms of technological advancements compared to the US and rapidly developing China. The problem is not the regulation and restriction of non-ethical and biased AI systems, but rather how they are calibrated. Striking a balance between innovation enablement and risk mitigation is essential. Alternately, the potential imbalance could result in asymmetric power dynamics, which could increase technological dependence on non-European actors.

AI has the potential to affect our perceptions, experiences, learning, and creativity, as well as the operations of academia and industry, by integrating into numerous aspects of our lives. Consequently, it is very important for the EU to influence the future of AI before it is too late, rather than positioning itself as a downstream adopter and regulator of technologies developed elsewhere.

AI could constitute an independent subject for further research and literature; hence, we will not delve into additional details in this monograph. However, we emphasize the significance of child-specific protections and regulations regarding AI. For example, given ChatGPT's capacity to shape the ideas and opinions of users, particularly children, it necessitates additional restrictions for the underage user group. OpenAI announced that some sensitive matters will be handled with greater care, if age verification mechanisms indicate that a user is under 18. These matters include images that contain gore and violence, conversations that may encourage

[31] Regulation (EU) 2024/1689 of the European Parliament and of the Council of 13 June 2024 laying down harmonised rules on artificial intelligence and amending Regulations (EC) No 300/2008, (EU) No 167/2013, (EU) No 168/2013, (EU) 2018/858, (EU) 2018/1139 and (EU) 2019/2144 and Directives 2014/90/EU, (EU) 2016/797 and (EU) 2020/1828 (Artificial Intelligence Act), OJ 2024 L 1689, 12.07.2024, pp. 1–144.

[32] Congress.gov, Regulating Artificial Intelligence: U.S. and International Approaches and Considerations for Congress, Library of Congress, 8 February 2026, https://www.congress.gov/crs-product/R48555.

risky or harmful behavior, sexual, romantic, or violent role play, and content that promotes for extreme beauty standards, unhealthy eating habits, or body shaming. The individual will have the option to verify their age with a government-issued identification, if the age estimation is inaccurate.[33]

In the same notice it also claims that advertisements will not be shown if age prediction mechanisms indicate that a user is a child.[34] We advocate that the minimum standard for AI tools to process children's data should be the avoidance of targeted advertising, user behavior profiling, and manipulatively directing them to consume in specific ways. We endorse such responsible advancements and recommend a cautious approach regarding the interaction of AI solutions with children including teenagers. We will collectively observe in the near future whether these promised actions are actually carried out.

Ultimately, we have demonstrated that while the GDPR and COPPA provide important legal foundations for protecting children's privacy and personal data, safeguarding children in digital environments remains a dynamic and evolving challenge. The risks, opportunities, and regulatory gaps that impact children and teenagers are constantly being reshaped by the rapid advancements in technology, particularly the expansion of AI and other data-driven systems. Despite the pace of technological change, the key message of this monograph remains constant: meaningful online safety for children depends on shared responsibility. Law makers, judicial bodies, law enforcers, platform providers, developers, operators, parents, educators, and society at large must collectively assume accountability for designing, governing, monitoring, and using online technologies in ways that prioritize the rights, well-being, and best interests of the child. As an African proverb says, "*it takes a village to raise a child*[35]".

Reference

Reupert A, Straussner SL, Weimand B, Maybery D (2022) It takes a village to raise a child: understanding and expanding the concept of the "village". Front Public Health (10) 1–7

[33] OpenAI, Age prediction in ChatGPT (updated on 11 February 2026) https://help.openai.com/en/articles/12652064-age-prediction-in-chatgpt.

[34] OpenAI, Age prediction in ChatGPT (updated on 11 February 2026) https://help.openai.com/en/articles/12652064-age-prediction-in-chatgpt.

[35] "The phrase "it takes a village to raise a child" originates from an African proverb and conveys the message that it takes many people ("the village") to provide a safe, healthy environment for children, where children are given the security they need to develop and flourish, and to be able to realize their hopes and dreams. This requires an environment where children's voices are taken seriously and where multiple people (the "villagers") including parents, siblings, extended family members, neighbors, teachers, professionals, community members and policy makers, care for a child."

Reupert et al. (2022, p. 2).

Appendix

Main Legal Cases Examined

Case Title	Case Summary and Significance
Data Protection Commission (Ireland), Decision on the Inquiry into Meta Platforms Ireland Limited (Instagram), Inquiry Ref IN-20-7-4	This case concerned the treatment of children's personal data on Instagram, operated in the EU by Meta Platforms Ireland Limited and investigated by the Data Protection Commission The Data Protection Commission found that, between 2018 and 2020, Instagram set teenagers' accounts to public by default and allowed child users of business accounts to make contact details publicly visible. These design choices were held to place an unreasonable burden on children to manage their own privacy and to fall short of the GDPR's requirements on transparency, data protection by design and by default, and risk assessment. Following intervention by the European Data Protection Board, the Data Protection Commission adopted its final decision in September 2022, ordering compliance and imposing a €405 million fine After the period covered by the inquiry, Instagram changed its settings so that teenage accounts are now private by default, reflecting a shift toward stronger baseline protection for children's privacy

(continued)

A. Alkış Tümtürk, *Online Privacy and Data Protection of Children in the European Union and the United States*, Ius Gentium: Comparative Perspectives on Law and Justice 141, https://doi.org/10.1007/978-3-032-27534-9

(continued)

Case Title	Case Summary and Significance
Data Protection Commission, Decision on the inquiry into TikTok Technology Limited regarding the processing of children's personal data, DPC Inquiry Reference IN-21-9-1	The TikTok case is one of the most significant GDPR enforcement actions concerning the protection of children's personal data. Following a binding decision of the European Data Protection Board, the Irish Data Protection Commission imposed a €345 million administrative fine on TikTok Technology Limited for GDPR infringements relating to the processing of minors' data. The decision focused in particular on TikTok's practice of setting children's accounts to public by default, the lack of clear and age-appropriate privacy information, and the use of interface design choices that nudged users toward less protective settings. The enforcement did not remain confined to a financial sanction but led TikTok to introduce changes to its platform design, including safer default privacy settings for younger users, broadly reflecting the approach adopted in the Instagram case discussed above. The case therefore demonstrates once again how regulatory enforcement can result in tangible improvements in children's online environments, rather than operating solely as a punitive measure
Data Protection Commission (Ireland), Decision on the Inquiry into TikTok Technology Limited, Inquiry Ref. IN-21-9-1	From a child-focused perspective, this case is noteworthy because, although it is not exclusively about child data, TikTok's large user base of children results in a significant volume of children's data, including identifiers, preferences, social interactions, and behavioural information. Considering the previous TikTok case, even if the platform's front-end features including interface design and account settings were enhanced to better safeguard children, this does not necessarily imply that TikTok would be compliant without implementing appropriate protections concerning data flows and back-end data governance. The substantial sanction of €530 billion underscores that data transfers constitute the primary safety concern under EU law
United States of America (on behalf of the Federal Trade Commission) v. Epic Games, Inc Case No. 5:22-cv-00518-BO (U.S. District Court for the Eastern District of North Carolina)	In 2022, the Federal Trade Commission (FTC) found that Epic Games violated the Children's Online Privacy Protection Act (COPPA) by collecting personal information from children under the age of 13 without obtaining verifiable parental consent The FTC also raised concerns about Epic's default communication settings, which allowed child users to engage in voice and text chat and could expose them to contact with strangers In addition, the FTC alleged that Epic employed certain interface design practices, commonly referred to as "dark patterns", that made it easy for users, including minors, to make unintended in-game purchases or made it difficult to cancel transactions or obtain refunds. Although these allegations were legally distinct from the COPPA violations, they formed part of the broader regulatory action against the company Epic Games agreed to resolve the case through a settlement that included a $275 million civil penalty for COPPA violations, described at the time as the largest of its kind, as well as a separate $245 million commitment to refund consumers for improper in-game charges. Under the settlement, Epic was required to strengthen its parental consent mechanisms, revise default settings for child users, delete previously collected children's data unless valid consent could be verified, and modify its interface design to prevent deceptive purchasing practices

(continued)

(continued)

Case Title	Case Summary and Significance
Fed. Trade Comm'n v. Google LLC Case No 1:19-cv-2642	The case between Google-YouTube and the FTC concerns YouTube's infringement of the Children's Online Privacy Protection Act (COPPA). In 2019, the Federal Trade Commission (FTC) determined that YouTube had gathered personal information from children under 13 years old without parental consent, violating COPPA regulations. Consequently, Google consented to a historic settlement of $170 million with the FTC. This case prompted YouTube to implement more stringent policies, requiring notification of data subjects prior to data collection and offering them the choice to opt in or opt out of personalized advertisements We attempted to demonstrate that the requirement for parental consent in the decision may not be consistently effective, as YouTube can be accessed without logging in to an account. In that scenario, the platform was unable to distinguish between an adult and a child for age verification purposes. The platform should require login credentials from users, similar to Facebook and Instagram, to access its services. Additionally, we attempted to elucidate the benefits of limiting platforms for marketing and profiling-related processes. However, parents should also be constrained in their sharing on platforms, as it may pose greater long-term risks to children than targeted advertisements
United States of America (on behalf of the Federal Trade Commission) v. Disney Worldwide Services, Inc. and Disney Entertainment Operations LLC Case No. 2:25-cv-08223 (U.S. District Court for the Central District of California)	Disney agreed to pay a $10 million penalty in December 2025 as it didn't label some YouTube videos as "Made for Kids". Due to this failure, YouTube didn't put in place the protections that are required for content aimed at children. Under the settlement, Disney is required to bring its practices into compliance by ensuring that parents are informed, and that valid parental consent is obtained whenever children's information is collected. The agreement also obliges Disney to establish an internal review process to correctly designate "Made for Kids" content on YouTube, unless the platform either moves away from creator-based labelling or adopts reliable age-assurance technologies capable of determining users' ages or age categories
Regina v. Aydin Coban (The Amanda Todd case)	The Amanda Todd case is widely known as the tragic incident involving Amanda Michelle Todd, a Canadian teenager who committed suicide after being a victim of cyberbullying and online harassment The Amanda Todd case was selected to underscore the critical importance of the right to be forgotten and the rigorous application of laws by police and courts. Had such a right been in place and effectively enforced, Amanda Todd might not have faced the relentless online harassment that contributed to her tragic fate. This case highlights the necessity of adopting and enforcing robust legal protections to safeguard the well-being of children and teenagers in the digital age

(continued)

(continued)

Case Title	Case Summary and Significance
Sidis v. F-R Publishing Corporation Case 113 F.2d 806	William James Sidis, an American child prodigy, gained fame for his extraordinary intellectual abilities, entering Harvard University at age 11 and becoming known for his remarkable mathematical and linguistic talents. As he grew older, Sidis sought to live a private life. However, in 1944, *The New Yorker* published a profile titled "Where Are They Now?" that delved into his personal life, leading Sidis to sue the magazine for invasion of privacy. In the case Sidis v. F-R Publishing, the United States Court of Appeals for the Second Circuit ruled against Sidis, stating that as a public figure, his right to privacy was diminished regarding matters of legitimate public interest. The court recognized Sidis's desire for privacy but deemed the article permissible due to his earlier prominence This case is frequently cited in discussions about the balance between privacy rights and freedom of the press, highlighting the tension between an individual's desire for privacy and public curiosity. In our research, we explored whether parents should have the authority to designate a child as a public figure and where children's rights to self-determination fit within this context This relatively old case was chosen to highlight the persistence of privacy issues across time and regulatory changes. It demonstrates that fundamental questions surrounding privacy remain unchanged despite evolving legal contexts
Murray v. Express Newspapers Ltd (CA) Case EWCA Civ446	J.K. Rowling and her husband took legal action against a newspaper that published their son's image without consent. Initially, the trial court ruled in favour of the newspaper, citing Article 10 of the European Convention on Human Rights, which protects freedom of speech and expression. Dissatisfied with this decision, Rowling and her husband appealed, arguing that their son's right to privacy under Article 8 should outweigh the newspaper's freedom of expression Upon appeal, the Court of Appeal recognized the importance of balancing Article 8 (right to privacy) and Article 10 (freedom of speech). In this case, the court concluded that the child's right to privacy should take precedence. This ruling supports the argument that Article 17(3)(a) of the right to be forgotten, which exempts "exercising the right to freedom of speech and information," should not apply when the data subject is a child The case highlights the significance of the right to be forgotten in protecting children's privacy rights. It ensures that children can regain control over their personal data without compromising freedom of expression. This decision sets a precedent for prioritizing children's privacy in the digital age and underscores the importance of safeguarding their rights in an increasingly interconnected world
Schrems v. Data Protection Commissioner C-362/14 (Schrems I)	This case originated when Max Schrems, an Austrian privacy activist, filed a complaint against Facebook's data transfer practices from the EU to the US. The European Court of Justice (ECJ) invalidated the EU-US Safe Harbor agreement in 2015, stating that it did not adequately protect EU citizens' data privacy rights when transferred to the US

(continued)

(continued)

Case Title	Case Summary and Significance
Data Protection Commissioner v. Facebook Ireland Limited, Maximillian Schrems C-311/18 (Schrems II)	This case revolved around the validity of the Standard Contractual Clauses (SCCs) used by companies like Facebook to transfer personal data from the EU to countries with less stringent data protection laws, particularly the United States. The ECJ's ruling in 2020 invalidated the EU-US Privacy Shield framework, citing concerns about US surveillance practices, and upheld the use of SCCs, but with certain conditions The reason for examining the Schrems I and II cases was to explore the recent history of transatlantic data transfers and their significance in international data protection and privacy law, especially concerning exchanges between the EU and the US. These cases highlight the evolving legal landscape and challenges surrounding the transfer of personal data across borders, shedding light on key issues such as data privacy, surveillance practices, and the adequacy of data protection frameworks

Bibliography

Articles

Alkis A (2021) Investigating the usefulness of online age verification methods. Studia Iurisprudentiae Doctorandorum Miskolciensium 1:8
Alkis A (2022) The impact of the privacy shield's invalidation on the EU-US dataflows. Studia Iurisprudentiae Doctorandorum Miskolciensium 1:34
Alkis-Tümtürk A (2022) Uncertain future of transatlantic data flows: will the United States ever achieve the 'adequate level' of data protection? Hung J Legal Stud 63(3):294–311
Auxier B, Anderson M, Perrin A, Turner E (2020) Children's engagement with digital devices, screen time. Pew Res Center 2
Barron JH (1979) Warren and Brandies, the right to privacy, 4 Harv. L. Rev. 193 (1890): demystifying a landmark citation. Suffolk Univ Law Rev 13(4):910
Bignami F, Resta G (2018) Human rights extraterritoriality: the right to privacy and national security surveillance. GWU Law School Public Law Res Paper 2017–67, forthcoming in Benvenisti E, Nolte G (eds) Community interests across international law. OUP 10, 18
Bontrager P, Roy A, Togelius J, Memon N, Ross A (2018) Deepmasterprints: generating masterprints for dictionary attacks via latent variable evolution. In: IEEE 9th international conference on biometrics theory, applications and systems, pp 1–9
Bratman B (2002) Brandeis and Warren's the right to privacy and the birth of the right to privacy. Tenn Law Rev 69(3):629
Bunn A (2019) Children and the 'right to be forgotten': what the right to erasure means for European children, and why Australian children should be afforded a similar right. Media Int Aust 170(1):41
Business Europe, DIGITALEUROPE, European Round Table for Industry, European Automobile Manufacturers Association (2020) Schrems II: impact survey report, 1–14. https://www.digitaleurope.org/resources/schrems-ii-impact-survey-report/
Ceruzzi P (1996) From scientific instrument to everyday appliance: the emergence of personal computers, 1970–77. Hist Technol 13(1):1–31
Chander A (2020) Is data localization a solution for Schrems II? J Int Econ Law 23(3):781

A. Alkış Tümtürk, *Online Privacy and Data Protection of Children in the European Union and the United States*, Ius Gentium: Comparative Perspectives on Law and Justice 141, https://doi.org/10.1007/978-3-032-27534-9

CHOC (Children's Hospital of Orange County) (2022) The COVID-19 vaccine for kids under 12: what parents should know. https://health.choc.org/the-covid-19-vaccine-for-kids-under-12-what-parents-should-know/

Clearwater A, Hughes JT (2013) In the beginning—an early history of the privacy profession. Ohio State Law J 74(6):899

Cory N, Dick E, Castro D (2020) The role and value of standard contractual clauses in EU–US digital trade. Inf Technol Innov Found 13

Dasgupta D, Roy A, Nag A (2017) Multi-factor authentication: more secure approach towards authenticating individuals. In: Advances in user authentication. Springer International Publication, p 186

Donovan S (2020) 'Sharenting': the forgotten children of the GDPR. Peace Hum Rights Gov 4(1):43

Evans YN (2020) One-sided social media relationships and the impact of advertising on children. Pediatrics 146(5):1–2

Fredrickson BL, Roberts TA (1997) Objectification theory: toward understanding women's lived experiences and mental health risks. Psychol Women Q 21(2):179–180

Frison-Roche MA (1995) Remarques sur la distinction de la volonté et du consentement en droit des contrats. RTD civ:574

Gellert R, Gutwirth S (2013) The legal construction of privacy and data protection. Comput Law Secur Rev 29(5):524

Gioia F, Griffiths MD, Boursier V (2020) Adolescents' body shame and social networking sites: the mediating effect of body image control in photos. Sex Roles 83:773, 776, 781

Hall HK (2018) Oversharenting; is it really your story to tell. John Marshall J Inf Technol Priv Law 33(3):132

Harrison K, Fredrickson BL (2003) Women's sports media, self-objectification, and mental health in black and white adolescent females. J Commun 53(2):228

Hill JF (2014) The growth of data localization post-snowden: analysis and recommendations for US policymakers and business leaders. The Hague Institute for Global Justice, Conference on the Future of Cyber Governance 32

Hong H (2005) Dismantling the private enforcement of the privacy act of 1974: Doe v. Chao. Akron Law Rev 38(1):76–77

Ivers EA (2021) Using state-based adequacy now, national adequacy over time to anticipate and defeat Schrems III. BC Law Rev 62:2589–2591

Jensen ML, Dinger M, Wright RT, Thatcher JB (2017) Training to mitigate phishing attacks using mindfulness techniques. J Manag Inf Syst 34(2):599

Kalven H Jr (1966) Privacy in tort law—were Warren and Brandeis wrong? Law Contemp Probl 31(2):327

Keltie H (2020) Sharenting and the (potential) right to be forgotten. Ind Law J 95:1006

Lee J (2015) SB 568: does California's online eraser button protect the privacy of minors? UC Davis Law Rev 48(3):1203

Legrand P (1997) The impossibility of 'legal transplants. Maastricht J Eur Comp Law 4(2):111

Lievens E, Verdood V (2018) Looking for needles in a haystack: key issues affecting children's rights in the General Data Protection Regulation. Comput Law Secur Rev 34(2):274

Linn E (2017) A look into the data privacy crystal ball: a survey of possible outcomes for the EU-US privacy shield agreement. Vand J Transnatl Law 50:1312–1313

Livingstone S, Byrne J (2015) Challenges of parental responsibility in a global perspective. In: Gasser U (ed) Digitally connected: global perspectives on youth and digital media. Berkman Center Res Publ, pp 26–29

Livingstone S, Stoilova M, Nandagiri R (2019) Children's data and privacy online: growing up in a digital age. An evidence review. London School of Economics and Political Science, London, p 35

Livingstone S, Stoilova M, Nandagiri R (2020) Data and privacy literacy: the role of the school in educating children in a datafied society. In: The handbook of media education research, p 415

Lukács A (2016) What is privacy? The history and definition of privacy. In: Keresztes G (ed) Tavaszi Szél 2016 Tanulmánykötet I. Doktoranduszok Országos Szövetsége, Budapest, p 258. https://publicatio.bibl.u-szeged.hu/10794/7/3188699.pdf

Macenaite M, Kosta E (2017) Consent for processing children's personal data in the EU: following in US footsteps? Inf Commun Technol Law 26(2):160

MacMillan C (2022) COVID-19 vaccine authorized for kids ages 5 to 11: what parents need to know. Yale Med. https://www.yalemedicine.org/news/covid-vaccine-for-ages-5-to-11

McCrohan KF, Engel K, Harvey JW (2010) Influence of awareness and training on cyber security. J Internet Commerce 9(1):24–27

McKay C (2016) Complying with international data protection law. Univ Cincinnati Law Rev 84(2):446–447

Mei P (1993) The EC proposed data protection law. Law Policy Int Bus 25(1):305

Meier EP, Gray J (2014) Facebook photo activity associated with body image disturbance in adolescent girls. Cyberpsychol Behav Soc Netw 17(4):200, 202

Milkaite I, Lievens E (2019) The GDPR child's age of consent for data processing across the EU–one year later. Better Internet for Kids 1–7

Minkus T, Liu K, Ross KW (2015) Children seen but not heard: when parents compromise children's online privacy. In: Proceedings of the 24th international conference on World Wide Web, p 777

Nascimbeni F, Vosloo S (2019) Digital literacy for children: exploring definitions and frameworks. UNICEF off Glob Insight Policy, Scoping Paper 1:10

Newman M, Swift M, Gladicheva V (2020) GDPR and CCPA start to bare teeth as privacy protection goes global. Bus Law Int 21(3):276

Ouvrein G, Verswijvel K (2019) Sharenting: parental adoration or public humiliation? A focus group study on adolescents' experiences with sharenting against the background of their own impression management. Child Youth Serv Rev 99:320

Palmer VV (2011) Three milestones in the history of privacy in the United States. Tulane Eur Civ Law Forum 26:71

Patel DR, Cabral MD, Ho A, Merrick J (2020) A clinical primer on intellectual disability. Transl Pediatr 9(Suppl 1)

Patel O, Lea N (2019) EU-UK data flows, Brexit and no-deal: adequacy or disarray? UCL Eur Inst Brexit Insights 10

Pearce G, Platten N (1998) Achieving personal data protection in the European Union. JCMS 36(4):531

Polonetsky J (2009) Online age verification for our children: a report on the tools and resources available for safeguarding the first generation of digital natives. In: 31st International Conference of Data Protection and Privacy Commissioners, pp 3–4

Prins C (2006) When personal data, behavior and virtual identities become a commodity: would a property rights approach matter? Scripted 3(4):280

Radesky J, Chassiakos YL, Ameenuddin N, Navsaria D (2020) Digital advertising to children. Pediatrics 146(1):2

Radin MJ (2002) Incomplete commodification in the computerized world. In: Elkin-Koren N, Netanel NW (eds) The commodification of information. Kluwer Law International, The Hague, pp 17–18

Reitz JC (1998) How to do comparative law. Am J Comp Law 46(4):621

Reupert A, Straussner SL, Weimand B and Maybery D (2022) It takes a village to raise a child: understanding and expanding the concept of the "village". Front Public Health 1–7

Richards NM (2013) The dangers of surveillance. Harv Law Rev 126(7):1952–1958

Roedder JD (1999) Consumer socialization of children: a retrospective look at twenty-five years of research. J Consumer Res 26(3):183–213

Sandfuchs B (2021) The future of data transfers to third countries in light of the CJEU's judgment C-311/18–Schrems II. GRUR Int 70(3):246

Schwartz PM (2011) Regulating governmental data mining in the United States and Germany: constitutional courts, the state, and new technology. William Mary Law Rev 53(2):368

Schwartz PM, Peifer KN (2017) Transatlantic data privacy law. Geo Law J 106:132–137 cited in Schwartz PM (2019) Global data privacy: the EU way. NYUL Rev 94:771–773

Sebastian MJ (2014–2015) The European Union's general date protection regulation: how will it affect non-EU enterprises? Syracuse J Sci Technol Law 31:222–223

Selby J (2017) Data localization laws: trade barriers or legitimate responses to cybersecurity risks, or both? Int J Law Inf Technol 25(3):230

Shah S, Mehtre BM (2015) An overview of vulnerability assessment and penetration testing techniques. J Comput Virol Hacking Techn 11:27–49

Smahel D, Machackova H, Mascheroni G, Dedkova L, Staksrud E, Ólafsson K, Livingstone S, Hasebrink U (2020) EU Kids Online 2020: survey results from 19 countries. EU Kids Online 30

Sorensen S (2016) Protecting children's right to privacy in the digital age: parents as trustees of children's rights. Children's Legal Rights J 36(3):156–157

Steinberg SB (2017) Sharenting: children's privacy in the age of social media. Emory Law J 66(4):876–877

Svantesson D (2020) Data localisation trends and challenges: considerations for the review of the privacy guidelines. OECD Digital Econ Papers 301:15

Szabó MD (2005a) Kísérlet a privacy fogalmának meghatározására a magyar jogrendszer fogalmaival. Inf Társadalom 5(2):46

Szabó MD (2005b) Kísérlet a privacy fogalmának meghatározására a magyar jogrendszer fogalmaival. Inf Társadalom 5(2):44

Talley VA (2019) Major flaws in minor laws: improving data privacy rights and protections for children under the GDPR. Ind Int'l Comp Law Rev 30(1):145

Thierer A (2007) Social networking and age verification: many hard questions; no easy solutions. Progress & Freedom Foundation Progress on Point Paper 14(5):3

Thompson EC (2018) The incident response strategy. Cybersecurity incident response: how to contain, eradicate, and recover from incidents 65–70

Thouvenin F (2021) Informational self-determination: a convincing rationale for data protection law? J Intellect Prop Inf Technol Electron Commerce Law 12(4):248

Tümtürk AA (2022) Implications of parental sharing of children's personal data online. ArsBoni Jogi Folyoirat X(1–2):11. https://arsboni.hu/wp-content/uploads/2022/09/Arsboni-foly%C3%B3irat_2022_1_2.pdf

Tümtürk AA (2022b) The threshold age for children's online consent in light of the Watson/Legrand debate: is legal transplant possible in the digital era? J Comp Law 17(1):243

van der Hof S (2016) I agree, or do I: a rights-based analysis of the law on children's consent in the digital world. Wis Int Law J 34:412–414

van der Hof S, Lievens E (2018) The importance of privacy by design and data protection impact assessments in strengthening protection of children's personal data under the GDPR. Commun Law 23(1):20

Van der Maelen C (2019) The coming-of-age of technology: using emerging tech for online age verifications. Delphi 2:115

Van Hoecke M (2015) Methodology of comparative legal research. Law Method 13–16

Váradi S (2021) Legal challenges of processing health data in the shadow of COVID-19 in the European Union. Forum Acta Juridica Et Politica 11(4):358–362

Verswijvel K, Walrave M, Hardies K, Heirman W (2019) Sharenting, is it a good or a bad thing? Understanding how adolescents think and feel about sharenting on social network sites. Children Youth Serv Rev 104:104401, 104407

Wald C (2016) The secret history of ancient toilets. Nature 533(7604):457

Wang FY (2020) Cooperative data privacy: the Japanese model of data privacy and the EU-Japan GDPR adequacy agreement. Harv J Law Tech 33:690–691

Warmund J (2000) Can COPPA work—an analysis of the parental consent measures in the children's online privacy protection act. Fordham Intellect Prop, Media Entertain Law J 11(1):192–193

Warren SD, Brandeis LD (1890) The right to privacy. Harv Law Rev 4(5):193–220

Watson A (2000) Legal transplants and European private law. Electron J Comp Law IV:13

Books

Blackstone W, Jones WC (eds) (1916) Commentaries on the laws of England. Bancroft-Whitney Co., San Francisco, pp 2430–2431

Craig P (2011) The evolution of EU law, 2nd edn. Oxford University Press, Oxford, p 335

Custers B, Sears AM, Dechesne F, Georgieva I, Tani T, Van der Hof S (2019) EU personal data protection in policy and practice. TMC Asser Press, Springer, The Hague, p 1

Dash S (2004) The intruders: unreasonable searches and seizures from King John to John Ashcroft. Rutgers University Press, p 9

Elkin-Koren N, Netanel NW (eds) (2002) The commodification of information. Kluwer Law International, The Hague, pp 17–18

Keeton WP et al (1984) Prosser and Keeton on the law of torts, 5th edn. West Publishing Co, St. Paul, pp 850–851

Naef T (2023) The global reach of the right to data protection. In: Data protection without data protectionism. Eur Yearb Int Econ Law, vol 28. Springer, pp 21

Watson A (1974) Introduction to legal transplants. In: Legal transplants: an approach to comparative law. pp 21

Westin AF (1967) Privacy and freedom. Atheneum, New York, pp 1–487

Legal Texts

U.S.C. § 45(a)(1) (1994): "Unfair methods of competition in or affecting commerce, and unfair or deceptive acts or practices in or affecting commerce, are hereby declared unlawful."

CFR Part 312 Children's Online Privacy Protection Act; Final Rule, 15 U.S.C. §§ 6501–6506, Federal Register Vol. 64, No. 212, 03.11.1999, pp 59888–59915

U.S.C. 2258A (2011) (Reporting requirements of electronic communication service providers and remote computing service providers) (a)

CFR 201 Data Protection Review Court; Final Rule, 28 U.S.C §§ 509, 510–512, Federal Register Vol. 87, No. 198, 14.10.2022, pp 62303–62308

U.S.C.§ 552a(b)-(f)

U.S.C. 1801 et seq

Act C of 2012 on the Criminal Code (Magyar Büntető Törvénykönyvről szóló 2012. évi C. törvény) (1 January 2023) Section 204(1)(a,b,c) and (2)(a) [Translated by Nemzeti Jogszabálytár], https://njt.hu/jogszabaly/en/2012-100-00-00

Act V of 2013 on the Civil Code (2013. évi V. törvény a Polgári Törvénykönyvről) (1 July 2021), Section 4:191(1)(a) and Section 4:193(1) [Translated by Nemzeti Jogszabálytár], https://njt.hu/jogszabaly/en/2013-5-00-00

Article 29 Data Protection Working Party, Adequacy Referential, 18/EN WP 254 rev01, Adopted on 28 November 2017, Last Revised and Adopted on 6 February 2018, pp 1–9

Article 29 Data Protection Working Party, Guidelines on Automated individual decision-making and Profiling for the purposes of Regulation 2016/679, 17/EN WP251rev.01, Last Revised and Adopted on 6 February 2018, pp 1–37, 26

Article 29 Data Protection Working Party, Opinion 03/2014 on Personal Data Breach Notification, 693/14/EN WP 213, Adopted on 25 March 2014, pp 5–6

Article 29 Data Protection Working Party, Opinion 4/2007 on the concept of personal data, 01248/07/EN WP 136, Adopted on 20th June 2007, pp 1–26

Article 29 Working Party, Guidelines on consent under Regulation 2016/679 17/EN WP 259 rev.01, Adopted on 28 November 2017, Last Revised and Adopted on 10 April 2018, 1–31

Assembly, UN General, Convention on the Rights of the Child, United Nations, Treaty Series 1577, no. 3 (1989), pp 1–23

Berliner Beauftragte für Datenschutz und Informationsfreiheit: Nach „Schrems II“: Europa braucht digitale Eigenständigkeit, Pressemitteilung, 711.424.1, 17 Juli 2020. https://www.datenschutz-berlin.de/fileadmin/user_upload/pdf/pressemitteilungen/2020/20200717-PM-Nach_SchremsII_Digitale_Eigenstaendigkeit.pdf

Biometric Information Privacy Act (BIPA) of 2018, 740 ILL. COMP.STAT. 14/1–99

California Consumer Privacy Act (CCPA) of 2018, CAL. CIV.CODE §§ 1798.100–1798.199.100

California Family Code, §§ 6750–6753 (1939), commonly known as *Coogan's Law*

Charter of Fundamental Rights of the European Union, OJ C 326, 26.12.2012, pp 391–407, Article 7–8

Charter of Fundamental Rights of The European Union, OJ C 364, 18.12.2000, pp 1–22, Article 11. It became legally binding as EU primary law with the Lisbon Treaty(*) in 1 January 2009

CJEU, Judgment in Case C-311/18 Data Protection Commissioner v Facebook Ireland and Maximillian Schrems, Press Release No 91/20, 16 July 2020, pp 1–3. https://curia.europa.eu/jcms/upload/docs/application/pdf/2020-07/cp200091en.pdf

Commission Decision of 26 July 2000 pursuant to Directive 95/46/EC of the European Parliament and of the Council on the adequacy of the protection provided by the safe harbour privacy principles and related frequently asked questions issued by the US Department of Commerce, OJ L 215, 26.07.2000, pp 7–47

Commission Decision of 5 February 2010 on standard contractual clauses for the transfer of personal data to processors established in third countries under Directive 95/46/EC of the European Parliament and of the Council, as amended by Commission Implementing Decision (EU) 2016/2297 of 16 December 2016 OJ L 344/ 100, 17.12.2016, pp 100–101

Commission Implementing Decision (EU) 2016/1250 of 12 July 2016 pursuant to Directive 95/46/EC of the European Parliament and of the Council on the adequacy of the protection provided by the EU-U.S. Privacy Shield, OJ L 207/1, 12.07.2016, 1–112

Commission Implementing Decision (EU) 2019/419 of 23 January 2019 pursuant to Regulation (EU) 2016/ 679 of the European Parliament and of the Council on the adequate protection of personal data by Japan under the Act on the Protection of Personal Information, OJ L 76, 19.3.2019, pp 1–58

Commission Implementing Decision (EU) 2021/1772 of 28 June 2021 pursuant to Regulation (EU) 2016/679 of the European Parliament and of the Council on the adequate protection of personal data by the United Kingdom under the Act on the Protection of Personal Information, OJ L 360, 11.10.2021, pp 1–68

Commission Staff Working Paper, Impact Assessment, SEC (2012) 72 final, p 68, https://www.europarl.europa.eu/cmsdata/59702/att_20130508ATT65856-1873079025799224642.pdf

Congress.Gov, Constitution Annotated Analysis and Interpretation of the US Constitution, Fourth Amendment Searches and Seizures, Amdt4.3.1 Overview of Unreasonable Searches and Seizures, https://constitution.congress.gov/browse/essay/amdt4-3-1/ALDE_00013715/

Congress.gov, Regulating Artificial Intelligence: U.S. and International Approaches and Considerations for Congress, Library of Congress, 8 February 2026, https://www.congress.gov/crs-product/R48555

Consolidated version of the Treaty on the Functioning of the European Union, OJ C 326, 26.10.2012, pp 47–390, Article 288

Consolidated versions of the Treaty on European Union and the Treaty on the Functioning of the European Union Consolidated version of the Treaty on European Union Consolidated version of the Treaty on the Functioning of the European Union Protocols Annexes to the Treaty on the Functioning of the European Union Declarations annexed to the Final Act of the Intergovernmental Conference which adopted the Treaty of Lisbon, signed on 13 December 2007 Tables of equivalences, OJ C 202, 7.6.2016, pp 1–388, Article 5(4)

Council of Europe, Convention 108+ Convention for the protection of individuals with regard to the processing of personal data, ETS No. 108 (2018) https://www.europarl.europa.eu/meetdocs/2014_2019/plmrep/COMMITTEES/LIBE/DV/2018/09-10/Convention_108_EN.pdf

Council of Europe, Convention for the Protection of Individuals with Regard to the Automatic Processing of Individual Data, 28.01.1981, ETS No. 108 amended as Council of Europe, Convention 108+ Convention for the protection of individuals with regard to the processing of personal data, ETS No. 108 (2018) https://www.coe.int/en/web/data-protection/convention108-and-protocol

Council of Europe, European Convention for the Protection of Human Rights and Fundamental Freedoms, as amended by Protocols Nos. 11 and 14, 4 November 1950, ETS 5, https://www echr.coe.int/documents/convention_eng.pdf

Court of Justice of the European Union, The Court of Justice declares that the Commission's US Safe Harbour Decision is invalid, Press Release, 117/15, Judgment in Case C-362/14 Maximillian Schrems v Data Protection Commissioner, 6 October 2015, 1–3

Data Protection Commission Ireland, Children Front and Centre, Fundamentals for a Child-Oriented Approach to Data Processing-Draft Version for Public Consultation, December 2020, 33

Directive (EU) 2015/1535 of the European Parliament and of the Council of 9 September 2015 laying down a procedure for the provision of information in the field of technical regulations and of rules on Information Society services OJ L 241, 17.9.2015, pp 1–15

Directive 95/46/EC of the European Parliament and of the Council of 24 October 1995 on the protection of individuals with regard to the processing of personal data and on the free movement of such data, OJ L 281, 23.11.1995, pp 31–50

EDPB, Guidelines 04/2021 on codes of conduct as tools for transfers, 22 February 2022, 1–16, https://edpb.europa.eu/system/files/2022-03/edpb_guidelines_codes_conduct_transfers_after_public_consultation_en_1.pdf.

EDPB, Guidelines 05/2020 on consent under Regulation 2016/679 Version 1.1, Adopted on 4 May 2020, Updated on 13 May 2020, 1–33 para. 129

EDPB, Guidelines 07/2020 on the concepts of controller and processor in the GDPR Version 2.1 Adopted on 07 July 2021, pp 1–51. https://www.edpb.europa.eu/system/files/2023-10/EDPB_guidelines_202007_controllerprocessor_final_en.pdf

EDPB, Guidelines 07/2022 on certification as a tool for transfers, version 2.0, 14 February 2023, 1–19, edpb_guidelines_07–2022_on_certification_as_a_tool_for_transfers_v2_en_0.pdf (europa.eu)

EDPB, Opinion 5/2023 on the European Commission Draft Implementing Decision on the adequate protection of personal data under the EU-US Data Privacy Framework (28 February 2023), pp 1–54, https://edpb.europa.eu/system/files/2023-02/edpb_opinion52023_eu-us_dpf_en.pdf (last visited 29 September 2023)

EDPB, Recommendations 01/2020 on measures that supplement transfer tools to ensure compliance with the EU level of protection of personal data Version 2.0, 18.06.2021, 3. https://edpb.europa.eu/system/files/2021-06/edpb_recommendations_202001vo.2.0_supplementarymeasurestransferstools_en.pdf

EDPB, Recommendations 01/2020 on measures that supplement transfer tools to ensure compliance with the EU level of protection of personal data Version 2.0, 18.06.2021, 3. https://edpb.europa.eu/system/files/2021-06/edpb_recommendations_202001vo.2.0_supplementarymeasurestransferstools_en.pdf

EDPB, Why a good additional technical safeguard is hard to find- A response to the consultation on the EDPB draft recommendations 01/2020 on measures that supplement transfer tools to ensure compliance with the EU level of protection of personal data, 2 https://edpb.europa.eu/sites/default/files/webform/public_consultation_reply/response_sto_edpb_recommendations.pdf

EDPB Statement, Statement 1/2025 on Age Assurance Adopted on 11 February 2025, pp 1–11

European Commission, Adequacy decisions: How the EU determines if a non-EU country has an adequate level of data protection' (13 January 2018) https://ec.europa.eu/info/law/law-topic/data-protection/international-dimension-data-protection/adequacy-decisions_en

European Commission, Amended Proposal for a Council Directive on the Protection of Individuals with Regard to the Processing of Personal Data and on the Free Movement of Such Data, Preamble, COM(92) 422 final - SYN 287, OJ C 311/30, 27.11.1992, pp 30–61

European Commission, Annex to the Commission Implementing Decision on standard contractual clauses for the transfer of personal data to third countries pursuant to Regulation (EU) 2016/679 of the European Parliament and of the Council, Brussels, 4.6.2021, C(2021) 3972 final, 6, Clause 8.6 "Sensitive Data"

European Commission, Commission Implementing Decision (EU) 2021/915 of 4 June 2021 on standard contractual clauses between controllers and processors under Article 28(7) of Regulation (EU) 2016/679 of the European Parliament and of the Council and Article 29(7) of Regulation (EU) 2018/1725 of the European Parliament and of the Council, OJ L 199/18, 7.6.2021, pp 18–30

European Commission, Commission Implementing Decision (EU) 2021/914 of 4 June 2021 on standard contractual clauses for the transfer of personal data to third countries pursuant to Regulation (EU) 2016/679 of the European Parliament and of the Council, OJ L199/31, 7.6.2021, pp 31–61

European Commission, Commission Implementing Decision of 10.7.2023 pursuant to Regulation (EU) 2016/679 of the European Parliament and of the Council on the adequate level of protection of personal data under the EU-US Data Privacy Framework, OJ C (2023) 4745, 10.07.2023, 1–64

European Commission, Commission Staff Working Document, Accompanying the document Communication from the Commission to the European Parliament and the Council Data protection as a pillar of citizens' empowerment and the EU's approach to the digital transition - two years of application of the General Data Protection Regulation, Brussels, 24.6.2020, SWD(2020) 115 final, pp 1–52, 17

European Commission, Communication from the Commission to the European Parliament, The Council, The European Economic and Social Committee and the Committee of the Regions a Digital Decade for children and youth: the new European strategy for a better internet for kids (BIK+), Brussels, 11.5.2022 COM (2022) 212 final, 6

European Commission, Communication from the Commission to the European Parliament and the Council Data protection as a pillar of citizens' empowerment and the EU's approach to the digital transition - two years of application of the General Data Protection Regulation, Brussels, 24.6.2020, COM (2020) 264 final, pp 1–18

European Commission, Communication from the Commission to the European Parliament and the Council Exchanging and Protecting Personal Data in a Globalised World, COM/2017/07 final, 10.01.2017, 7

European Commission, Data protection: Commission adopts adequacy decisions for the UK (28 June 2021) https://ec.europa.eu/commission/presscorner/detail/ro/ip_21_3183

European Commission, Directorate-General for Communications Networks, Content and Technology, Center for Law and Digital Technologies (eLaw) and LLM, Mapping age assurance typologies and requirements – Research report, Publications Office of the European Union, 2024, pp 1–64, https://data.europa.eu/doi/https://doi.org/10.2759/455338, at 7

European Commission, eID, What is eID?, https://ec.europa.eu/digital-building-blocks/wikis/display/DIGITAL/eID

European Commission, Proposal for a Council Directive Concerning the Protection of Individuals in Relation to the Processing of Personal Data, COM(90) 314 final – SYN 287, OJ C 277/3, 5.11.1990, pp 3–12

European Commission, Proposal for a Regulation of the European Parliament and of the Council amending Regulation (EU) No 910/2014 as regards establishing a framework for a European Digital Identity, Brussels, 3.6.2021 COM (2021) 281 final 2021/0136 (COD)

European Commission, Shaping Europe's digital future, Electronic Identification, https://digital-strategy.ec.europa.eu/en/policies/electronic-identification

European Commission, Trade, EU trade relationships by country/region, Countries and Regions, United States, https://policy.trade.ec.europa.eu/eu-trade-relationships-country-and-region/countries-and-regions/united-states_en#:~:text=The%20European%20Union%20and%20the,and%20investment%20partner%20by%20far

European Data Protection Board, Approved Binding Corporate Rules, https://edpb.europa.eu/our-work-tools/accountability-tools/bcr_en?page=1

European Data Protection Supervisor (EDPS), Data Protection, https://edps.europa.eu/data-protection/data-protection_en

European Union Agency for Fundamental Rights, Council of Europe, European Court of Human Rights, European Data Protection Supervisor: Handbook on European data protection law (2018), 28, https://www.echr.coe.int/Documents/Handbook_data_protection_ENG.pdf

Executive Order No. 14086, vol. 87 no. 198 Federal Register, 14.10.2022, pp 62283–62297, Section 2(c)(i)(B)

Family Educational Rights and Privacy Act of 1974, 20 U.S.C. § 1232g (1974)

Foreign Intelligence Surveillance Act of 1978, 50 U.S.C. §§ 1801–1885, 25.10.1978, §1801(h) "Minimization procedures"

FTC, Court Approves Order Requiring Disney to Pay $10 Million to Settle FTC Allegations the Firm Enabled the Unlawful Collection of Children's Personal Data (31 December 2025) https://www.ftc.gov/news-events/news/press-releases/2025/12/court-approves-order-requiring-disney-pay-10-million-settle-ftc-allegations-firm-enabled-unlawful

GDPR.EU, What is GDPR, the EU's new data protection law?: History of GDPR: https://gdpr.eu/what-is-gdpr/

Guidelines 2/2018 of the European Data Protection Board (EDPB) on derogations of Article 49 under Regulation 2016/679 7 (May 25, 2018), 4–5, https://edpb.europa.eu/sites/default/files/files/file1/edpb_guidelines_2_2018_derogations_en.pdf

Health Insurance Portability and Accountability Act. Pub. L. No. 104–191, 110 Stat.1936 (1996)

Hessisches Datenschutzgesetz of 7 October 1970, Gesetz- und Verordnungsblatt für das Land Hessen Teil I, No. 41, 625 of 12 October 1970

N.Y. Sess. Laws 1903, ch. 132, §§ 1–2, amended by N.Y. Civ. Rights Law, §§ 50–51 (McKinney 1909)

Online Eraser Button Law: S.B. 568, 2013 LEG. 2013–14 SESS. (Cal. 2013), https://leginfo.legislature.ca.gov/faces/billNavClient.xhtml?bill_id=201320140SB568

Personal Information Protection Commission: Amended Act on the Protection of Personal Information (Tentative Translation) (June 2020) https://www.ppc.go.jp/files/pdf/APPI_english.pdf

Privacy Act of 1974, Pub. L. No. 93–579, 88 Stat. 1896, as amended 5 U.S.C.§ 552a

Regulation (EU) 2016/679 of the European Parliament and of the Council of 27 April 2016 on the protection of natural persons with regard to the processing of personal data and on the free movement of such data, and repealing Directive 95/46/EC (General Data Protection Regulation), OJ 2016 L 119, 04.05.2016, pp 1–88

Regulation (EU) 2022/2065 of the European Parliament and of the Council of 19 October 2022 on a Single Market for Digital Services and amending Directive 2000/31/EC (Digital Services Act) OJ L 277, 27.10.2022, pp 1–102

Regulation (EU) 2024/1183 of the European Parliament and of the Council of 11 April 2024 amending Regulation (EU) No 910/2014 as regards establishing the European Digital Identity Framework, OJ 2024 L 1183, 30.04.2024, pp 1–64

Regulation (EU) 2024/1689 of the European Parliament and of the Council of 13 June 2024 laying down harmonised rules on artificial intelligence and amending Regulations (EC) No 300/2008, (EU) No 167/2013, (EU) No 168/2013, (EU) 2018/858, (EU) 2018/1139 and (EU) 2019/2144 and Directives 2014/90/EU, (EU) 2016/797 and (EU) 2020/1828 (Artificial Intelligence Act), OJ 2024 L 1689, 12.07.2024, pp 1–144

S.B. 568, 2013 LEG. 2013–14 SESS. (Cal. 2013), https://leginfo.legislature.ca.gov/faces/billNavClient.xhtml?bill_id=201320140SB568

S.836 - 119th Congress (2025–2026): Children and Teens' Online Privacy Protection Act. Congress.gov, Library of Congress, 27 January 2026, https://www.congress.gov/bill/119th-congress/senate-bill/836, Section 2(a)(17)

S.1748 - 119th Congress (2025–2026): Kids Online Safety Act. Congress.gov, Library of Congress, 14 May 2025, https://www.congress.gov/bill/119th-congress/senate-bill/1748

Telephone Consumer Protection Act of 1991, 47 U.S. Code § 227 (1991)

The White House: Fact Sheet: President Biden Signs Executive Order to Implement the European Union-U.S. Data Privacy Framework (7 October 2022), https://www.whitehouse.gov/briefing-room/statements-releases/2022/10/07/fact-sheet-president-biden-signs-executive-order-to-implement-the-european-union-u-s-data-privacy-framework/

Treaty of Lisbon, Amending the Treaty on European Union and the Treaty establishing the European Community, OJ C 306, 17.12.2007, pp 1–271

U.S. Const. amend. I: "Congress shall make no law respecting an establishment of religion, or prohibiting the free exercise thereof; or abridging the freedom of speech, or of the press; or the right of the people peaceably to assemble, and to petition the government for a redress of grievances."

U.S. Const. amend. XIV section 1.1: "All persons born or naturalized in the United States, and subject to the jurisdiction thereof, are citizens of the United States and of the State wherein they reside. No State shall make or enforce any law which shall abridge the privileges or immunities of citizens of the United States; nor shall any State deprive any person of life, liberty, or property, without due process of law; nor deny to any person within its jurisdiction the equal protection of the laws."

U.S. Government Publishing Office (GPO): The Constitution of the United States of America Analysis and Interpretation Centennial Edition Interim Edition: Analysis of Cases Decided by the Supreme Court of the United States to June 27, 2016, 112th Congress 2nd Session, Document No: 112–9, pp 1–2835, 1285 et seq

UN Commission on Human Rights, Convention on the Rights of the Child, E/CN.4/RES/1990/74, 07.03.1990

United Nations Committee on the Rights on the Child (2013) General Comment No. 14 on the right of the child to have his or her best interests taken as a primary consideration (art. 3, para. 1). CRC/C/GC/14, p 18, para. 84

Working Party's Working Document on the Transfers of personal data to third countries: Applying Articles 25 and 26 of the EU Data Protection Directive, DG XV 1998 D/5025/98 WP12

Legal Cases

BVerfG, Order of the First Senate of 15 December 1983 - 1 BvR 209/83 -, paras. 1–214, BVerfGE 65, 1 - 71 Volkszählung

Case 113 F.2d 806, Sidis v. F-R Pub. Corporation (No. 400), Judgment of the Court of Appeals for the Second Circuit, New York, 22 July 1940

Case 148/78, Pubblico Ministero v Ratti [1979] ECR 1629, EU:C:1979:110, p 1636

Case C-131/12 Google Spain SL and Google Inc. v Agencia Española de Protección de Datos (AEPD) and Mario Costeja González EU:C:2014:317
Case C-311/18 Data Protection Commissioner v Facebook Ireland Limited and Maximillian Schrems EU:C:2020:559
Case C-362/14 Maximillian Schrems v Data Protection Commissioner EU:C:2015:650
Case C-404/92 P X v Commission [1994] ECR I-4737, paragraph 17
Case C-450/06 Varec [2008] ECR I-581, EU:C:2008:91, para. 48
Case C-507/17 Google LLC v Commission nationale de l'informatique et des libertés (CNIL) EU:C:2019:772
Case C-62/90 Commission v Germany [1992] ECR I-2575, paragraph 23
Case C-80/06, Carp v. Electricité de France (EDF) [2007] ECR I-4473, EU:C:2007:327, para. 20
Case EWCA Civ446, Murray v Express Newspapers plc and another, Judgment of the Court of Appeal, England and Wales, 7 May 2008, 512
Data Protection Commission, Decision on the inquiry into Meta Platforms Ireland Limited, formerly Facebook Ireland Limited, regarding the processing of children's personal data on the "Instagram" social media network, DPC Inquiry Reference IN-20–7–4, adopted 2 September 2022
Data Protection Commission, Decision on the inquiry into TikTok Technology Limited regarding the processing of children's personal data, DPC Inquiry Reference IN-21–9–1, adopted 8 September 2023
Data Protection Commission, Decision on the inquiry into TikTok Technology Limited regarding transfers of personal data to China and related transparency obligations under the GDPR, DPC Inquiry Reference IN-21–9–2, adopted 30 April 2025
Dudgeon v. the United Kingdom judgment on 22 October 1981, no. 7525/76 para. 40–41
European Data Protection Board, Decision 2/2022 on the dispute arisen on the draft decision of the Irish Supervisory Authority regarding Meta Platforms Ireland Limited (Instagram) under Article 65(1)(a) GDPR, adopted 28 July 2022
European Data Protection Board, Decision 2/2023 on the dispute arisen on the draft decision of the Irish Supervisory Authority regarding TikTok Technology Limited under Article 65(1)(a) GDPR, adopted 2 August 2023
Fed. Trade Comm'n v. Google LLC, No. 1:19-cv-2642 (D.D.C. 2019) and Fed. Trade Comm'n v. Google LLC, No. 1:19-cv-02642, Stipulated Order for Permanent Injunction and Civil Penalty Judgment (D.D.C. 2019)
Free Speech Coalition, Inc. v. Paxton, 606 U.S. (2025)
Free Speech Coalition, Inc. v. Anderson, No. 23–4104 (10th Cir. 2024), appeal from No. 2:23-cv-00287-TS (D. Utah, 2023)
Free Speech Coalition, Inc. v. Rokita, No. 1:24-cv-00980-RLY-MG (S.D. Ind. June 10, 2024) (order granting preliminary injunction June 28, 2024)
Free Speech Coalition, Inc. v. LeBlanc, No. 2:23-cv-02123, 2023 (E.D. La. Oct. 4, 2023), appeal docketed, No. 23–30780 (5th Cir. 2023)
Free Speech Coalition, Inc. v. Skrmetti, No. 2:24-cv-02933 (W.D. Tenn. Dec. 30, 2024)
Free Speech Coalition, Inc. v. Moody, No. 4:24-cv-00514 (N.D. Fla. filed Dec. 16, 2024)
Griswold v. State of Connecticut, 381 U.S. 479 (1965) 484–86. https://tile.loc.gov/storage-services/service/ll/usrep/usrep381/usrep381479/usrep381479.pdf
Hurbain v. Belgium judgment (Grand Chamber) on 4 July 2023, no.57292/16 para. 255 et seq
Hurbain v. Belgium judgment on 21 June 2021, referral to the Grand Chamber 11 October 2021, no.57292/16 para. 132 et seq
Klass and Others v. Germany judgment on 6 September 1978, no. 5029/71 para. 41
Leander v. Sweden judgment of 26 March 1987, no. 9248/81 para. 46–48
Niemietz v. Germany judgment on 16 December 1992, no. 13710/88 par. 28–33
Peck v The United Kingdom No 44647/98
Powell and Rayner v. the United Kingdom judgment of 21 February 1990, no. 9310/81, para. 41
Société Colas Est and Others v France, no. 37971/97

Szabó and Vissy v. Hungary judgment 12 January 2016, no. 37138/14 para. 73
United States of America (on behalf of the Federal Trade Commission) v. Apitor Technology Co., Ltd., Case No. 3:25-cv-07363 (U.S. District Court for the Northern District of California)
United States of America (on behalf of the Federal Trade Commission) v. Cognosphere, LLC and Cognosphere Pte. Ltd., Case No. 2:25-cv-447 (U.S. District Court for the Central District of California)
United States of America (on behalf of the Federal Trade Commission) v. Disney Worldwide Services, Inc. and Disney Entertainment Operations LLC, Case No. 2:25-cv-08223 (U.S. District Court for the Central District of California)
United States of America (on behalf of the Federal Trade Commission) v. Epic Games, Inc. Case No. 5:22-cv-00518-BO (U.S. District Court for the Eastern District of North Carolina)
United States of America (on behalf of the Federal Trade Commission) v. Iconic Hearts Holdings, Inc. and Hunter Rice, Case No. 2:25-cv-09310 (U.S. District Court for the Central District of California)

Websites

A Parent and Carer's Guide to Instagram: Manage Privacy, 15–16 https://www.internetmatters.org/wp-content/uploads/2021/11/UK_Instagram_-parent_and_carer_guide_to_instagram.pdf
AEPD (Spanish DPA), Risk Management and Impact Assessment in the Processing of Personal Data, (Jun 2021), https://www.aepd.es/es/documento/risk-management-and-impact-assessment-in-processing-personal-data.pdf
Apple, Siri: https://www.apple.com/siri/
Apple, Use Face ID on your iPhone or iPad Pro: https://support.apple.com/en-us/HT208109#:~:text=Tap%20Set%20Up%20Face%20ID,your%20head%2C%20tap%20Accessibility%20Options
BBC News, Edward Snowden: Leaks that exposed US spy programme, 17 January 2014, https://www.bbc.com/news/world-us-canada-23123964
BBC News: Amanda Todd: Dutchman sentenced for fatal cyber-stalking (15 October 2022) https://www.bbc.com/news/world-us-canada-63218797
BBC, Parents of teenager who took his own life sue OpenAI, Published 27 August 2025, https://bbc.com/news/articles/cgerwp7rdlvo
BEUC (The European Consumer Organisation), Making European Digital Identity as Safe as It Is Needed, https://www.beuc.eu/sites/default/files/publications/beuc-x-2022-016_eidas_position_paper.pdf,1
Britannica, Joe Biden, https://www.britannica.com/biography/Joe-Biden
Brooke Auxier, Monica Anderson, Andrew Perrin and Erica Turner, Children's engagement with digital devices, screen time, Pew Research Center, (2020). 2. https://www.pewresearch.org/internet/2020/07/28/childrens-engagement-with-digital-devices-screen-time/
CBC News: Amanda Todd's parents recall teenager's anguish at recurring social media torment (7 Jun 2022) https://www.cbc.ca/news/canada/british-columbia/todd-sextortion-trial-coban-1.6480477
CBC News: Parents, Dutch police investigator testify in trial of man accused of cyberbullying Amanda Todd, (11 Jun 2022) https://www.cbc.ca/news/canada/british-columbia/amanda-todd-week-one-1.6485200
Children may also have bank accounts with the consent of their parents or guardians. For instance: HSBC, Children's Bank Accounts: https://www.hsbc.co.uk/current-accounts/products/children/

CNIL (French DPA), Analyse d'impact relative à la protection des données: publication d'une liste des traitements pour lesquels une analyse est requise (6 Nov 2018), https://www.cnil.fr/fr/analyse-dimpact-relative-la-protection-des-donnees-publication-dune-liste-des-traitements-pour

CNIL (French DPA), Privacy Impact Assessment (PIA) Methodology, (February 2018), https://www.cnil.fr/sites/cnil/files/atoms/files/cnil-pia-1-en-methodology.pdf

CNIL, Sharing photos and videos of your child on social networks: what risks (28 November 2025), https://www.cnil.fr/en/sharing-photos-and-videos-your-child-social-networks-what-risks

CNIL, The open source PIA software helps to carry out data protection impact assessment, (30 June 2021), https://www.cnil.fr/en/open-source-pia-software-helps-carry-out-data-protection-impact-assessment

CNN, 'You're not rushing. You're just ready:' Parents say ChatGPT encouraged son to kill himself, Published 25 July 2025, Updated 20 November 2025, https://edition.cnn.com/2025/11/06/us/openai-chatgpt-suicide-lawsuit-invs-vis

Council of Europe, Chart of signatures and ratifications of Treaty 108, https://www.coe.int/en/web/conventions/full-list?module=signatures-by-treaty&treatynum=108

Data Protection Commission Ireland, List of Types of Data Processing Operations which require a Data Protection Impact Assessment, pp 1–6, https://www.dataprotection.ie/sites/default/files/uploads/2018-11/Data-Protection-Impact-Assessment.pdf

euCONSENT, A summary of the achievements and lessons learned of the euCONSENT project and what comes next (7 Dec 2022) https://euconsent.eu/a-summary-of-the-achievements-and-lessons-learned-of-the-euconsent-project-and-what-comes-next/

euCONSENT, Building a Safer Internet: The Journey to AgeAware® (9 January 2025) https://euconsent.eu/building-a-safer-internet-the-journey-to-ageaware/

EuConsent, Digital Age of Consent under the GDPR: https://euconsent.eu/digital-age-of-consent-under-the-gdpr/#:~:text=As%20per%20Article%208%20of,at%20least%2016%20years%20old'

euCONSENT, euCONSENT's first large scale pilot (18 Mar 2022) https://euconsent.eu/euconsents-first-large-scale-pilot/

euCONSENT, euCONSENT's first large scale pilot: How about parental consent? Which Parental Consent Providers were involved? How was the process? (18 Mar 2022) https://euconsent.eu/euconsents-first-large-scale-pilot/

euCONSENT, euCONSENT's first large scale pilot: What did the participants have to do? (18 Mar 2022) https://euconsent.eu/euconsents-first-large-scale-pilot/

euCONSENT, FAQ: What is euCONSENT?, https://euconsent.eu/faq/

euCONSENT, Interoperability through AgeAware from euCONSENT (24 June 2025) https://euconsent.eu/interoperability-through-ageaware-from-euconsent/

Euractive: Schrems: round three (4 November 2022) https://www.euractiv.com/section/digital/podcast/schrems-round-three/

European Commission, Binding Corporate Rules (BCR), https://ec.europa.eu/info/law/law-topic/data-protection/international-dimension-data-protection/binding-corporate-rules-bcr_en

European Commission, Blueprint for an age verification solution to help protect minors online (9 October 2025) https://digital-strategy.ec.europa.eu/en/factpages/blueprint-age-verification-solution-help-protect-minors-online

European Commission, European Commission and United States Joint Statement on Trans-Atlantic Data Privacy Framework (25 Mar 2022) https://ec.europa.eu/commission/presscorner/detail/en/ip_22_2087

European Commission, New European strategy for a Better Internet for Kids – Questions and Answers, 11 May 2022, 12. How will the new strategy address age verification?, https://ec.europa.eu/commission/presscorner/detail/en/QANDA_22_2826

European Commission, Questions & Answers: EU-U.S. Data Privacy Framework (7 Oct 2022) https://ec.europa.eu/commission/presscorner/detail/en/QANDA_22_6045

European Commission, Standard Contractual Clauses, https://ec.europa.eu/info/law/law-topic/data-protection/international-dimension-data-protection/standard-contractual-clauses-scc_en

European Commission, Study on the impact of marketing through social media, online games and mobile applications on children's behaviour (1 Mar 2016) https://commission.europa.eu/publications/study-impact-marketing-through-social-media-online-games-and-mobile-applications-childrens-behaviour_en

European Commission, Trans-Atlantic Data Privacy Framework (25 Mar 2022), https://ec.europa.eu/commission/presscorner/detail/en/FS_22_2100

European Commission, Types of EU law, Types of EU legal acts: Directives, Types of EU law (europa.eu)

European Commission, Types of EU law, Types of EU legal acts: Regulations, https://commission.europa.eu/law/law-making-process/types-eu-law_en

European Commission, What does data protection 'by design' and 'by default' mean?, https://commission.europa.eu/law/law-topic/data-protection/reform/rules-business-and-organisations/obligations/what-does-data-protection-design-and-default-mean_en

European Data Protection Supervisor (EDPS), Data Protection: Privacy- a fundamental right, https://edps.europa.eu/data-protection/data-protection_en

European Data Protection Supervisor (EDPS), Data Protection: What is data protection?, https://edps.europa.eu/data-protection/data-protection_en

European Data Protection Supervisor (EDPS), Data Protection: What is privacy?, https://edps.europa.eu/data-protection/data-protection_en

European Data Protection Supervisor (EDPS), Opinion on the Communication from the Commission on "A comprehensive approach on personal data protection in the European Union", OJ C 181/01, 22.06.2011, p 1, https://edps.europa.eu/data-protection/our-work/publications/opinions/comprehensive-approach-personal-data-protection_en

European Parliamentary Research Service (EPRS), Update on the state of play of the EU-US data transfer rules, Members' Research Service, 14–20. https://www.europarl.europa.eu/RegData/etudes/IDAN/2018/625151/EPRS_IDA(2018)625151_EN.pdf

Facebook data policy includes Instagram terms as well, but you may also check it here: Instagram, Help Centre, Data Policy: How do we operate and transfer data as part of our global services? https://help.instagram.com/155833707900388

Facebook Help Center, How to Report Things, How do I report a child under the age of 13 on Facebook?: https://www.facebook.com/help/157793540954833/?helpref=uf_share

Facebook, Data Policy: How do we operate and transfer data as part of our global services? https://m.facebook.com/privacy/policy/version/20220104/

Facebook, Help Centre, Safety Resources for Parents: How to request data from your underage child's Facebook account? https://www.facebook.com/help/173734372685099/?helpref=uf_share

Facebook, Privacy Policy: How do we transfer information?, https://www.facebook.com/privacy/policy?section_id=9-HowDoWeTransfer

Facebook, Safety Centre, Online Child Protection: Our Policies https://www.facebook.com/safety/onlinechildprotection

Facebook, Sign Up: https://www.facebook.com/signup

Federal Trade Commission, Complying with COPPA: Frequently Asked Questions, Verifiable Parental Consent, How do I get parental consent?: https://www.ftc.gov/business-guidance/resources/complying-coppa-frequently-asked-questions#I.%20Verifiable%20Parental%20Consent, FAQ I.4

Federal Trade Commission, Complying with COPPA: Frequently Asked Questions, H. General Audience and Teen Sites or Services, 1, https://www.ftc.gov/business-guidance/resources/complying-coppa-frequently-asked-questions#I.%20Verifiable%20Parental%20Consent

Federal Trade Commission, FTC Staff Sets Forth Principles For Online Information Collection From Children, July 1997, https://www.ftc.gov/news-events/news/press-releases/1997/07/ftc-staff-sets-forth-principles-online-information-collection-children

Federal Trade Commission, Fortnite Video Game Maker Epic Games to Pay More Than Half a Billion Dollars over FTC Allegations of Privacy Violations and Unwanted Charges, Press

Release (19 December 2022) https://www.ftc.gov/news-events/news/press-releases/2022/12/fortnite-video-game-maker-epic-games-pay-more-half-billion-dollars-over-ftc-allegations

Federal Trade Commission, Privacy Online: A report to Congress, June 1998, https://www.ftc.gov/sites/default/files/documents/reports/privacy-online-report-congress/priv-23a.pdf

Federal Trade Commission, Verifiable Parental Consent and the Children's Online Privacy Rule: https://www.ftc.gov/business-guidance/privacy-security/verifiable-parental-consent-childrens-online-privacy-rule

Federal Trade Commission: Complying with COPPA: Frequently Asked Questions, Why does COPPA apply only to children under 13? What about protecting the online privacy of teens?, https://www.ftc.gov/business-guidance/resources/complying-coppa-frequently-asked-questions

For more information about OneTrust platform and their automated data protection impact assessment system: OneTrust, products> PIA and DPIA Automation, https://www.onetrust.com/products/pia-and-dpia-automation/

FRA (European Union Agency for Fundamental Rights), Consenting to medical treatment without parental consent, https://fra.europa.eu/en/publication/2017/mapping-minimum-age-requirements-concerning-rights-child-eu/consenting-medical-treatment-without-parental-consent#:~:text=However%2C%20where%20a%20medical%20intervention,is%20set%20at%2015%20years

FRA (European Union Agency for Fundamental Rights), Minimum age requirements related to rights of the child in the EU, Social rights; Employment; Education; Alternative care; LGBTI and Mobility: https://fra.europa.eu/en/publications-and-resources/data-and-maps/minag?dataSource=MINAG_en_62756&media=png&width=740&topic=group05&question=MINAG_HE01&plot=MAP&subset=NONE&subsetValue=NONE&answer=MINAG_HE01&year=2017

FRA, Minimum age requirements related to rights of the child in the EU, Marriage and sexual consent; Citizenship; Political Participation; Religion; Health: https://fra.europa.eu/en/publications-and-resources/data-and-maps/minag?dataSource=MINAG_en_62756&media=png&width=740&topic=group05&question=MINAG_HE01&plot=MAP&subset=NONE&subsetValue=NONE&answer=MINAG_HE01&year=2017

Fun Brain, Privacy Policy: https://www.funbrain.com/privacy-policy

Fun Brain: https://www.funbrain.com/

Galexia, http://www.galexia.com.au

Global News: Exclusive: Mountie who worked Amanda Todd case speaks for first time (10 Aug 2022) https://globalnews.ca/news/9050914/amanda-todd-officer-speaks/

Google Family Link https://families.google/familylink/

Google Family Link, Privacy Notice for Google Accounts and Profiles Managed with Family Link, for Children under 13 (or applicable age in your country) ("Privacy Notice"): Information Google Shares https://families.google.com/familylink/privacy/child-policy/

Google, Help Centre: Age requirements on Google Accounts, Find your country's age requirement, https://support.google.com/accounts/answer/1350409?hl=en#zippy=%2Ceurope

Google, Privacy & Terms, When Google shares your information https://policies.google.com/privacy?hl=en-US#infosharing

Google, Products, https://about.google/products/

Google, Safety and Security, How we detect, remove and report child sexual abuse material, Susan Jasper (28 Oct 2022), https://blog.google/technology/safety-security/how-we-detect-remove-and-report-child-sexual-abuse-material/

Google, Sign Up: https://accounts.google.com/signup/v2/webcreateaccount?flowName=GlifWebSignIn&flowEntry=SignUp

Global Privacy Enforcement Network, 2025 Global Privacy Enforcement Network sweep focuses on the protection of children's privacy (3 November 2025) https://www.privacyenforcement.net/content/2025-global-privacy-enforcement-network-sweep-focuses-protection-childrens-privacy

Global Privacy Enforcement Network, Authorities Listings, https://www.privacyenforcement.net/authorities-listings
Global Privacy Enforcement Network, Our mission, (https://www.privacyenforcement.net/content/our-mission
Happify, Legal, Happify™ Privacy Policy: Last Updated July, 2020, https://www.happify.com/public/legal/#legal
HSBC Voice ID, https://www.hsbc.com.hk/ways-to-bank/phone/voice-id/
ICO, Data protection by design and default, at What is data protection by design?, and at What is data protection by default?, https://ico.org.uk/for-organisations/guide-to-data-protection/guide-to-the-general-data-protection-regulation-gdpr/accountability-and-governance/data-protection-by-design-and-default/#dpd3
ICO, Data protection by design and default, How does data protection by design and by default link to data protection impact assessments (DPIAs)?, https://ico.org.uk/for-organisations/guide-to-data-protection/guide-to-the-general-data-protection-regulation-gdpr/accountability-and-governance/data-protection-by-design-and-default/#:~:text=A%20DPIA%20is%20a%20tool,by%20design%20and%20by%20default
ICO, Rights related to automated decision making including profiling, https://ico.org.uk/for-organisations/uk-gdpr-guidance-and-resources/individual-rights/individual-rights/rights-related-to-automated-decision-making-including-profiling/
If we search on LinkedIn or other job search platforms, we may come across several announcements for open positions such as data protection/privacy officer, data privacy specialist, privacy operations specialist, and so on: LinkedIn, Privacy Officer jobs in Hungary: https://www.linkedin.com/jobs/search/?geoId=100288700&keywords=privacy%20officer&location=Hungary
Information Commissioner's Office (ICO), The benefits of data protection laws, https://ico.org.uk/for-organisations/sme-web-hub/the-benefits-of-data-protection-laws/#:~:text=And%20you%20have%20to%20protect,discrimination%20or%20even%20physical%20harm
Information Commissioner's Office (ICO), What rights do children have?, When may a child exercise these rights on their own behalf?, https://ico.org.uk/for-organisations/guide-to-data-protection/guide-to-the-general-data-protection-regulation-gdpr/children-and-the-uk-gdpr/what-rights-do-children-have/
Information Commissioner's Office (ICO), When do we need to do a DPIA?, What does the ICO consider likely to result in high risk?, point (9), https://ico.org.uk/for-organisations/uk-gdpr-guidance-and-resources/accountability-and-governance/data-protection-impact-assessments-dpias/when-do-we-need-to-do-a-dpia/
Instagram Help Center, How to Report Things, Report a child under 13 on Instagram, https://help.instagram.com/2922067214679225/?helpref=hc_fnav
Instagram Help Centre, Recommendations on Instagram, https://help.instagram.com/313829416281232/?helpref=uf_share
Instagram Help Centre, Sharing to other social networks, https://help.instagram.com/169948159813228
Instagram, Help Centre, Community Guidelines, https://help.instagram.com/477434105621119/?helpref=uf_share
Instagram, Kids Diana Show (image posted on 21 Aug 2021) https://www.instagram.com/p/CSeZgdHjkVF/?hl=tr
Instagram, Privacy Policy, How do we transfer information?, https://privacycenter.instagram.com/policy/?section_id=9-HowDoWeTransfer
Johnson & Johnson, Privacy Policy: Contacting us https://www.jnj.com/corporate/privacy-policy
Johnson & Johnson, Privacy Policy: Use by Minors https://www.jnj.com/corporate/privacy-policy
Max Schrems, https://schre.ms/
Meta AI, Powered by AI: Instagram's Explore recommender system (25 Nov 2019), https://ai.meta.com/blog/powered-by-ai-instagrams-explore-recommender-system/
Meta Newsroom: What Our Research Really Says About Teen Well-Being and Instagram (26 Sept 2021) https://about.fb.com/news/2021/09/research-teen-well-being-and-instagram/

Meta, Child sexual exploitation, abuse and nudity, https://transparency.fb.com/en-gb/policies/community-standards/child-sexual-exploitation-abuse-nudity/?source= https://www.facebook.com/communitystandards/child_nudity_sexual_exploitation

Meta, Community Standards Enforcement Report, Second Quarter 2021 (18 Aug 2021), https://about.fb.com/news/2021/08/community-standards-enforcement-report-q2-2021/

Meta, Empowering Parents, Protecting Teens: Meta's Approach to AI Safety (17 October 2025, updated on 23 January 2026), https://about.fb.com/news/2025/10/teen-ai-safety-approach/

Meta, Facebook Community Standards, Child sexual exploitation, abuse and nudity, Policy rationale, https://transparency.fb.com/en-gb/policies/community-standards/child-sexual-exploitation-abuse-nudity/

Meta, Facebook Community Standards, https://transparency.fb.com/en-gb/policies/community-standards/?source= https://transparency.fb.com/en-gb

Meta, How Meta uses AI to better understand people's ages on our platforms (22 June 2022) https://tech.facebook.com/artificial-intelligence/2022/6/adult-classifier/

Meta, Online Child Protection: Tools and Technology https://about.meta.com/actions/safety/online childprotection

Meta, Safety Centre, Online Child Protection, https://about.meta.com/actions/safety/onlinechildprotection

Mr. Alkohol (Coctails&Drinks), https://mralkohol.hu/

MyFitnessPal Privacy Policy, https://www.myfitnesspal.com/privacy-policy

MyFitnessPal, Sign Up: https://www.myfitnesspal.com/account/create

NBC News, Hackers are leaking children's data — and there's little parents can do, 10 September 2021, by Kevin Collier, https://www.nbcnews.com/tech/security/hackers-are-leaking-childrens-data-s-little-parents-can-rcna1926

Nemzeti Adatvédelmi és Információszabadság Hatóság (NAIH), GDPR 35 (4) Mandatory DPIA List, List of Processing Operations Subject to DPIA GDPR 35 (4), points (2), (19), and (20), https://www.naih.hu/data-protection/gdpr-35-4-mandatory-dpia-list

Nemzeti Adatvédelmi és Információszabadság Hatóság (NAIH), GDPR 35 (4) Mandatory DPIA List, List of Processing Operations Subject to DPIA GDPR 35 (4), points (2), (19), and (20), https://www.naih.hu/data-protection/gdpr-35-4-mandatory-dpia-list

NOYB, European Commission Gives EU-US Data Transfers Third Round At CJEU, 10 July 2023, https://noyb.eu/en/european-commission-gives-eu-us-data-transfers-third-round-cjeu

OpenAI, Age prediction in ChatGPT (updated on 11 February 2026) https://help.openai.com/en/articles/12652064-age-prediction-in-chatgpt

OpenAI, Our approach to advertising and expanding access to ChatGPT (16 January 2026) https://openai.com/index/our-approach-to-advertising-and-expanding-access/

OpenAI, Retiring GPT-4o, GPT-4.1, GPT-4.1 mini, and OpenAI o4-mini in ChatGPT (29 January 2026) https://openai.com/index/retiring-gpt-4o-and-older-models/

Pew Research Center, Children's engagement with digital devices, screen time, https://www.pewresearch.org/internet/2020/07/28/childrens-engagement-with-digital-devices-screen-time/

Pew Research Center, Connection, Creativity and Drama: Teen Life on Social Media in 2022 (16 Nov 2022) https://www.pewresearch.org/internet/2022/11/16/connection-creativity-and-drama-teen-life-on-social-media-in-2022/

Pew Research Center, Connection, Creativity and Drama: Teen Life on Social Media in 2022: Teens have a range of definitions for digital privacy (16 Nov 2022) https://www.pewresearch.org/internet/2022/11/16/connection-creativity-and-drama-teen-life-on-social-media-in-2022/

Pew Research Center, Parenting Children in the Age of Screens: Parents' attitudes – and experiences – related to digital technology (28 Jul 2020) https://www.pewresearch.org/internet/2020/07/28/parents-attitudes-and-experiences-related-to-digital-technology/

Pew Research Center, Teens' views about social media: In their own words: Teens explain what they think social media companies do with their data (16 Nov 2022) https://www.pewresearch.org/internet/2022/11/16/2-teens-views-about-social-media/

Rachel Sandler: CDC Will Collect Personal Data On Vaccine Recipients, Raising Privacy Concerns, Forbes, 8 Dec 2020, https://www.forbes.com/sites/rachelsandler/2020/12/08/cdc-will-collect-personal-data-on-vaccine-recipients-raising-privacy-concerns/?sh=2ac8021d50ec

Statista: Most popular social networks worldwide as of January 2023, ranked by number of monthly active users (in millions), https://www.statista.com/statistics/272014/global-social-networks-ranked-by-number-of-users/

The Guardian, Boy, 12, Steals Credit Card and Goes on Bali Holiday after Fight with Mother (23 Apr 2018): https://www.theguardian.com/australia-news/2018/apr/23/boy-12-steals-credit-card-and-goes-on-bali-holiday-after-fight-with-mother

The Guardian, Fake fingerprints can imitate real ones in biometric systems – research, 15 Nov 2018: https://www.theguardian.com/technology/2018/nov/15/fake-fingerprints-can-imitate-real-fingerprints-in-biometric-systems-research

The Guardian, Google and AI startup to settle lawsuits alleging chatbots led to teen suicide, Published 8 January 2026, https://www.theguardian.com/technology/2026/jan/08/google-character-ai-settlement-teen-suicide

The Guardian: Couple who screamed at their kids in YouTube 'prank' sentenced to probation (12 Sept 2017) https://www.theguardian.com/us-news/2017/sep/12/youtube-parents-children-heather-mike-martin

The International Trade Administration (ITA), U.S. Department of Commerce, Data Privacy Framework Program, https://www.dataprivacyframework.gov/s/

The International Trade Administration (ITA), U.S. Department of Commerce, Data Privacy Framework Program, Data Privacy Framework (DPF) Program Overview, https://www.dataprivacyframework.gov/s/program-overview

The New York Times, A Dad Took Photos of His Naked Toddler for the Doctor. Google Flagged Him as a Criminal, Published 21 Aug 2022, Updated 21 Jun 2023, https://www.nytimes.com/2022/08/21/technology/google-surveillance-toddler-photo.html

The New York Times, Alan F. Westin, Who Transformed Privacy Debate Before the Web Era, Dies at 83 (22 Feb 2013) https://www.nytimes.com/2013/02/23/us/alan-f-westin-scholar-who-defined-right-to-privacy-dies-at-83.html

The Wall Street Journal, Facebook Knows Instagram Is Toxic for Teen Girls, Company Documents Show (14 Sept 2021) https://www.wsj.com/articles/facebook-knows-instagram-is-toxic-for-teen-girls-company-documents-show-11631620739?mod=hp_lead_pos7

The Wall Street Journal, Julie Jargon, How 13 Became the Internet's Age of Adulthood? (18 Jun 2019): https://www.wsj.com/articles/how-13-became-the-internets-age-of-adulthood-11560850201

Today, Have a social media account for your baby? 40 percent of millennial moms do (18 Oct 2014) https://www.today.com/parents/have-social-media-account-your-baby-40-percent-millennial-moms-%201D80224937

Twitter, BlogHer: "So I Posted Photos of My Kid Online and This is Where They Ended Up http://ow.ly/2uSjRn" (14 Feb 2013) https://twitter.com/blogher/status/302079107901046784

U.S. Department of State, Archive, Progress & Freedom Foundation https://2001-2009.state.gov/p/io/unesco/members/48807.htm

Ügyfélkapu: https://ugyfelkapu.gov.hu/

UNICEF, More than 175,000 children go online for the first time every day, tapping into great opportunities, but facing grave risks (6 Feb 2018), https://www.unicef.org/press-releases/more-175000-children-go-online-first-time-every-day-tapping-great-opportunities

United Nations, Office of the United Nations High Commissioner for Human Rights (OHCHR): Children's right to privacy in the digital age must be improved (15 Jul 2021) https://www.ohchr.org/en/stories/2021/07/childrens-right-privacy-digital-age-must-be-improved

UpcoMinds, AgeCheck, JusProg, Lisal Expert, Revealing Reality, AGEify, Aston University, London School of Economics and Political Science, Leiden University, Digie, AVPA, John Carr,

https://euconsent.eu/partners/

YouTube help, Manage privacy settings, Understanding the basics of privacy on YouTube apps https://support.google.com/youtube/answer/10364219?hl=en#:~:text=YouTube%20does%20not%20sell%20your,results%2C%20and%20serving%20relevant%20ads. (For their privacy policy they direct you to the above-mentioned Google Privacy Policy)

YouTube Help, YouTube Policies, Child Safety Policy: Content Featuring Minors, https://support.google.com/youtube/answer/2801999?hl=en&ref_topic=9282679#zippy=%2Ckorhat%C3%A1ros-tartalom%2Ckiskor%C3%BAakat-megc%C3%A9lz%C3%B3-tartalom%2Ccontent-featuring-minors

YouTube Help, YouTube Policies, Child Safety Policy: What happens if content violates this policy, https://support.google.com/youtube/answer/2801999?hl=en&ref_topic=9282679#zippy=%2Ckorhat%C3%A1ros-tartalom%2Ckiskor%C3%BAakat-megc%C3%A9lz%C3%B3-tartalom%2Ccontent-featuring-minors

YouTube Help, YouTube Policies: Child Safety Policy, https://support.google.com/youtube/answer/2801999?hl=en&ref_topic=9282679#zippy=%2Ckorhat%C3%A1ros-tartalom%2Ckiskor%C3%BAakat-megc%C3%A9lz%C3%B3-tartalom%2Ccontent-featuring-minors

YouTube Kids Privacy Notice: Information we share https://kids.youtube.com/t/privacynotice

YouTube Kids: An application specially designed for children https://www.youtube.com/kids/

YouTube Official Blog, Extending our built-in protections to more teens on YouTube, (29 July 2025) https://blog.youtube/news-and-events/extending-our-built-in-protections-to-more-teens-on-youtube/

YouTube, Building content recommendations to meet the unique needs of teens and pre-teens, https://services.google.com/fh/files/misc/vibe-expansion-gtm-casestudy.pdf

YouTube, Newsnercom channel: Barber Pranks Kid By Pretending He's Cut His Ear Off, https://www.youtube.com/watch?v=0TSNKp4XsOU

YouTube, Ryan's World Channel: Christmas Morning 2016 Opening Presents with Ryan ToysReview, https://www.youtube.com/watch?v=WyOkjW5FqBU

YouTube, Simply Allie Channel: Night Time Routine of a Mom 2021 // Mom Of 3 // Preschooler, Toddler and Infant, https://www.youtube.com/watch?v=Dx7Ty0Yg2-k

YouTube, Storyhive Channel: Yoga for Kids!, https://www.youtube.com/watch?v=X655B4ISakg

YouTube, Terms of Service, General Terms and Conditions: Who can use the service?, Age requirements https://kids.youtube.com/t/terms

YouTube, Thesomebodytoknow channel: My story: Struggling, bullying, suicide, self-harm, available at: https://www.youtube.com/watch?v=vOHXGNx-E7E

YouTube, Vlad and Niki's Channel: Vlad and Nikita play with Toy Cars - Collection video for kids, https://www.youtube.com/watch?v=NtzftGb0EcM

The manufacturer's authorised representative in the EU is Springer Nature Customer Service Centre GmbH, Europaplatz 3, 69115 Heidelberg, Germany. If you have any concerns regarding our products, please contact ProductSafety@springernature.com

Printed and bound by CPI Group (UK) Ltd, Croydon, CR0 4YY
17/09/2026
02218462-0001